SUCCESSFUL FUNDRAISING

SUCCESSFUL FUNDRAISING

A Handbook of Proven Strategies and Techniques

*William K. Grasty
and Kenneth G. Sheinkopf*

Charles Scribner's Sons · New York

Copyright © 1982 William K. Grasty and Kenneth G. Sheinkopf

Library of Congress Cataloging in Publication Data

Grasty, William K.
Successful fundraising.

Bibliography: p.
Includes index.
1. Fundraising—Handbooks, manuals, etc.
I. Sheinkopf, Kenneth G., 1945– . II. Title.
HG177.G72   658.1'522   82–5647
ISBN 0–684–17493–6   AACR2

1 3 5 7 9 11 13 15 17 19   F/C   20 18 16 14 12 10 8 6 4 2

Printed in the United States of America.

To the hundreds of thousands of volunteers and professionals who keep nonprofit organizations alive and thriving. May you one day be heard to say, "Thanks, but we don't need any more money this year."

To give away money is an easy matter,
and in any man's power.
But to decide to whom to give it,
and how large and when,
and for what purpose and how,
is neither in every man's power—
nor an easy matter.
Hence it is that such excellence is rare,
praiseworthy, and noble.

ARISTOTLE

Contents

Preface and Acknowledgments

The difference between baseball great Pete Rose and a minor leaguer might be explained by the way Rose does the few fundamental things perfectly, while the bush leaguer does many things imperfectly. The same is true of fundraisers. There are simple, basic fundamentals that any fundraiser can master. You can learn how to write a direct mail letter, how to manage the elements of an annual fund campaign, how to establish a deferred giving program, how to organize and train volunteers, and how to employ all the other methods of fundraising that create a "climate of acceptance" among your organization's various publics. You can do these things very professionally, or you can just make amateur stabs at them.

The top bracket of fundraisers (or "development officers," as they are now often known) is made up of creative people—idealists, if you will—who are able to use their heads as well as their feet, who know how to get the most out of themselves and from others, and who look upon fundraising as a business. For that's what it is—a big business. During 1980 our country's businesses, foundations, and private citizens donated a record $47.74 billion to a wide variety of philanthropic causes. But perhaps most encouraging, at a time when inflation was hitting record heights, when more and more people were feeling the pinch of a recession, unemployment, staggering interest rates, and the many other effects of a weak economy, nearly 85 percent of the total given to charities—$39.93 billion—came from individuals.

Whether you are a paid professional or a part-time volunteer, you will be able to do a better job raising money for your organization if you understand what the business is all about, what makes people donate their money, for this is clearly a business about people.

There is no doubt that the decade of the 1980s is going to be a difficult one for fundraisers. Giving is not keeping pace with inflation (it did until 1979!); changing social conditions are affecting the public's perception of many charities; dramatic media accounts of fraudulent fundraisers are making many people skeptical of the entire giving process; cutbacks in federal and local aid have created a crisis; and the rising costs of fundraising, from postage to printing, are making many campaigns ineffective. A more thorough knowledge of fundraising techniques is essential to help you better cope with a rapidly changing economy. Our annual giving programs, capital campaigns, special projects, challenge gifts, and unique efforts are going to have to work a lot harder to reach our goals.

This book was written to help organizations seeking funds, both large and small, reach a new measure of achievement. It is both a primer and a practical guide for individuals and groups involved in the gamut of fundraising activities and is designed to supply theory and techniques to aid in solving the problems that invariably crop up in the context of raising funds. It will help you master the basic principles of the business and will also introduce you to some of the most successful and innovative strategies. Case study materials and examples that illustrate the techniques abound throughout the book.

No ONE CAN CLAIM to have written a book completely unaided. We are obviously indebted to the experiences of many men and women, the results of years of hard work raising funds for charitable organizations.

We wish, therefore, to express our obligation for the thoughts and suggestions gathered from the successes (and failures) of our colleagues. These ideas and comments, now packed into two filing cabinets in our office, include voluminous digests of books and articles, notes on speeches heard at fundraising conferences, folder after folder of case studies and techniques, and innumerable bits of wisdom gleaned from hundreds of conversations held in taxis, airplanes, buses, offices, and hotel lobbies. To these authors, colleagues, and friends, we remain in debt. Whenever possible, we have acknowledged in the text the source of the material, and we greatly appreciate the cooperation we received from fundraisers around the country in all types of nonprofit organizations.

We also want to acknowledge in particular the assistance and ideas of John J. Schwartz, president of the American Association of Fund-Raising Counsel; Donald L. Lemish, vice-chancellor for institutional advancement and planning at East Carolina University; John E. Dolibois, vice-president for development and alumni affairs at Miami University; Adelaide Snyder, vice-president for university relations and public affairs at Florida Atlantic University; Cynthia L. Snyder, director, CASE Reference Center; and the research staffs at the Foundation Center Library in Washington, the University of Central Florida Library, and Independent Sector. Equally important were the contributions of our colleagues at the University of Central Florida and our staff specialists, Evelyn Alford and Sandy Cherepow, who assisted in typing and preparing the manuscript.

Katherine Heintzelman and the editorial and production staff at Charles Scribner's Sons should also be credited with assistance in the completion of this book. We are grateful for their excellent contributions, suggestions, and ideas.

Finally, our love to Sue and Jeff Grasty and to Blanche, Adam, and Jeff Sheinkopf, who tolerated the many distractions this work created. They often asked when we would finish this book. At last we can show them . . . it is done.

William K. Grasty
Kenneth G. Sheinkopf

PART ONE

THE MECHANICS OF FUNDRAISING

The first chapter in this section deals with the people who must set the sense of direction and style for the fundraising program: the president, the chief development officer, the board of trustees, volunteers, and outside consultants. The ideal caliber, potential, and role of each of these people is discussed in detail.

Shifting from people to programs, Chapter 2 examines the annual fund campaign in all its complexity. Because many practitioners do not fully understand the philosophy and mechanics behind an annual fund drive, they tend to be anxious about or suspicious of the program. This is understandable, but not acceptable. The annual fund campaign involves principles, methods, and techniques that work in all fundraising programs. With this kind of background, you can greatly increase your chances of success. Here, then, is the basic course for the beginner and a strong refresher for the professional.

The final chapter in this section covers gift clubs. Some of the suggestions are minor, some major, but each can trigger a significant difference in the giving habits of donors and their loyalty to the organization.

1

Organization and Leadership

When the board of trustees of Yale University was looking for a president for the institution some years ago, a distinguished alumnus suggested the following job description:

> Yale's next president must first of all be a Yale man and a great scholar . . . also a social philosopher who has at his fingertips the solution to all the world's problems from Formosa to birth control. He must be a good public relations man and be an experienced fund raiser. He must be a man of the world, yet he must also have great spiritual qualities—a great administrator who can delegate authority. He must be a great leader, not too far right, nor too far to the left, and of course, not too much in the middle. He must be a man of iron health and stamina; a young man but also mature and full of wisdom. . . . You have no doubt realized there is only one who has most of these qualifications. But there is a question even about him. "Is God a Yale man?"[1]

It was not too long ago that the top official of an organization did all the fundraising—whether the president of the college or the pastor of the church. Whatever the reason for the "begging mission," it was generally a supreme crisis, in crucial times, and it called for a person who could combine the fervor of an Old Testament prophet with the happy gift of the humorist, and do justice to both.

Now things have changed somewhat. The crises may still be supreme, and the times may still be critical. But the chief executive, no matter what title he or she holds, can no longer be a one-person show, traveling hither and yon like the circuit rider of old, calling on friends and parishioners and former benefactors. Although still the institution's most effective fundraiser, the chief executive is now assisted by the board of trustees, the development office, hard-working volunteers, and when needed, outside consultants.

THE ROLE OF THE PRESIDENT OR CHIEF EXECUTIVE

Volumes have been written on the job of a president, but, as Richard D. Cheshire, president of the University of Tampa, has put it, his or her basic responsibilities are to plan, promote, and preside.[2] John Kemeny, former president of Dartmouth College, notes that the president should be an institution's most important fundraiser, but he or she will also be its most frustrating one because a president "is the most useful—yet scarcest—resource."[3]

The president cannot be viewed solely as the chief decision maker. Rather, he or she is the chief planner—of people, of time, of space, and of money. As for the decision process, that is a responsibility that should be delegated to senior officers. The president should be available, however, to hear decisions and refine them if necessary. As Irma L. Rabbino of Mount Holyoke has said, "The president is the star of the show, the Hamlet, and whoever takes the part must be prepared to be on stage for a good portion of the play. The presidential role also parallels that of the architect who conceives and creates a beautiful building. The architect may contract out the actual work to builders, but the dream schemes are his (or hers)."[4]

When it comes to defining and planning the essential function of the development operation, there is no question that the chief executive should be involved. The president *is* the institution. As the leader, the president *is* critical to a successful fundraising program—he or she is the one who sets the tone, the direction, and the pace. What the president says and does is what donors grasp.

Donors expect results, and the more positive the results, the more donor confidence is enhanced.

Hiring the Chief Development Officer

Since the president must both set and monitor the fundraising objectives, the first priority is to hire a person capable of drafting (for presidential review and modification) a plan that sets forth very specific objectives and the ways and means of their accomplishment. This process starts with the chief development officer.

Keep in mind that development is not just a title or job description calling for fundraising. It is a philosophy or way of life for the entire organization. The chief development officer must become actively involved in the total life of the institution. Only by knowing the ideals, needs, structure, and people of the institution will he or she be able to establish a rapport with outsiders.

While every institution will have different needs, which perhaps demand certain specific qualities in a development officer, some generalizations are in order. Every chief development officer should have a track record that demonstrates the following:

- A strong background in fundraising and a deep commitment to the task.
- A strong record in management, especially in dealing with a volunteer leadership.
- The ability to be not only a fundraising technician but also a fundraising diplomat. The chief development officer must know the techniques of public relations, communications, and related activities.
- The qualities of honesty, integrity, compassion, and tolerance.
- Initiative in carrying out responsibilities.
- The ability to handle failure without discouragement.
- The ability to relate well to the organization's constituents— to speak their language, know their problems, understand their needs.
- Creativity: the ability to look at problems in new ways and from different perspectives to seek out the best solutions.
- Perhaps most of all, the willingness to work. We all have heard stories of people "suddenly" giving huge sums of money to

charitable organizations. When asked why, they often reply, "Nobody asked me to give before." Your fundraiser should see that a lot of asking takes place.

A president who obtains the services of such a person is fortunate. While this ideal candidate is usually difficult to find (at times impossible), every president should remember that, given time, most of the skills can be learned. Good common sense and character traits cannot.

The working relationship between a president and the chief development officer must be one of candor and openness. A close personal relationship is not nearly as necessary as a strong professional one. Each officer must understand the other—the aspirations, strengths, weaknesses, and even the quirks so often ingrained in each.

Presidential Expectations

As with every other resource available to a president, he or she should expect certain kinds and levels of performance from the chief development officer and staff. H. Sargent Whittier, Jr., of St. Lawrence University, enumerates these "standard procedures":

1. The president should not have to be involved in any development activity which can be carried out by the staff.
2. The president should insist that all activities in which he or she is involved be preceded by a full written briefing on the nature of the event, its purpose, and the background of the people to be involved. Such briefings should also include instructions about how to get to the scene of the activity and suggestions for appropriate topics to be covered.
3. The president should expect the staff to handle all follow-up details, such as letters to key participants for his or her signature, file memos, and critiques.
4. The president should expect to be kept fully and promptly informed about changes in the involvement or status of key individuals, both prospects and donors, including their gifts.
5. The president should expect to know the status of all fundraising programs to whatever extent desired.
6. The president should expect professional staff work that places

the presidency in the best public light and prevents the president from appearing to be less than fully informed or effective.[5]

Two unfortunate situations can sometimes occur in the relations between president and chief development officer. Many presidents find it difficult to delegate the authority their chief development officers need to fulfill their obligations. Many find it difficult to admit that there is someone else quite as capable (maybe even more so) of doing the development job as they are. This can be an enormous problem, as the president cannot have fundraising as his or her major responsibility and still handle all the other phases of institutional leadership. Conversely, it must also be said that many presidents are saddled with development people who cannot handle their assignments well. This is why it is so important to define areas of responsibility and to ensure that the best possible people are working on the development team.

THE ROLE OF THE DEVELOPMENT OFFICE

Some development operations are quite large, with two dozen or more professional people, and an appropriate number of auxiliary staff and clerical help. This is particularly true in large educational institutions, where the development organization includes all those offices and personnel assigned to work with the publics vital to the institution. The chief development officer at an educational institution sometimes coordinates activities in areas as diverse as government relations, student recruitment, community services, and foundations. Regardless of the number of areas overseen by the development operation, there are but two main functions: *public relations*, building acceptance of the organization and its goals through press, TV, radio, publications, community exhibits, and special events; and *fundraising*, dealing with all aspects of alumni activities, firms and corporations, special gifts prospects, deferred giving, foundations, and capital projects.

The essential task of the development office, by whatever name it is called, is to help the organization's chief executive secure the needed resources to enable the institution to fulfill its mission. To this end, every activity must be evaluated on the basis of whether or not it is helping to achieve this goal.

It is going to cost you some money to raise money, of course. Setting up a development program entails certain initial costs that may not be totally recovered for some time. You will need some staff, an expense budget, and additional support for public relations and related areas. The costs will be highest and the dollar return lowest during the first year or so, but a well-planned program should start paying dividends after that first year.

Different types of fundraising incur different levels of costs. It is not unusual to spend one dollar or more for every dollar of annual fund money raised the first year, but you then have the basis of an ongoing campaign at little extra cost. Capital fundraising appears to many people to cost little since goals are usually so high, but there are still substantial investment expenses. And the costs of a planned giving program often seem higher than any others because most deferred gifts don't begin paying off for three to five years. Ongoing programs, however, have few expenses when compared to the great potential they offer.

Once a program has begun, the following general costs can be used as indicators of what others spend to raise money: annual fund appeals, 11 to 37 cents per dollar raised; capital gifts programs, 5 to 11 cents per dollar; corporate gifts, 3 to 11 cents; foundation gifts, .5 to 2 cents; and deferred gifts, .6 to 3 cents per dollar raised (these programs are discussed in detail in later sections).[6] A 1981 study of the major charitable organizations showed that fundraising costs averaged 11 to 25 percent of their dollars raised. The American Cancer Society, for example, currently spends about 12 percent of their total income on fundraising. The American Heart Association spends 14 percent, the American Lung Association spends 25 percent, and the National Multiple Sclerosis Society spends 13 percent.[7]

So assuming you're given an adequate budget to set up your office, you're ready to begin the research. Start by collecting all the information you can about your organization—its background, purpose, achievements. Find out what is unique (if anything) about it—why it should be supported. Begin building the case for support. Try to ascertain the giving potential of your constituency —how much can they reasonably be asked to give—and how much you think they will actually give. Ask yourself if there is enough potential at this time to make a fundraising program worthwhile. Then get ready to go to work.

Responsibilities of the Development Officer

The development officer has certain responsibilities common to all chief administrators. We have already identified one such duty as working under the policies and procedures established or approved by the president. Other duties are selecting personnel for the office, coordinating the work, recommending the budget, and training the paid staff and volunteer workers.

In addition, the development officer has three specific responsibilities that relate solely to his or her own areas of operation.

1. The development officer is responsible for the *organization of the departments under his or her jurisdiction*. This is accomplished by:
    a. Drawing up a table of organization complete with committees and volunteers.
    b. Preparing the calendar of work for the year in cooperation with the staff.
    c. Developing all job descriptions for the staff.
    d. Developing sound departmental policies that promote the interest and loyalty of the staff.
2. The development officer is responsible for the overall *public relations program of the institution*. This is accomplished by:
    a. Interpreting the institution's major goals, financial and otherwise, to its various publics and gaining acceptance for them.
    b. Planning all publications of a promotional nature.
    c. Developing a program of press and media relations to disseminate news and information.
3. The development officer is responsible for all *fundraising policies and activities*. This is accomplished by:
    a. Organizing both the annual programs for current operations and the long-range programs for capital projects.
    b. Initiating a program to obtain support through wills and bequests.
    c. Identifying all possible sources of voluntary private gift support for fundraising purposes and needs.
    d. Establishing all methods of solicitation by *anyone* connected with the institution, including giving or withholding

permission to solicit any individual, business, corporation, or foundation.

e. Maintaining an orderly process to acknowledge, record, and recognize any gift received.

Because development activities are so difficult to measure—at least until you get the year-end final totals—many practitioners suggest using a "management by objectives" (MBO) system to provide for measurement of your program. Using MBO techniques, you can schedule and structure activities so that progress can be evaluated throughout the year. You have probably set year-long goals, such as the amount of money to be raised, the number of gifts needed. By setting up day-to-day and week-to-week objectives, you can tell how each phase of your campaign is progressing, how your mailings are doing, how the phone campaign has contributed to the overall goal, and so on.

For example, you want to raise $100,000 from local corporations this year. You could set the following goals: the development director will call on the top 25 corporations during the first six months of the year; the chief executive of your organization will personally call or visit the top ten corporations outside your area but within your state; direct mail appeals will be sent to 100 corporations by the end of the third quarter of the year. Now you have specific sub-goals to aim for, and you can tell if you are not getting these things done long before the year is over.

Managing Volunteers

It has been said that a president or a vice-president for development can shout to a prospective donor and not be heard, but the right volunteer can whisper and produce results.[8]

Your job as chief development officer is to find these "right" volunteers, teach them about your organization, train them in the basics of fundraising and solicitation, match them with the best prospects, and then turn them loose.

Volunteers are used today for everything from proposal writing to personal solicitation; from ranking prospects to hosting special events; and from answering the telephone to making phonothon calls. The American Association of Fund-Raising Counsel reported in 1980 that 24 percent of the American people—37 mil-

lion people over the age of thirteen—volunteer their time and
effort for organizations. It also noted a Gallup study that found
seven out of ten adults willing to serve in their communities, in
neighborhood betterment activities, or in the performance of social
services.[9]

Estimates place volunteer time at more than six billion hours of
work each year. Many of America's largest nonprofit organizations
could not continue their services if volunteers were not available.
The American Heart Association, for example, has more than
2,300,000 fundraising volunteers; the American Cancer Society,
1,800,000; and the Boy Scouts, more than 1,100,000.[10]

A recent article in *Ms.* magazine pointed out the most common
problems organizations face with volunteers, including their not
asking for the gift, beating around the bush, being dishonest, begging, apologizing or demanding, not knowing the financial side of
their program, and underestimating giving potential.[11] If you adequately prepare your volunteers for their job, you can avoid most
of these common weaknesses.

How many volunteers do you need? Most experts suggest following the "one-for-five rule." This means that each volunteer
should be given no more than five prospects to solicit, and leaders
should have no more than five workers to supervise. This is especially important for you to control, since typical results find about
a third of the volunteers doing all the work assigned, another third
completing some of their work, and the other third never getting
any of the job done. Your task is to watch over these people—
especially that last third—and be ready to reassign their work to
others who will complete it.

Remember that volunteers are not substitutes for your professional staff. But if you can train them to use their skills, their
ideas, and their contacts (especially their contacts), volunteers can
play important roles in furthering your development effort.

To keep them active and helpful, you need to keep them involved. Assign them specific duties. Put them on committees. Give
them their own responsibilities. One college president has put it
succinctly: "For enlisting and holding effective workers and donors, there are three magics. The first magic is participation. The
second magic is participation. And the third magic is participation."[12] Keep your volunteers involved, and you'll have good
workers.

Consultant Arthur Frantzreb explains, "Most volunteers give of their time and talent in proportion to their estimate of their value to the institution, their confidence in the management, and their loyalty, faith, and gratitude for benefits received by themselves and society."[13] If you make your volunteers feel that they are part of the team and that their work is really important, you'll have a far more successful program than if you just treated them as people "hanging around." And looking at the staffing needs of most development programs, it is clear that volunteer help is not only welcome, but is badly needed.

THE ROLE OF THE TRUSTEES

Of all the publics important to any institution, none is more important than the board of trustees. Every board should be composed of individuals who are willing to be actively involved in fundraising, and who can do the job effectively. If they cannot do it effectively, then they should be willing to give the necessary time to learn.

The old saying that a trustee should provide "work, wealth, and wisdom" is still true. Alas, however, trustees who will bring these three things to the institutional program are not to be found marching four abreast down the street. When one is discovered who can provide the time and talents needed, he or she is usually already taken by at least five other institutions and organizations. The hard, cold fact, as Frank Ashmore, formerly Executive Director of the American College Public Relations Association, has pointed out, is that "most trustees are grown, not born—and you'll probably have to grow your own."[14]

Selecting and Enlisting the Trustee

Never speculate. Before appointing any person as trustee, investigate his or her potential to be of service. The fact that the prospect is prestigious or affluent is never enough. His or her influence and resources could turn out to be committed elsewhere.

Each selectee should be chosen because of special qualifications for a specific board responsibility. Hundreds of highly qualified individuals are available if one will only search for them. The mistake is often made of selecting an individual who is already spread too thin because of activity in other organizations. As Paul Davis says, "Better to select a trustee who will be a major force in one institution, rather than a minor force in many."[15]

Once the right trustee is selected, it is the responsibility of the president to work with the board chairman and the chief development officer to be certain that the candidate fully understands what the responsibilities are, including fundraising. No invitation to serve should be issued until this matter is out on the table, perfectly clear. To do otherwise is to render a disservice to the selectee and to the institution.

Once a trustee is approved or elected, he or she should be fully oriented to the institution. In addition to board meetings, visits and sessions with key institutional leaders should be scheduled. Social activities provide learning opportunities. Publications are another source.

Trustees are one of the keys to successful fundraising, and only when they are fully oriented to the institution can they become qualified salespersons. Their effective performance as fundraisers comes only after sufficient exposure to the institution —to its aims, its values, its plans, its financial need, its people and their aspirations.

Trustees and the Chief Development Officer

In working with trustees, every development officer should fulfill the responsibility to inform, guide, and, where necessary, stir the board into action. Of all the constituents a development officer may encounter, it is the trustees who, in the long haul, will play the most significant part in any major undertaking. No development officer will ever achieve a full measure of success without the intelligent, vigorous, and often sacrificial support of the board of trustees.

Trustees are never to be considered pawns to be moved about at will. They are to be consulted on significant problems. To return to the "wealth, work, and wisdom" concept, you can expect neither wealth nor work until you first ask for wisdom. Trustees are not just patrons. They are participants, and it is the development officer's task to assist them to become all that they can become.

Such an undertaking calls for an incredible amount of service from the development officer. The development office must provide full data on the development program and the people each trustee will solicit. When an effort pays off, a trustee wants the donor to be properly thanked and recognized, and needs to be properly recognized for having obtained the gift.

Trustees can do more than solicit gifts. They can be asked to screen and assign prospects. They can help plan the campaign. They can use their influence to help the appropriate person at the institution gain entree to business and corporation heads, to the right person at foundations. In short, the number of activities for which they can be of help is limitless.

One of the best ways to keep trustee involvement is to place your board members on committees. You can set up a number of different committees, ranging from annual giving and deferred gifts to special projects, community awareness, endowment committees, and others. By having board members on more than one of these, you will keep them involved in different facets of the organization's operation.

H. Sargent Whittier, Jr., has offered suggestions on the chief development officer's relationship with trustees. Here is a summary of Whittier's comments.

Get the endorsement of top trustees at the beginning. Before you accept the position as development officer, be sure to meet with those board members most involved in fundraising. You will want the opportunity to meet and assess the top leaders with whom you will be working.

Serve the president first. Your relations with trustees depend on your relationship with the president. In dealing with trustees, you will operate on three levels—as the development officer, as a member of the president's staff, and as a personal friend. Avoid raising issues with trustees that you have not first discussed with the president.

Thoroughly understand how policy is made and implemented at your institution. Be careful not to interfere in the functions of other officers at your institution. You must sense when and how to bring issues that fall outside your area of responsibility to the attention of the president and your other colleagues.

Get to know your trustees personally and professionally. You need to understand each trustee's views, interests, and circumstances if you are to be effective.

Keep trustees out front. Avoid the temptation to put yourself front and center. Giving trustees the leadership role strengthens their commitment.

Involve trustees in development planning. They must have sufficient knowledge and command of the data to represent the program effectively.

Keep trustees fully informed. Trustees, through their business and professional contacts, have spheres of influence. They must receive regular news about your fundraising progress.

Encourage trustees to solicit their peers. Staff members should not ask trustees for a gift except under unusual circumstances. Trustees deserve to be asked by other trustees.

Learn how to handle the hard questions. As your relationship with trustees grows, they will lean on you for information and advice. Always respond openly, but exercise judgment when offering suggestions. If the question is out of your area or you are unsure about the facts or institutional position, say so and suggest instead that the trustee discuss the issue with a more appropriate officer.

Back institutional policy. Once a decision has been made by the president, back that decision fully and without equivocation. There is no place in our business for attempts to undermine or change decisions through the back door.[16]

THE ROLE OF THE CONSULTANT

There may come a time when outside professional counsel is needed. When and if it comes, the president must be involved. He or she must support the need for outside help, be confident of the firm selected, and expect to benefit just as much or more as do the development staff and the trustees.

Michael Radock of the University of Southern California has noted that outsiders can challenge your staff with innovative ideas and alternative choices. Consultants can help a president evaluate the administrative staff, report to trustees on staff productivity, suggest changes for new administrators to make, and, in general, provide expert advice in establishing new programs and services.[17]

The use of consultants is not a new aspect of the fundraising business. Scott M. Cutlip of the University of Georgia and San Diego State University's Allen H. Center note that professional fundraisers have been around since after World War I, "when the potential of American philanthropy was realized for the first time." They add that estimates show that outside agencies help raise 25 cents of every philanthropic dollar.[18] Before using such counsel, however, you need to weigh the advantages and disadvantages. Such firms bring expert know-how and skilled personnel, along with knowledge of proven techniques, but they also may hurt staff morale and weaken some support since these outsiders are now sharing in the proceeds.

In selecting outside consultants, the first step is to know exactly what you want and what kind of changes will come about as a result of the work. The more specific you can be in identifying the area of operations that needs help, the more specific you can be about the type of help needed. Keep in mind that outside consultants will not raise money for you. Their job is to help *you* raise it.

Perhaps you want a survey done on the attitude of the public toward your institution. The consultant can collect the information, analyze it, and make recommendations. Perhaps your board of trustees needs training in what a board does and the roles of board members. A consultant can be most helpful. Perhaps your donor record and acknowledgment system is in a sorry state. A consultant may recommend an entirely new system or a new records clerk.

The most familiar assignments, of course, are related to fundraising. Here, consultants can offer very specific advice on specialized projects designed to reach corporations or foundations, or on the feasibility of conducting a capital campaign. In this latter instance, a qualified consulting firm can provide the answers to such important questions as:

1. Do you have a valid need that can be sold to constituents?
2. Are the board of trustees, the president, the development staff behind the project enough to give their time and talents?
3. Are the right leaders available? Will they work for your organization?
4. Do you know how much money can be raised?
5. Are you certain that you know how to run the campaign?

Finding the Consulting Firm

Once you have decided what kind of help you want, you can begin to look at the available firms. A good place to start is to ask other similar organizations in your area for referrals. Another source is the American Association of Fund-Raising Counsel (AAFRC). The professional organization to which you belong should also be able to provide names of consulting firms. You are seeking reliability, experience, and reputation, so choose carefully.

Once you have several names to choose from, write and request copies of their promotional literature so you can start identifying the services each firm provides. Also ask the firm to identify its clients. Ask for a *complete* list so that you can call these former clients about the services. Look at their client list to see whether the firm has experience in working with organizations of your type and size. If they have worked primarily with large organizations with large budgets—and you are a small organization with an even smaller budget—you have a right to know this. Without this knowledge, you could receive recommendations that you could not financially handle.

Always interview consultants as you would a prospective employee for your organization. In the interview process notice how well the consultant (often it will be a team) communicates. All the experience possible will do you no good if the consultant cannot communicate. Finally, be wary of anyone you think is telling you what they think you want to hear.

Drawing the Contract

The final steps are to negotiate the specifics of service, set a schedule, and agree on a fee (professional consultants *never* work on a commission). These specifics should be put in the contract so there can be no misunderstandings at a later time. Include in the contract the exact problem to be solved, what is to be done, the persons responsible for completing each and every aspect of the work by what time, and how much it will cost and when payment is required.

It is also advisable to stipulate some midpoint date for evaluation so that both parties can assess the progress made and, if necessary, terminate or alter the agreement. The contract should always include the desired result. Avoid using vague terms. Clearly specify what is expected.

You may wish to consult an attorney to minimize the risk of any misunderstandings. Essentially, the more effort put into formalizing the contract, the less time, effort, and money you may have to spend should disagreements arise.

Used wisely, consultants can help your institution gain increased acceptance from those publics vital to it. Increased acceptance leads to increased funds for current operations and capital growth.

Perhaps the role of the consultant has best been stated by Harold J. Seymour in his book *Designs for Fund-Raising*: "The most important function of consultation is not to play the wizard, but simply to provide at stated intervals the perspective that is possible only with triangulation. Perspective in turn leads to confidence, and confidence is the one biggest thing in the whole fundraising process—always worth taking plenty of pains to find."[19]

To conclude this chapter we would like to repeat that the president, the trustees, and the chief development officer set the style and provide the direction for the institution they serve. This calls for dedicated, capable, imaginative, and knowledgeable men and women.

The president is the organization. More than anyone else, he or she sets the climate in which fundraising takes place. Trustees are members of the development team. They should all be donors. They must all be fundraisers. The development officer aids in the interpretation of the philosophy and goals of the institution so as to actively involve the institution's publics in the achievement of those goals. The development officer insures continuity of effort toward the institution's long-term advancement. He or she trains and manages the volunteers who are essential to the fundraising effort. Development counsel is available for analysis and recommendations, when needed.

2 The Annual Fund

The story is told of a violent snowstorm and a helicopter carrying a rescue team to within one mile of a mountain cabin that had been buried deep in snowdrifts. It took hours for the rescue team to struggle on foot through the deep drifts, and another hour to shovel away the snow blocking the entrance to the cabin. When a lone mountaineer responded to the knock at the door, one of the rescuers joyously shouted, "Are you there? We're from the Red Cross." A moment or two of silence followed before a weak voice came from inside: "Well, it's been a pretty tough winter. I don't see how we can give anything this year."

Many charitable organizations find themselves in the position of that rescue team. Their job is to provide a service or answer some vital community need, yet they are often perceived as constantly conducting fund drives and asking for money. Yet without these private funds, many organizations could not provide much beyond their most basic programs and services. Most find that it takes constant support to fill the gap in each year's budget. When someone gives in 1982, it only means that they are needed as much, or more, in 1983. Giving is truly an annual process.

It is clear that no fundraiser can be all things to all people and take on every fundraising activity that is suggested or imposed by well-meaning advisors. Unfortunately, many fundraisers don't know this and so are inclined to say "yes" to any idea that poses the possibility of raising a few dollars. With the institution needing money to survive, and needing it in a fairly steady stream, the development officer, often out of frustration, moves from one event to another—from barbecues to bingo, from cookbooks to concerts—to anything that will generate donations.

There is nothing wrong with raising money by holding special events. Obviously, if the need is for a few hundred or a few thousand dollars, a special fundraising event—even a series of events —can often generate the income. However, when the need is for hundreds of thousands or even several million dollars, a comprehensive plan *must* be designed to fit the need.

Fortunately, such a strategy exists. It is known in the fundraising business as the annual fund campaign.

Started in 1890 by Yale University, the annual fund is a program that consistently (annually) solicits gifts from all elements of a constituency.

In 1890, the Yale Alumni Fund raised $11,000. Ninety years later, the program topped $12 million in one year's efforts. Also, by June 1979, a special five-year campaign at Yale raised $374 million.[1] Impressive as these figures are, they do not begin to tell the story. Over the years, and by following Yale's example, colleges and universities across the country have begun their own annual fund programs, and by vigorous and creative effort have made one of the most telling contributions ever to the business of raising funds. John G. Johnson, vice-president for development at Carnegie-Mellon University, insists that it is through annual giving that "the academic community has received an increasing flow of unrestricted dollars accompanied by a genuine spirit of concern on the part of alumni. It is largely through annual giving that our institutions carry on the endless process of educating the educated about education."[2]

As evidence of the impact of annual giving in colleges and universities, the *Chronicle of Higher Education* reported that for the year 1977–78 alone, more than $445 million in gifts was received through annual fund appeals.[3] Considering that this figure applies only to the 1,065 schools reporting, there is evidence enough to say that annual giving is a significant strategy to be considered by an institution or agency seeking dollars. Whether you are working in education, culture, health, welfare, religion, or allied fields, an annual giving campaign can be used successfully to achieve the full potential of an existing program.

THE PHILOSOPHY

In a certain sense, an annual fund campaign is not a campaign at all, but more of a philosophy. This philosophy, simply stated, is that an all-inclusive, coordinated strategy can better concentrate effort and produce results than can a series of special campaigns.

The scenario of annual giving—with minor variations—involves excellent record-keeping; setting goals; establishing an organization; writing a case statement; identifying, evaluating, and cultivating prospects; preparing materials; recruiting volunteers; planning meetings and events; publicizing the campaign; the actual solicitation; receipts and acknowledgments; rewards and recognition; evaluation; and planning for the next year's annual fund drive.

If all of this seems rather formidable, it is because this *is* a major effort. But this is also what fundraising is all about. It is the commitment of time and self, and an understanding of the methods used, that separates the professional from the amateur—the successful fundraiser from the one who just comes close.

TYPES OF GIFTS

Before suggesting methods and techniques important to an annual fund drive, it seems prudent to mention the four tiers of giving (they start at the bottom and work upward).

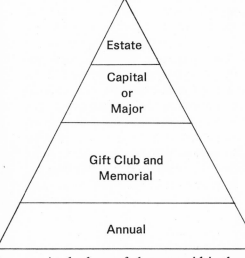

Estate

An even smaller number of donors who provide gifts that generally await future use.

Capital or Major

An even smaller number of donors with sufficient assets to make large gifts.

Gift Club and Memorial

A smaller number of donors belonging to gift clubs. Also donors who make gifts in memorial, in honor, or on special occasions.

Annual

A large number of donors making relatively small gifts.

At the base of the pyramid is the annual gift. This is generally for current year needs, and is the gift for "now"—the immediate annual cash gift for current operations. In this category you will find a large number of donors who make relatively small gifts—gifts of from $10 to $100. If your organization does not handle gift clubs or memorial gifts (the second level), then annual gifts of $250, $500, $1,000, even $5,000 are not unusual, although the number of donors making such gifts will be few.

The second tier—gift club and memorial giving—is there for a good reason. Over the years, experience has dictated that anytime an institution embarks on a quest for funds—whether annual, capital, or both—the success of the venture will *always* depend on the commitments of relatively few donors. Because of this, many nonprofit organizations have instituted gift clubs, which are important tools within the annual fund. Whereas a donor might not give $10 or $25 or $50 annually to an organization, that same donor may give the same organization $100 or $500 or $1,000 annually for the privilege of joining a club from which he or she derives satisfaction (and benefits) from membership.

Memorial gifts come from what might be termed the "never giver." This does not mean that annual givers or club members do not make memorial gifts from time to time. Nevertheless, the majority of gifts in *memorial* (for the deceased) and in *honor* (for the living) come from persons who are not interested in annual giving or club membership. Memorial giving is thus an attractive option to these donors. If your institution is not seeking this type of gift, steps should be taken to do so. Not only will you perform a very valuable service to the donor, you can also add a significant dollar dimension to your annual fund.

The capital or major gift is *sacrificial* giving. This gift is above and beyond the annual or club gift. Often it is a multiyear pledge of a relatively large sum of money for capital needs and special project purposes.

An estate gift, the so-called deferred gift, is generally a lump-sum bequest or trust arrangement that is realized at a future time.

Often the question arises as to what you do with the annual fund during a capital campaign. The answer is simply to conduct them simultaneously—even to the extent, perhaps, of including deferred giving. According to age and assets, a donor can be solicited for an annual gift, or a capital gift, or a deferred gift, or for a gift combining all these categories. In any event, thought should be given before sacrificing annual giving during a capital drive. A better approach is to keep it going by making it a component of the capital campaign. If a person gives $100 annually, consider asking for $1,000 ($100 annual and $900 capital).

Each of these tiers of giving is discussed in greater detail in later chapters.

INITIAL CONSIDERATIONS

Just as no diver should go headfirst into the water without knowing or testing its depth, no development professional should embark on a campaign without first putting together an effective fundraising plan. Here are four considerations to resolve before tackling those other elements that make the program work:

Adequate preparation time. Noah didn't wait to start building the Ark until he felt the first drops of rain. Similarly, you cannot launch your program without time to determine your needs, set your goals, establish an organization, prepare the case for support and the promotional materials, and do all the other tasks that must be done to achieve a reasonable success.

For example, if you plan to run your campaign on a calendar year—January 1–December 31—planning should begin months in advance, perhaps the previous summer. Once undertaken, this means that halfway through the campaign, time must be set aside to plan the next one. Adequate preparation time is a continuing consideration never to be overlooked.

Adequate budget. It takes money to raise money, and there is no point in going into a campaign unless expense dollars are available. The cost of raising money can be very high, especially in the early years. No matter how good you are, you won't raise a great deal at the very beginning. You must generate public sympathy for your organization and your case for support before you can raise more than relatively modest sums.

It may cost you as much to fund the development program as you generate through fundraising in the first year. The second year should see as much as a 50 percent drop in costs. Subsequently, this figure should drop to a range of 10 to 15 cents on the dollar.

In figuring your budget, thousands of dollars can be saved if you use a little persistence and gather advance information. For example, you need to know how many and what kind of promotional pieces to print during the year and when the publications are to appear. Discussion with your printer about types of paper, scheduling, avoiding unusual sizes and shapes, and prudent use of color may bring about some cost-saving alternatives. Other budget items to consider are mailing costs, travel, phone, duplicating, and advertising.

Adequate leadership. Leadership, both lay and professional, is a necessity if you are to have an effective campaign. If it is not available, the campaign usually fails. At best, it can only be partially successful.

It is essential that you have the support of your president or chairman, and that he or she is prepared to assume personal leadership in the cultivation and solicitation of large and important gifts.

In like fashion, your board of trustees or advisors is important to a sound program. Not only should the members be a substantial source of income, but they should have at least one responsibility or assignment in carrying out the campaign to a successful conclusion.

Another prerequisite is the recruitment of strong volunteer leadership to chair and serve as your committees. The most successful fundraising volunteers are those who are or have been involved in your institution. Unless a dedicated corps of volunteers is there to participate, the results will be less than magic.

Finally, you and your staff (if you have one) must devote the required time and energy to the campaign. In this regard, it is not unusual for members of the staff to lack experience or skills. Or if they have too many other duties, they cannot devote the time necessary for good fundraising. There is nothing to be done in this difficulty except to add professionals (if needed) or to free the staff from other tasks so they can devote themselves to the campaign.

Adequate constituency relations. An effective campaign depends on many people being informed of the good work your agency or institution is doing. In short, effective fundraising takes the person that good public relations has cultivated and directs him or her toward the goal of contributing some money and some time to the welfare of your institution.

Sometimes, however, the work, even the good quality of work done by an organization, is unknown to that organization's publics. In this instance, and even though every other element for a fund drive exists, entering the campaign might severely jeopardize its success. The purpose of the campaign is to raise money, and if there is no cultivated constituency prepared to support the drive for funds, the first step should be to carry out a fundamental but carefully planned public relations program.

In and of itself, a good and positive public relations program will not make or break a fundraising effort, but it can certainly create an atmosphere (though not overnight) for raising funds. It is this positive environment that will encourage an institution's publics to support it financially. (See Chapter 7 for a discussion of the public relations campaign.)

Assuming, then, that adequate preparation time has been scheduled, that an adequate budget is approved, that adequate and dedicated leadership is available, and that your institution has an existing constituency that could generate substantial dollar support, you are ready to look at those elements necessary to a successful annual fund campaign.

PLANNING AND ORGANIZATION

Research and Records

If there were no other reason for keeping good records on your alumni, members, parishioners, patients, patrons, and prospects, the annual giving program would provide it. Unfortunately, many institutions fail at adequate record-keeping until the need for funds forces a change. Obviously, you cannot raise funds from lost alumni, unknown parishioners, anonymous prospects, or those about whom you have little information.

As stated elsewhere in this book, how you collect and record donor prospect information is unimportant. That you do it is essential.

Donors. A donor already on the books is your starting point for action. A simple giving record for every contribution should be readily available—whether the donor is an individual, a business, a corporation, a foundation, or whatever.

Usually the front and back of a 5″ × 8″ card is sufficient space to record the necessary data. For quick identification you might

use different-colored cards—blue for major donors, white for corporations and businesses, green for gifts under $100, and so on. Here is the basic information you will want to record:

1. Name, address, business and home telephone numbers. If the gift is from a corporation, business, or foundation, you will want the key contact person and the names of the corporate officers and/or directors.
2. To what did he/she give?
3. How much? On what date?
4. Type of gift (cash, securities, etc.).
5. Was a pledge involved? What are the terms?
6. Areas of donor interest.
7. Giving record by year. How much? When?
8. Connection with the institution; that is, is the donor an alumnus, parent, patient, staff, etc.?
9. How was the appeal made? Personal, mail, phone?
10. Did the donor receive any special giving recognition? What? When?

The next step is to do a *development profile* and maintain it yearly. You will want to record the following information by year:

• How much money have you raised year by year?
• What was the percentage increase or decrease in these years?
• How much of the money was unrestricted?
• What is the giving percentage of your constituency; that is, how many alumni, parents, businesses, corporations, friends, actually give to your institution? How much do they give?
• What is the size of their average gifts?
• What was your budget for the years in question?
• What was the size of your staff?

With this information in good order, attention can be given to identifying, researching, and evaluating key prospects. Keep in mind that donors already on your books also qualify as prospects for larger gifts.

Identifying prospects. Because annual giving is the fundamental element of a fundraising program, the majority of donors will make relatively small gifts to your cause, because you make it clear to the donor that you will be back again next year for a similar gift. In identifying your prospects, however, you cannot afford to spend time researching the ten-dollar donor. The cost will clearly exceed the benefits. As a result, the 80/20 rule should be kept firmly in mind—that 80 percent of the money will come from 20 percent of the donors.

In locating prospects, you should seek names from every possible source. You should review key lists such as country club and golf club directories, United Way contributor lists, *Who's Who*, and chamber of commerce memberships.

Be creative. Check as many sources as you can. Go through the files in your local newspaper's "morgue." Check local property rolls, tax stamps, probate records, and plat books. (Plat books are usually available from property tax offices, real estate and development offices, land contractors, title companies, and so on. They not only give a description of the land with its actual features, they tell who owns the land.) Go through proxy statements, area histories, social registers. Read the obituaries—some of your prospects will die, some will become prospects when members of their family die. Daniel Lynn Conrad of the Institute for Fund Raising suggests you find people who are in the right "time windows"—people who have just received money, whose company has just gone public, who have just been promoted or sold large amounts of real estate, whose health is failing or whose heirs have died, or who are looking for new investments.[4]

Above all, make sure your information is accurate. Don't assume someone can or cannot give because of hearsay. If no information is available on a prospect, don't give up. Keep checking registers and books—even the zip code directory can point you to clusters of wealthy people.

Rating prospects. Once you have your master list in order, you will need committees to go through the rating process. While a single committee can handle the task, a better job can be done with two committees. The first is for general screening of the list. The second refines the names even further. Since all work must be done in strictest confidence, no fanfare should accompany the appointing of these committees.

Committee members should be peers of the prospects they will be ranking—people of approximately equal standing and who belong to the same societal groups as the prospects (for example, bankers rate bankers, lawyers rate lawyers, and so on). The committee as a whole will then know about most of the prospects. Seven to ten committee members are usually sufficient to handle several hundred names an hour, and a session should last no longer than two hours. A single chairman should serve both committees. When the first screening ends, that committee should be thanked and dissolved. The chairman then continues with the second committee. An institutional staff member should always be present both to serve the committee and to keep it on track.

The first level of the rating process is the general screening level. At this session, all you need on your master list are the prospects' names and addresses. Start the session by setting a dollar level, then ask this question about each prospect: If asked by the right person, at the right time, for the right cause, could this prospect make an annual gift of, say, $100?

Ask this question name-by-name, then follow by asking about a $250 gift, $500, $1,000, and so forth to find the correct level. While this session is being conducted, the staff people should be taking notes and assigning the prospect a rating as agreed on by the committee.

Additional information needed during this first screening are answers to questions about the prospect's civic interests, family, and business, as well as who should ask for the gift.

What will finally emerge at the end of this first session is the giving potential of all your prospects. There may be many prospects rated as "unknown" or "don't bother to ask." Nevertheless, they remain prospects as "least likely to contribute," and should be carried forward to the second-level screening. Additionally, you will discover that some prospects will be discounted as annual givers but rated as possible one-time major givers. It is not unusual for a committee to come up with something like this for a prospect: "He's good for $1,000, but I wouldn't ask for that. I'd go for at least $5,000. Get him to kick the program off. If he does, his interests can be cultivated for an annual gift next year."

With such information, you may have prospects for annual gifts and prospects for major gifts. This will put you in good stead when it comes time to put your annual fund committees together and begin the solicitation process.

The second rating session is when you really get down to business. With this new committee it is essential that peers rate. peers —people of one giving level rating others at that same level. The process is followed as in the first screening, a name-by-name review. In addition, you should collect some very specific resource information. Here is a sample of the kind of background data you should be interested in for every prospect:

1. Age—date and place of birth.
2. Education—college or graduate school—class.
3. What is known about spouse? If a wife, maiden name important. Interests, positions held in community activities, business, if any.
4. Names of children and birth dates.
5. Honors and achievements, civic activities, clubs, religious preferences, political activities.
6. Special interests (art, athletics, etc.)
7. Does the prospect know anything about the institution? What does he/she think about it? Any gripes?
8. Who knows the prospect well and could provide further information, perhaps solicit?
9. Can this prospect be considered for a volunteer position?
10. Financial data—estimates of individual or family *annual* income. Additional information for capital purposes about any known securities, stock, partnerships, foundations, real and personal property. Additional information for estate purposes—the value of all assets.

Once this committee finishes its work, it should be dissolved. With the rating profiles in hand, you will have predictive information on:

- Persons who should be asked for an annual gift of $100, $250, $500, etc.
- Persons who should be asked only for a major gift—$1,000, $2,500, $5,000, etc.
- Persons who are likely to contribute, but in a small way—$10, $25, $50.
- Persons who are rated as *least likely* to contribute anything. For this group, a decision will have to be made whether to include them in the solicitation.

You will also have pertinent data about each prospect: age, education, family, business, estimate of annual income, overall wealth, civic and charitable interests, and who should solicit the gift. The more you know about the prospect, the better you can match him or her to someone with similar interests, vocation, attitudes, and so on. Your presentation will thus be more closely tailored to the prospect's own needs and interests.

All information should be summarized on a prospect cultivation form, a sample of which is on page 31.

In asking for and researching background information, collect no more information than you need, keep only the information that can be used, and put it in one place, where it can be easily retrieved. Some basic resources to use when completing prospect identification and research are your local newspaper, *Who's Who in America* and similar reference materials, *Standard and Poor's Register of Corporations, Directors, and Executives,* as well as personal contact and observations.

Finally, in collecting data on alumni, parents, church members, and other "in-house" constituencies, you should consider writing a questionnaire and asking them to supply the needed information. If you decide to go this route (sooner or later you will, if you are serious about raising funds), then the questionnaire should be an attractive piece, modest in length, and designed so as to get answers to questions about age, education, civic membership, children, range of yearly income, what areas of the school, church, etc. the person is interested in, and so forth.

Always give a reason for sending the questionnaire. This adds to the chances of a better-than-average return. You might state that the questionnaire is being sent to collect data on a certain program or to get a profile of the graduates, class by class. In this regard, some opinion questions should be placed in the questionnaire that will give the person an opportunity to state how he/she feels about the growth and development of the institution.

In summary, the task of identifying, screening, and rating prospects and current donors is not an easy one. Nor is it truly scientific, for in the final analysis, only the prospect will determine whether he or she will give, and how much. Nevertheless, without information on a donor's past performance and predictive information as to how a prospect is likely to perform when approached at the right time, by the right person, for the right cause, the

PROSPECT CULTIVATION SUMMARY

Date Prepared _____

1. *Identification*

   Name _____

   Address (home) _____ Telephone _____

   _____

   (business) _____

   _____ Telephone _____

   (business title) _____

2. *Information*

	Birthdate	College	Year Graduated	Religious Affiliation
Prospect				
Spouse				
Family				

   General Remarks:

3. *Interests*

   Religious, cultural, civic, political _____

   _____

   At (your institution) _____

   _____

4. *Involvement* (with your institution)

   Past _____

   Potential _____

   Known well by _____

5. *Gifts*

Date	Amount	Purpose	Potential
_____, 19____	$ _____ for _____		Annual $ _____
_____, 19____	$ _____ for _____		Special $ _____
_____, 19____	$ _____ for _____		Bequest $ _____
_____, 19____	$ _____ for _____		Other $ _____

   Outstanding Pledges:

   _____, 19____ $ _____ for _____

   _____, 19____ $ _____ for _____

   _____, 19____ $ _____ for _____

6. *Who Should Solicit* _____

chances for a successful fund campaign are immeasurably reduced.

Cultivating prospects. The cultivation process begins the moment a prospect is identified. Good research makes cultivation possible. Because prospects must get to know your institution, they should be added to your mailing lists for periodic and systematic contact.

Another cultivation move is to add prospects to your invitation lists. When you have a function reasonable for prospects to attend, invite them. Even if it is nothing more than planting a tree, get them there to watch the hole being dug.

Prospect research and cultivation never end. Because these people are your top 20 percent, go so far as to assign members of your board, and even your president, to the prospects. Give them the background information you have collected on each name, and explain fully the importance of contact and cultivation in preparation for solicitation.

G. T. Smith, president of Chapman College, has put the importance of cultivating prospects into a unique perspective: "Fund raising is frankly more psychological than financial, for the human spirit and its aspirations are our primary concern. If we are successful in expanding the *human* resources of our institutions, the necessary *financial* resources will not be difficult to secure."[5]

Goals and Objectives

Too often, goal-setting ranges from the president walking in one day and saying, "Next year I want one million dollars," to doing an extensive market analysis of the charitable dollar limit of your entire geographical region, and then guessing about how much of it you think you can get.

For an institution to have broad-based giving support, it is essential that the leaders—the president, the trustees or advisors, and representatives from all constituent groups—have a say in establishing the needs and goals of the institution. They must also agree on a plan of action to meet the needs and goals, all within a specified time frame.

The first step is to determine where you are and where you want to go. This study will translate into "needs"—for facilities, personnel, equipment, salaries, expenses, and special funds such as unrestricted money, scholarships, loans, research, and the like. Make sure you are not adopting a "wish list." What you want is a rock bottom "need" list.

With refinement, your needs can be put into dollar figures. These dollars then become "gift opportunities" to which you want the public to respond.

With this information, you now have the beginnings of the case statement (to be discussed later in this chapter), which presents the unique mission of your institution, its needs, and compelling reasons to support it.

Next, a time frame is needed, and with it the amount of money to be raised each year. (Unless you are an established institution with a long track history, it is best to start with a three-year plan: last year, this year, next year.) Whatever time frame you decide on (whether it is a three-year, five-year, or other length plan) it should contain successive yearly goals for the annual fund, and if a capital campaign is needed, those yearly goals as well. You should also note staff and budget needs for each year of the drive.

With such information in hand, you are ready to ask—and answer, we hope—two key questions: "Where is the money to come from?" and "How much can my institution reasonably expect to get?"

If you have followed the procedures discussed previously, this information is already available to you from your development profile, which is the year-by-year review of your institution's gift support. This history of dollars raised and donors categorized by group, dollar amount, and average size of gifts is the best clue you have as to what will happen in the future. In essence, you have a profile of your base support—support that has taken perhaps years to develop and grow. It is reasonable to assume, then, that this base support will not change dramatically unless positive steps are taken by your institution.

You have also identified, researched, and rated your prospects. Some are prospects for annual gifts, others for one-time major gifts, others are rated as "least likely" to give.

The two groups together, donors and prospects, can tell you where you can expect the money to come from, and how much.

Applying what is known as the five-to-one rule (you need $500,000 in potential cash value to actually get $100,000 in gifts), you now have an estimate of how much money you could receive.

To crystallize your efforts, you will want a planning model to put your objectives in perspective. The sample three-year planning model on the next page is a good one.

The Case Statement

In the simplest of terms, the case statement is your institution's sales pitch. It tells your customers (donors and prospects) who you are, what you are trying to do, and why. It is also a good internal document to help you, your board, and your volunteers better focus attention on your group's policies and plans.

It presents the institution's objectives and needs in no-nonsense terms. It states as clearly and as persuasively as possible the reasons a person should invest in your institution, and the benefits that will result. It gives history, purpose, and plans. And it tells how your organization differs from other similar ones.

Without a strong case, you are in trouble. People generally do not make large or continuing gifts to a cause they don't understand. Nor do they give just because they get a tax deduction or simply because you say you need the money. Need it for what? Why? Long-time fundraiser and former college professor Howard R. Mirkin suggests that the reason for support should be broader than the organization—people support causes, programs, and facilities, not institutions.[6]

Think of your case statement as a well-planned, carefully prepared motivational presentation that will impress your prospect. Keep these things in mind:

- Whatever the need, it must be related to the community you serve. This is the first principle of selling. Your approach to the prospect must be in the prospect's interest.
- The need must be real and readily demonstrated. And it must have a sense of urgency—it must be supported *now*.
- The need, even though real and readily demonstrated, must be worth supporting. Donors must be convinced of this or you will likely receive only token support.

PLANNING MODEL

Factors	3 Years Ago	2 Years Ago	Last Year	Goal for Current Year	Goal for Year 2	Goal for Year 3
Total Dollars Raised						
Percentage Increase/Decrease						
Donors Number of alumni giving Number of parents giving Number of friends giving Number of businesses giving etc.						
Average Size of Gift Alumni Parents Friends Businesses etc.						
Special Consideration Past and future gift clubs (by dollar levels) Challenge gifts (amount—who for) Special projects (minicampaigns) Capital campaign (starting when)						
Budget						
Size of Staff						

- You must show that the need cannot be met without your prospect's support; that is, the institution cannot, within itself, meet the need.
- You must be prepared to show exactly how the funds will be spent. If you need to furnish a new hospital wing, tell what items are needed and how much each will cost.

In preparing the case, there is no substitute for thoroughness. While you can possibly do the research, planning, and writing yourself, you should consider using a committee to help in the preparation. Often the members can provide more reasons for confidence in what you are "selling" and the ability to sell it than you can alone.

If you decide to use a committee, then select persons who know the institution and the community. Ask your budget officer, who knows your institution's financial status. Get someone who readily knows the institution's policies and goals. Get representatives from your in-house constituents, such as alumni, parents, staff, and trustees. Appoint a community leader or two—a person or persons who support the work of your institution (or will, after they have heard your story). Also appoint a writer who is closely associated with the institution and skilled not only in what to say, but how to say it.

Only one person should write the actual case document. Possibly you, the development officer, should do the first draft. If you have good writing skills, then you can consider doing the finished product. By and large, however, an experienced writer (your committee member) should do the copy.

Once the case is written, the leaders of your organization should review it to make certain that it is an institutional statement completely acceptable to them. Quite often, case statements, without thorough review, turn out to be an inventory of the writer's pet ideas.

The case statement need not be long or elaborate, although sometimes it is. Say what needs to be said, and say it in simple, brief language that people can understand. Pictures and charts can always be used to advantage in illustrating the copy and tend to make the presentation much more interesting and appealing.

The case should be donor-oriented. Your prospective donor is far more interested in personal benefit than in your institution. As an example, consider the fact that you are reading this book because you suppose that some aspect of your life or job will be affected by something that is said here. If you decide that what we are saying is of no use to you, you will soon put this book aside or begin turning the pages in search of something more useful. In this regard, you are like every prospect who will read your institution's case statement, asking, "What use is this to me?"

Make your appeal, then, from the prospect's point of interest. Show that your institution's needs and wants are a good investment and that by helping your institution, your prospects will help themselves and the communities in which they live and work.

Here is a sample outline that you may want to refer to in putting your case together:

1. What does your organization do? Don't write a history of your institution. Instead, use this opening to tell your prospective donor just what kind of business you are in and the benefits that will result when he or she invests in your institution's future.

   Write from a position of optimism. Your organization is a successful enterprise that has identified some genuine community needs. State these needs and the rationale for the needs. Answer all important potential questions.

   In sum, follow consultant James G. Lord's advice: tell your prospective donor that "we are doing A and B. If we only had X (sigh), then we could also do C, D, and E."[7]

2. How can your prospects help you? If you are trying to sell the idea that you need scholarship money, you aren't selling scholarships, you are selling an opportunity to assist students. Why is this a smart investment for your prospect? Muster arguments that will encourage donors to get involved in helping your institution solve this need. Make your arguments persuasive and compelling, and back them up with proof and demonstration.

   Most donors are naturally cautious, and until statements made to them are convincingly proved, they will remain skeptical. Behind their reluctance to give is the feeling that they should not give their money until reasonably certain that the expenditure is sound. Therefore, whatever the need, whatever it is you are selling, should be packaged with just enough supporting proof to break up the clouds of doubt you will en-

counter. Use statistical data, case histories, personal testimony.
3. What does it cost? If you have prepared your presentation correctly, your prospects know who you are and what you stand for. They know that you provide a real service. They know there is a need to expand this service, and that if it is expanded, they and their communities will benefit. Now you are to tell them how much it costs, and that the price is fair.

Be very specific. Explain your plans for raising the necessary funds. Identify those people in leadership positions who are behind your project. Include the names of the key members on your fundraising team.

Tell your prospects exactly how much money you need, when you need it, and what their investments will accomplish. Show how gifts can be made. (Sometimes this information is not included in the case statement but is reserved for a separate document or booklet that explains how a person can give.)
4. What are the benefits? This is the final step and is essentially one of reconfirming that the donor will be satisfied with the results. Explain what would happen if your organization did not exist. Inspire confidence. Generate enthusiasm. Stimulate acceptance.

What will your case statement look like when it is finished? That depends on your needs and how you intend to solicit the funds. If it is a simple, direct appeal for funds, you might end up with a two-page letter. On the other hand, you might need an eight- to ten-page brochure. Some case statements take the form of a movie or slide presentation, especially when you are appealing to a captive audience. Others combine the written with the visual. It all depends on your needs and is something you and your committee must determine.

While it may seem redundant to speak again of preparation, a few additional thoughts are warranted.

In fundraising, there is no such thing as writing a case statement to appeal to pedestrians on a busy street. A pedestrian on a busy street is not a prospect, though he or she is a candidate for a public relations program that could generate some degree of interest in your institution. Thus all your fundraising efforts should be directed toward persons who already have some interest in your institution.

Since all your prospects will not have the same degree of interest and financial ability, you may want to develop several case statements to appeal to different groups of prospects. For example, if your institution is a university, the type of case statement you would prepare for alumni would be quite different from one you would write for the general community.

With alumni, you can expect to be dealing with an audience already sympathetic to your cause. This fact alone enables you to come directly to the point of stating the needs of the university, the plan to meet those needs, and how alumni can help.

For members of the community you will have to go into more detail, particularly pertaining to needs and plans. Your copy will have to be much more motivational. You will need to emphasize the economic, educational, and cultural advantages that your institution brings to the community.

Unfortunately, there is no ready solution to the problem of adapting your case statement to different audiences. Every effort means compromise, but you have a choice about the kinds of compromises to make. In this respect, you can more readily understand why records are so important, why donor and prospect research are so vital. With good records and research in front of you, audience analysis becomes the art of making intelligent decisions. You may provide a little something for everyone—an approach that politicians have to take—or you may direct your case statement to a particular group. In the final analysis, the choice becomes one of taking a good look at the different publics you serve and then asking two questions about each: *How much does this constituency know about my institution? How much does this constituency care about my institution?* How your donors and prospects stand in relation to these questions will tell you whether to go with one case statement or several, and how the case or cases should be written. Whatever strategy you choose, the most important thing is to know that you have a choice. The next important thing is to make that choice and not let your case statement be a matter of chance.

The Volunteer Organization: Recruitment and Training

Volunteers are the backbone of most nonprofit organizations. They sense community impulses, interpret institutional policy, and take on important assignments on behalf of the staff and chief executive of the institution. It is critical that their confidence be maintained, that their talents be effectively used, and that they be compensated (graciously thanked) for contributing to a worthwhile cause.

In recruiting your volunteer leadership, the first phase is to plan the basic campaign structure. At the very top of the organization is the annual fund chairman. Sometimes this position is held by a steering committee. Regardless, there should be *one person* who will make it all happen.

Search diligently for the best possible person for this position. Ideally, you should be looking for an individual with the following qualifications:

- A very successful business executive, who is widely known and admired in the community.
- A person who has done *important* volunteer work, who has "experience in the trenches," and who accepts great challenges.
- A person with a strong commitment to your institution and to achieving objectives.
- A person capable of making a large gift and also soliciting large gifts.
- A person who is inspired and who can help recruit and inspire other key volunteers.

Conduct your search in secret, or at least with as little fanfare as possible. Should the word get out that you are recruiting specific people for this top leadership post, and are being turned down, you will have great difficulty in completing the task.

When asking your top choice to take the job, don't do it by letter or phone. Instead, your president and chairman of the board should invite the prospect in person. They should know enough not to be discouraged if the prospect is reluctant to take the job. At the same time, under no circumstances should they do any arm-twisting or minimize the amount of work to be done. Serving as annual fund chairman takes effort, time, money, and commitment. That should be made clear from the very start.

Once your top choice accepts, you should immediately meet with him or her and set the plans for the campaign. The chairman should become involved in planning each step of the drive. In short, he or she should become as acquainted with the objectives and needs of the campaign as you are.

If you are going to have a total solicitation program—including perhaps trustees, gift club members, business and industry, alumni —you will need a chairman or captain for each "public" to be solicited. Your annual fund chairman should help in recruiting these volunteers. Here again, you must proceed cautiously in publicizing your "candidates" for each committee chair. And again you are looking for people available and willing to take part in your program—people who have good contacts with potential donors and important groups. Once these chairmen or captains are recruited, they, in turn, will help recruit the volunteers needed for their area of responsibility.

In determining how many volunteers are needed to complete your organizational structure, keep in mind that you should ask a worker to contact no more than five or six prospects. If you require more than this from your volunteer, the chances are he or she will bail out as soon as possible.

With your organization complete, the next step is to train your volunteers. Never simply assign jobs. If you expect volunteers to produce results, then you must provide some job training. Not only will this inspire and build confidence in your volunteers so that they will do a better job, but the training sessions will help you identify future candidates for leadership roles. In addition, one well-trained volunteer can help you train others, thus diminishing your workload.

How extensive your training sessions should be depends on how much money you need to raise, the complexity of your plans to raise it, the number of volunteers you have, their knowledge and experience of your institution, and what kinds of experience they have had in raising money. Such training sessions could run from one day to several days. Make your training sessions more or less like seminars in which full and open discussion can take place. Avoid turning these sessions into lectures, with you as the "teacher" standing in front of the "class" doling out great chunks of wisdom.

In training your volunteers, your first objective is to give them all the information they need to accomplish the task. This information is readily available to you because you have spent considerable time compiling it. It is what we have previously discussed—

your lists of donors and prospects and your case statement. Your second objective is to convincingly show your workers that you and your staff are behind them all the way, and are readily available for advice and help.

The training sessions should provide your volunteers with the following opportunities:

- To meet and know each other so as to work and win as a team.
- To hear the chief executive officer and others discuss the "state of the institution"—its purposes, programs, and policies.
- To fully understand the case statement—the goals, plans, and procedures; the needs of the institution and why these needs *must* be met.
- To understand the techniques to be used in soliciting gifts.
- To review the timing of the campaign, the materials to be used, pledge cards, and all reporting dates, deadlines, and procedures.

Once recruited and trained, volunteers should be provided with a volunteer solicitor's kit or notebook. Included will be all necessary background information, copies of the case statement, questions most likely to be raised by the prospects and appropriate answers, and information about gifts and tax deductions.

Finally, the volunteers will be given pledge cards for the prospects to be solicited. Generally, each team captain or committee chairman will make these assignments and distribute the cards. The pledge card or contribution form is a simple document that gives the donor's name and address, suggested gift amounts, plus a blank line for "other" amounts not suggested. If a pledge is intended, there is a space to note the amount and when the donor expects to complete the commitment. The pledge card is generally left with the donor by the volunteer solicitor, or, if used in a direct mail piece, it is enclosed with the appeal. A return envelope, preaddressed to the institution, is always included. Some organizations stamp the return envelopes; some do not. This is a decision you must make, depending on your budget. (See the case study examples included in this book for sample pledge cards.)

Thus, to establish a volunteer program, you must carefully identify volunteers, recruit, train, and provide them with assistance when and wherever needed. But there is one more fundamental step to take if you hope to keep your volunteer program alive from year to year. You must say thank you.

Like anyone else, volunteers need to be thanked for the job they do. Even if they fail, they still need that good word of appreciation. Recognition comes in many forms. A word of thanks from you, the chief development officer, a letter from your president or board chairman—these are a must. If you can afford it, consider an award on the order of a plaque, certificate, or book. It does not have to be expensive. Whatever you decide, it will mean a lot to your volunteer. Usually, he or she will work for you again next year.

To conclude this section, here are some tips to help you manage your volunteer labor force:

1. Stay in contact with your volunteers. Periodic progress reports should be the rule. If a problem develops, take time immediately to review and resolve the problem.
2. Do not call meetings simply to call meetings. Your volunteers' time is important. Use it wisely.
3. If a volunteer wants to quit the team, accept the resignation if it is legitimate. Replace him or her with someone else.
4. If you have a volunteer who is not pulling with the team, then you should consult with the team captain and the annual fund chairman about approaching this member. A friendly but frank conversation with the volunteer will usually resolve the difficulty. He or she will either resign or enter into the spirit and need of the campaign. The purpose of this meeting is to clear the air.
5. Always make your volunteers feel that they are an important part of the effort. They are.

In dealing with volunteers, who hold the key to your campaign's success in their effort, keep in mind the words of James F. Oates, retired chairman of Equitable Life who headed Princeton's $53-million campaign in the 1950s: the only attitude with which trustees had a right to go into a fundraising campaign, he insisted, was one that regarded failure as unthinkable.[8]

Finally, as a professional staff person, you should remember that your primary task is to help others lead and not do the leading yourself. Your job is to attend to details and to provide assistance and advice when it can be meaningful and helpful. When failure comes, and it will sometimes, acknowledge it but don't accept it. It's all a part of the day's work.

CAMPAIGN TECHNIQUES

Thus far our discussion has centered on the decisive amount of work that must be done before the public even hears that you plan to raise funds. Admittedly, the planning process is rigorous and not particularly exciting. But rigorous or not, it is work that must *precede* any actual solicitation of funds. The function of planning is not an end in itself. Its overriding purpose is the development of a course or courses of action that are realistic, attainable, and productive.

The success of a fundraising campaign depends on whether an organization can develop an adequate fundraising strategy. That strategy involves, foremost, the setting of goals and objectives, and the recruitment and organization of capable volunteers. Also required is the effective use of the following key techniques, which have consistently aided institutions in getting more gifts from donors and prospects.

Matching Gifts by Employees

Historically this kind of support has been the exclusive province of four-year colleges and universities. Now, however, some corporations will match gifts to hospitals, art groups, and the public media as well. A corporation with a matching gift program will match the contribution of its employees dollar-for-dollar up to a set figure; some companies will more than match them.

According to the Council for the Advancement and Support of Education (CASE), over 800 corporations now have some sort of matching gifts program. CASE publishes a handbook, *Matching Gift Details*, that gives the specifics for all matching gift corporations, including whether your institution qualifies for a gift, the maximum amount you may receive for a gift, and how and where to go about getting the corporate match.

A matching gifts program is an effective and easy way to stimulate gifts. If you purchase the CASE leaflet *Double Your Dollar*, and include it in at least one of your direct mail pieces, you will have an effective campaign reminder to alumni, parents, and friends that their gifts to your institution may be matched, if they work for a matching gift corporation. Many companies also match gifts from retirees and spouses.

Challenge Gifts

A challenge program makes a significant appeal to all constituencies, and adds another dimension to annual giving. Donors can be challenged at any time, provided you do not overdo the idea. However, experience teaches that the best time to issue a challenge is when annual giving has reached a plateau or is declining.

Russell V. Kohr of Kalamazoo College points out that challenge gifts offer three specific benefits: they establish a timetable, promote in-house campaigns of corporations with matching gift programs, and provide you with the opportunity to ask for gifts now from prospects who have indicated that your organization is in their wills. On the other hand there are drawbacks—the challenge must be a true one or it will lose its potency; it must be significant enough to attract attention; if a building is to be named for the challenger, the challenge must cover a significant part of the building's costs; and the challenge might persuade donors to make token gifts instead of the larger gifts they might make on their own.[9]

The challenge may be issued in many different ways—dollar-for-dollar, double-the-dollar, or whatever appeals to the challenger. Sometimes the challenge donor (with advice from you as to where the challenge is needed) will match only new gifts or increased gifts.

Challenges come from the following sources:

- Foundations often look favorably on proposals requesting a challenge grant. The Ford Foundation and Kresge are examples.
- The United States Government makes challenge offers. The National Endowment for the Humanities is an excellent source.
- Boards of trustees, directors, or advisors often challenge other constituencies.
- A distinguished alumnus or friend of the institution might issue a challenge. Sometimes several individuals band together in

issuing a challenge. Occasionally, the donor or donors wish to remain anonymous.

There are many ways to set up a challenge gift program. At the University of Chicago, a husband and wife team pledged $1 million to match new or increased gifts in 1975 (the goal was exceeded by more than 50 percent). A Wofford College trustee gave $1,000 for each percentage point of increase in annual giving (it went from 12 percent to more than 74 percent during his challenge period!). Each member of a challenge club at Nebraska Wesleyan University pledged $10 for every percentage point of increase over the previous record (the percentage went from 15 to 33). An anonymous Georgia Tech donor offered to match all new gifts and increases up to $100,000 ($138,000 in new gifts was received). A University of Pennsylvania donor matched each graduate's increase over his or her largest gift in the past 12 years (annual giving increased $600,000 that year). Many other plans are used, and most fundraisers report that even when the challenge ends, giving often continues at a higher level than before the challenge program began.[10]

How do you get a challenge gift? You go and ask for it. But the asking is much different than when seeking an outright gift.

Once you have identified those donors with the potential of making a challenge gift, your approach is specifically why you need the money, how much is needed, and how you would like the challenge issued—dollar-for-dollar, new gifts only, or some other approach. The bottom line is that you are not asking for any money up front. Only if and when the challenge is met will your donor be expected to give the amount agreed upon.

Any organization should be honored to receive a challenge gift, and as much promotion as possible should accompany the announcement. A brochure is an excellent way to highlight all the details and conditions of the challenge, including the deadline. A phonothon is also an ideal way to promote a challenge gift. Conditions can be easily explained, and specific questions readily answered.

The prompt and enthusiastic reporting of the results of a challenge is a must. If a challenge lags or is almost within reach, announcements to this effect inspire additional gifts.

Best of all, a successful challenge appeal raises a donor's

sights. In the years following, most will continue giving at the higher level.

Gift Clubs

A full discussion of gift clubs is found in the next chapter. For our purposes here, it is useful to point out that they are an excellent way to identify, attract, and gain lasting commitment from a good many donors. For many nonprofit organizations, the continued cultivation of major donors depends upon gift clubs.

Once the purpose, dollar level, constituency, and leadership of a gift club have been identified, the basic solicitation techniques are used. They are the tried-and-true methods that apply to all fundraising programs. They include high-quality, fully personalized invitations, active personal solicitation by the best qualified people, direct mail appeals, telephone follow-ups, and continuity. Also, the proper recognition of the gift club member is a major consideration. While recognition can take many forms, it should always be timely, in good taste, meaningful to the donor, and in proper relationship to the importance of the gift.

Reunion Giving

Used primarily by educational institutions, a reunion celebration is an excellent device for any organization that can muster a relatively large number of persons into a class. Once this is done, the necessary planning for a 5-, 10-, 15-, 20-, or 25-year reunion can begin.

The organization structure is really a minicampaign. A chairman or steering committee is needed, with captains for each division, such as special and major gifts. Decisions must be made as to whether gifts asked for will be restricted to some particular project, or if they will be unrestricted. If restricted, then several needs should be presented to the reunion class for their opinions. Whatever is decided, a class goal should be set, a scale of giving worked out, volunteers recruited from the class itself, and a time schedule provided for making the gifts. Use personal solicitation, direct mail, and the telephone in contacting the class. It is vitally important that your volunteers be provided with accurate background information on their classmates.

The best years for holding reunions have been found to be the tenth and twenty-fifth. Since a reunion takes a tremendous amount of staff energy and time, advance planning is essential. Committee organization should be in place as early as a year to a year and a half in advance of the actual reunion. This much time is needed to recruit the necessary class volunteers, set the events program, such as tours, dinners, and lectures, formulate the goal, and design and print the campaign literature.

Reunions are very special events and are excellent public relations tools. Make the most of any and every reunion-giving success story. Do everything possible to get people back to your organization for a visit. Even if many do not give, once they come "back to the campus," they tend to give later.

Lybunts and Sybunts (and Locusts)

A lybunt is a donor who gave Last Year But Unfortunately Not This year. A sybunt is a donor who gave Some Year But Unfortunately Not This year. A locust gives every seven years. Since the objective is to keep donors giving year after year, what to do about lybunts, sybunts, and the others always poses a problem. Estimates hold that 15 to 25 percent of the donors who gave last year will not give this year. Thus the development officer must get that many new donors, year after year, just to stay even. But is this progress?

Perhaps the best way to deal with the doubtful donor is to examine the three prime reasons people give one year but not the next, and then suggest an approach that might diminish the problem.

1. It may be that your lybunts and sybunts are one-time givers. This is not unusual. Some people prefer to spread their gifts around—one year to this organization, the next year to another, and so on. If this is so, accept the fact and move on.

2. It may be that they feel their gift really doesn't make any difference. The $10- to $25-donor often thinks this. The only answer is constant assurance that this is not true. Never, never forget a donor to your organization. Always look for ways to acknowledge and publicize gifts. You can never express too much appreciation.

3. It may be that they suffer the same malady that we do—they

are procrastinators. How do you pay your bills? Probably you first pay those that must be paid. The rest you put in order of importance and pay as long as the money lasts. When the money runs out, you put them off until next month, and then the next month, until finally you put them off permanently.

So what can be done about our cousin procrastinators? For every lybunt and sybunt who gives $500 or more, make a personal visit. Nothing else will do. Follow this visit with a thank-you letter.

For donors under $500, use the telephone. Make it a campaign. It will not be that expensive because your constituency is small, relatively speaking. A good time to telephone is just before you start your annual drive for funds or just before you end your annual drive. For example, if you receive no gift in 1982, call just before the end of the 1982 campaign or right at the beginning of the 1983 campaign. With success, and you will enjoy some, you can start off the 1983 campaign with a nice increase. Do the same for the 1984 campaign.

There is nothing wrong, of course, with using direct mail. However, since your prospect has not responded to direct mail in the past year or more, forego this method in favor of the personal visit and the telephone.

Corporate Support

Among the growing contributors to nonprofit organizations in the 1980s are corporations and big businesses. Every charitable organization can find an office (if only a branch office in the smaller towns) of a major American corporation or business. Educational institutions have long known the value of courting their support.

You can usually predict the chances of success in obtaining corporate gifts by asking some basic questions about the corporation, your organization, and your community: Is the organization within the geographical area of the corporation's area of interest? Does the company have a history of making charitable gifts? Are there relationships between your organization and the company (e.g., do you educate their employees, offer services for their families, maintain facilities for their use?). Do you have board contacts with the company's top executives?[11]

Robert L. Graze of the Independent College Funds of America told a fundraising conference several years ago that there were four main parts to a successful corporate appeal: You must present a convincing case that is balanced by reasoned optimism, tailored to the contributor, and whittled to the shortest effective length. He adds the importance of the "three G's" in corporate calls—get in, get the order, and get out.[12]

The interest of America's corporations in making their communities better places to live and work has helped produce significant funding for many charitable organizations. Because of the business background of many executives, their busy schedules, and their wide interests, you need to approach a corporation much as you do a foundation. But the general annual fund guidelines remain the same. Build your case. Research your prospects and match your case to their interests. Cultivate the corporations and remember their needs. Ask for the gift and show your appreciation when you get it. Consider that a 1980 report from the Clearinghouse on Corporate Social Responsibility, which gave information on 147 life and health insurance companies and their support of social programs and activities, reported more than $2 billion in "social investments." One main theme emerged from their giving interests: "Our feelings about company contributions," one company reported, "are to know the people involved and to be a part of what they are doing rather than just sending out a check."[13]

Finally, keep in mind the words of James A. Avery of Humble Oil and Refining, who offered some thought on corporate solicitation: "Fundraisers should not forget the importance of the word 'benefit' to the companies that give. Many donations made by corporations are funds donated because the corporations are getting something in return for this gift—buying a service or community atmosphere or improving an image. Thus corporate philanthropy is an *investment* of corporate funds, not a giving of them."[14]

Federated Fundraising

In federated campaigns several organizations join together to conduct a campaign and share the proceeds. The United Way, Community Chest, and other joint efforts have provided for the needs of many community organizations. Since local situations differ, you may want to consider carefully whether you wish to get involved in a federated effort.

There are some distinct benefits of these campaigns, including the coordination of solicitation, so that major donors can give one substantial gift instead of being asked to give to many organizations; costs are lower since they are shared and your work is not as likely to keep duplicating someone else's efforts; the top fundraisers in your community can work for everyone's needs; all groups, regardless of their size, can receive funds from these coordinated efforts, and you will need to have fewer volunteers and less effort from your own organization. On the other hand, be aware of some drawbacks, including the fact that *your* big donors are now making gifts that will be shared; your needs will be just a part of the total effort, thus reducing your own case statement; the organization of the campaign sets the budgets and payments, and has the control over the campaign and funds; your staff and volunteers will probably not be as committed as if it were your own campaign; and your other fundraising drives may now be more restricted because federated drives typically replace all other campaigns during the year.

In selecting one or more of the techniques or strategies previously discussed, every effort should be made to identify and use only those that have the greatest potential for success, given the climate of the community and availability of resources. For example, do not use the Reunion Giving idea unless reasonably assured that a good portion of your constituency can be targeted into a class or classes appropriate for the amount of time and effort that must be expended.

Once all the mechanics of the campaign are in place, there remain only three basic ways to approach donors: personal contact, direct mail, and the telephone. Since separate chapters are reserved for the discussion of direct mailing and phonothons, we will concentrate here on face-to-face fundraising.

Person-to-Person Solicitation

The best way to raise money is to ask for it, and the best method to use is person-to-person, eyeball-to-eyeball contact. Unfortunately, this "first principle" is often neglected by beginning (and even professional) fundraisers.

Many reasons are offered for this failing: bad weather, aches and pains, too much to do at the office, yesterday's failures, or even yesterday's big success—all these and dozens of other excuses can convince a soft fundraiser that this is not the day to make personal calls.

What happens? The fundraiser lets down and loses momentum. The next time he or she decides to go out, it's harder to get started, and much harder to keep going. It's also much easier to lay off another day, and harder still to "crank it up" again.

The biggest weakness in not making personal solicitation calls is the alibiing about why it shouldn't or can't be done. Don't make excuses. The truth, unvarnished and without reservation, is that substantial gifts come from making personal calls.

H. Perk Robins of the University of Georgia advises solicitors to call on the best prospects first—they will help set the pace of the campaign and strengthen the volunteer's confidence. He adds that the best way to use the telephone in a personal solicitation campaign is not to touch it.[15]

Professional fundraisers believe that if the constituents are close by, you should personally approach, if at all possible, anyone capable of giving $100 or more. Depending on the size of your constituency, you may have to set a higher figure. Regardless, take every opportunity available to personally call on your donors and prospects. It is the best way of all to let someone know how important he or she is to your organization and how meaningful the gifts.

Lynda Boyer of UCLA says that fundraising is really just like any type of sales job—you are selling your institution and yourself. She advises you to ascertain your group's particular strengths and unique qualities, and use these in your presentation. And when all else fails, use peer pressure. Tell the prospect how many others in his or her profession have given, and how much. Many businesses and professions are highly competitive, and donors may be more likely to give if they know a competing firm has also given.[16]

For the volunteer who is apprehensive, even fearful, about his or her ability to call on donors and prospects successfully, the following encouraging thoughts may prove helpful.

Keep the right mental attitude. We often hear that "we are what we eat." To that we should add, "we are what we believe," or "we raise what we ask for." Fundraising is the job of stimulating people to give. Therefore, any letdown in energy, enthusiasm, or optimism is certain to spell defeat. Never allow refusals or a series of opposing ideas to stack up in your mind until you become doubtful of your ability. The greatest single ingredient for calling on donors and prospects is enthusiasm. Constant vigilance over this factor is necessary to keep defeatism out.

Be prepared. This is not only the simple and sound motto for the Boy Scouts, it should be yours as well. A well-planned call, like a well-organized trip, should be carefully prepared. It calls for a thorough knowedge of your institution's needs and your prospect's ability to give, so that your confidence and sincerity will impress your prospect.

If you are in the habit of calling on donors and prospects cold, with little other thought in mind than that by the law of averages you will eventually get a good percentage of them to give, you are wasting time and energy. But thorough preparation before the call will give you something concrete to present and will result in increased gifts.

Approach every prospect from his or her interest. There is no good reason why prospects should give you money just because you want them to. There is much greater likelihood of their doing so when they see a personal benefit in making a gift. Talk about ways to meet "opportunities" rather than "needs." With experience, you will be able to sense the right approach for the prospect on each occasion—just how to fit your need to the prospect's need. Once you have your prospect's interest, you are well on your way to creative conviction. This atmosphere of conviction results in gifts.

More often than not, a fundraiser will run into the staller—a person inclined to hesitate or put off. This is no reason to panic or become discouraged and give up. Virtually every person in the world is indecisive at times. There can be a hundred reasons why a prospect wants to put off making a gift. The fact that he hasn't voiced a definite "no" indicates that he is at least partially sold.

Capitalize on this opportunity and *carefully* ask "Why?" If the reason given is lack of immediate funds, it is then possible to arrange for a pledge payable at a more convenient time, when your prospect will feel less strapped for money.

In any event, don't let the stallers stop you. Work in their interest for your interest.

Give your prospect a chance to talk. The most unconvincing fundraiser in the world is the one who won't stop talking. To talk on and on after the presentation has been made is the best way to lose a gift. No prospect will interrupt to say, "You can stop now, I'm sold." There must be occasional moments of silence to give the prospect a turn. This puts everything squarely up to the prospect, who now has to do something. Usually, he or she will throw up a protective armor of resistances. Meet them head-on, courteously, showing respect for each one. Just because a prospect offers objections—even criticisms—doesn't mean he will not make a gift. It could mean that he wants to hear your answer to his every negative thought.

When this occurs, don't reply in haste. A fast, snappy reply could give your prospect the idea that you are a "know-it-all." Instead, take it easy. Ponder a moment or two, then give a courteous, intelligent answer. Do not talk on and on. Spend no more than thirty seconds in answering the resistance. Once it is disposed of, focus your prospect's attention on a positive reason for making a gift that has nothing to do with his or her objections. This takes your prospect one step closer to making the gift.

Develop a thick skin. Not every prospect will have a happy and courteous disposition—depend on it. You will meet grouches, tough talkers, and short-tempered gorillas. Do not be offended or allow them to rub you the wrong way. Maybe they've had a bad night, or a hard day, or are simply testing you to see if you can take it. Almost never does the ranting, raving, sarcastic, and coldly indifferent type of prospect mean anything personal toward you. Therefore, keep your tongue and your patience in check. Hold your composure and soon your testy prospect will begin to calm down—if not on this visit, then on the next one. And there should always be a next one.

By so doing, you will eventually win the prospect's good will, and with it a relationship that results in a gift.

Put a little romance into your presentation. "Just the facts, ma'am," may have been all right for Jack Webb, but cold reasoning and facts do not always appeal to donors and prospects. Most of them want a little romance. In fact, it can be the best part of your call, if you will provide it.

When presenting your need for funds for your project, tell about the struggle to get where you are. Tell about the men and women who dreamed the dream, who sacrificed to see it come to reality. Tell about the lives that will be touched and made better because of its acceptance. Romance the idea, the project, the need. It may be the old appeal to a person's better nature, but it's a language all of us listen to and understand. Present the facts—yes. But sweeten them with a little romance.

Fundraising consultant Arthur Frantzreb says that personal solicitation involves three basic elements—the introduction (to establish common ground between you and the prospect), the argument (to inculcate sympathetic interests in the satisfaction of organizational needs and gift opportunities), and the summation (when you present specific gift ranges, opportunities, and a description of the gift's impact). Start with the strongest argument and proceed with logical reasoning.

Frantzreb advises you to listen and "let the prospect spin his or her own dream"; it is far more important to know when to close than when to begin. When the time arrives, prepare to leave.[17]

THE POST-CAMPAIGN

At its most basic, fundraising comes down to two fundamental questions: how do you start prospects giving, and how do you continue that giving? The answer to the first question is the basis for the material covered so far in this chapter. In response to the second question, we come to the post-campaign—equally as important as any other part of your entire program.

The post-campaign calls for a record system that will provide complete and accurate information—address changes, addition of names, receiving, recording, acknowledging, and reporting of gifts. There must be constant updating of files. A card must be made for every new donation and corrected for every repeat gift. Included must be the donor's name and preferred mailing address, company and position, date of contribution, and all other actions that transpire, such as the date of the thank-you letter.

Unless this record system is put in place and maintained, next year's campaign will be almost impossible to launch.

Acknowledge All Gifts and Pledges

When a person makes a gift, he or she wants to know that it arrived. You need to acknowledge its arrival promptly if you want the giver to contribute next year.

All gifts, regardless of size, should receive an official receipt. The receipt says that you care enough to acknowledge the gift officially and also indicates your business efficiency—an important consideration to the donor.

Make every effort to receipt the gift officially the day it is received. Generally, this is not difficult. During a campaign, however, when the number of gifts increase dramatically, it is still important to make that extra effort and receipt all gifts the day received. Each gift is from an *individual*, and it is the individual who must be recognized.

Always send receipts that are attractive and typed without errors (no strikeovers).

Like gifts, every pledge should be promptly acknowledged (no receipt at this point) with all the terms noted. A letter is sufficient.

When the time comes for the donor to fulfill a pledge, a pledge reminder should be sent. Do not make it read like a military order. A warm, courteous "This is to remind you . . ." is sufficient. Assure the donor that the gift is important, and that it does make a difference. Thank the donor graciously. Enclose a return envelope.

In case of lapsed pledges, which are particularly common with small pledges, send a "checkup on your pledge reminder." You have sent a reminder, now send a "checkup" letter. Ask if a mistake has been made. Did we forget to bill you? Did something happen to the mail? Always include a return envelope.

Donors set strange pledge times. Some say they will pay on the twentieth of a certain month (maybe after their tax time). Others want to be billed in six months. Still others make their pledge that day, but say they will pay every two weeks or every two months. Don't be surprised at any time they set to honor their pledge. Also, do not expect donors to remember. They expect you to remind them.

Partially in response to this situation, many charitable organizations are turning to preauthorized payments—checks approved by the donor in advance and cashed on a regular basis. Scott Van Batenburg of the Hartford National Bank and Trust Company notes that such groups as Yale University, the Republican National Committee, and the National Rifle Association are all using preauthorized payments in their fundraising efforts. It began in the early 1970s when a group of Boston College alumni wanted to set up a system so that graduates could automatically contribute to the annual fund on a monthly basis.[18] You might want to check with your local banks to see if they can help you set up a similar program for your donors.

Thank Each Donor Promptly

An official receipt is not sufficient appreciation for the gift. Many organizations use printed thank-you forms. This is acceptable, except for first-time contributors and other special cases. Every first-time contributor, regardless of the size of the gift, rates a special, personalized letter from the head of the institution. In addition, if the gift is restricted to a need or project headed by another person, that other person should also write and thank the donor for the gift.

If a contributor increases his or her gift, this rates a special letter acknowledging the increase. Finally, every major gift is to be acknowledged by a letter from the head of the institution. This is usually done with the $100-and-up gift.

As an added touch of appreciation, it is a good idea to set up a system that enables you at a later time to send another thank-you letter, reporting on what was done with the donor's money. Do this any time you can.

One more suggestion: since everyone checks his or her bank statement every month, get a rubber stamp made up. The stamp should say something like "Thanks again for your gift to (organization)." The letters should be fairly large. Stamp the message on the front of every check. When the donor reviews the bank statement, there is an additional thank-you for the gift. The Purdue Alumni Foundation, for example, stamps a bright red "Purdue Thanks You" across the face of each check it receives. Donors report that it makes the job of sorting through the month's canceled checks a bit more pleasant.

Increase the Donor's Interest in Your Institution

It is a fundamental truth in fundraising that a person interested in an organization is more than likely to contribute to its cause provided the cause is just. Interest stems from knowledge; therefore, anything you can do to increase a donor's knowledge about your organization will pay off.

Put the donor on your mailing list. Do not bombard him or her with material, but judiciously send newsletters, magazines, press releases, progress reports, and article reprints. Send invitations to lectures, talks, and open houses. The result will be increased interest and, it is hoped, a willingness to contribute more.

Jon Cosovich of Stanford University knows that happy donors are the best prospects for more gifts in the future. Stanford holds a number of activities for donors, including receptions and seminars, special events and exhibitions, football lunches, musicales, appointments to advisory boards and committees, and direct involvement in helping solicit gifts from their peers. For gifts related to specific academic areas, Stanford has the faculty member in charge of that area or department maintain regular contact with the donor; information on the faculty member's awards and honors is sent to the donor; dinners with the faculty are hosted by the president, and announcements of gifts and follow-up results are sent to the media, published in special books, and promoted by university publications.[19]

Return a Gift for a Gift

Depending on the size of the gift, send an appropriate gift in return. For gifts of $1 to $100, send something inexpensive—a decal, bookmarker, wallet calendar card, or certificate of appreciation. For larger contributors, present larger gifts. If a donor builds you a building, name it after her. If another donor furnishes a room, put up a plaque in his honor.

Most fundraisers advise spending between 1 and 3 percent of the contribution on a gift for the donor. This means you can purchase awards or plaques costing between $10 and $30 for a $1,000 donor, and spend $1 to $3 for a $100 donor.

Publicize the Donor's Generosity

Some donors wish to remain anonymous or do not like publicity; find out first. But most constituents like to see their names in print. If the gift is relatively large, hold a check presentation ceremony. Try for media coverage. If that is not possible, cover the event in your house and community publications. For all gifts, large and small, consider an honor roll or president's report.

The annual report tells your contributors what you did with their money. It should be brief and more statistical than subjective. In preparing the report, select only the high spots of your year's work. Use pictures and pie and bar graphs to break up the monotony of the text and list of names.

Include in your honor roll:

• An opening message from the head of your organization, expressing appreciation to all donors and including the "state of the institution" report.
• Messages from other key supporters—for example, the alumni association president, the chairman of your board of trustees, or the chairman of the annual fund.
• A listing of all donors—alumni and friends.
• A listing of all donors by gift clubs.
• A listing of matching gift companies.

The printing of the honor roll can be as elaborate and expensive as your budget will allow. Some organizations use newsprint to keep the cost down.

Prior to distributing the honor roll to your constituents, you might consider using the piece as a clean-up before the fiscal year ends. This is accomplished by sending constituents a "printer's copy" for proofreading and approval of the listing; this reminds those whose names are missing to send a gift.

An honor roll is an effective tool in keeping a constituency informed of an organization's goals, disappointments, and successes,

and in promoting larger gifts and renewals plus increased participation. Every organization, if at all possible, should have such
a publication and it should contain the listing of donors' names.

Hold a Wrap-Up Meeting

A retreat, if you can manage it, is a good idea. Its purpose is to
evaluate the past year's program and to make recommendations
for the coming year. Those who should attend are the development
staff, the president of the institution, representatives or the executive committee of the board of trustees, and key volunteers of the
annual giving program.

Every aspect of the campaign is reviewed: budget, mailings,
publicity, phonothon, what was good, what was bad, where money
was wasted, where money was well spent. Review every mailing
piece and every letter: which ones worked best? what ages responded best to a particular mailing? which months were most
productive? which areas of constituency concentration were the
most fruitful? Review all volunteers to determine who should be
asked to serve again and who should not.

At the conclusion of the meeting it is advisable to produce a
scrapbook of the campaign. Every office needs this if only as a
reference in future years.

Include in the scrapbook complete examples of your publicity
and mailings. Also include a detailed budget. Show expenditures
for every aspect of the campaign.

By following the six basic suggestions for handling the post-
campaign, ample opportunities exist for encouraging donors to
continue giving year after year. One question, however, often
troubles fundraisers: what should be done about a gift that
is unacceptable?

John Kemeny, formerly of Dartmouth College, suggests, "A
fund raiser does not just raise money for the institution, but raises
money for something the institution needs and wants." He explains
that there are several conditions under which he might send a gift
back. These include gifts for disreputable purposes (such as setting
up a program you don't believe in so the donor can, in effect, buy
the opinions of your faculty); funds for a new building for which
you won't be able to pay the operating costs; gifts for new pro-

grams that might run for three years or so, with your group expected to pick up the cost afterward. When donors make gifts for programs you are not in favor of or don't feel merit support, you run the risk of letting your donors determine the nature of your organization.[20]

James B. Martin notes that he has faced many of the same questions at the University of Kansas and has found it necessary to establish clear guidelines covering gifts and their uses. He points out that small gifts can sometimes cause problems. He once received a $25 check for the annual fund that was earmarked specifically to "tar and feather" a certain professor. Martin returned the check, noting that the university could not accept its restriction.[21] (Tongue-in-cheek, he adds that considering the cost of tar and feathers, the gift was really too small to do the job.)

Thus one annual drive ends and another begins. In reviewing the information presented in this chapter, remember:

1. An annual fund drive is annual. Don't skip a year for any reason.
2. Select the best possible people you can find to serve in the leadership positions of the campaign.
3. Develop your case for support.
4. Involve as many volunteers as possible. The more people who ask for money, the more money you will receive.
5. Work closely with each volunteer and provide every tool needed to get the job done. Be absolutely certain to give recognition when the campaign is over.

SUCCESSFUL APPROACHES

The following examples illustrate how a number of institutions have used various strategies and techniques to enhance their annual fund campaigns. They provide a range of ideas that call for a relatively small cash outlay.

Marion College's Brown Bag Mailer

Marion College (Marion, Indiana) proved that you can find inexpensive ways of raising money if you're willing to try unconventional approaches.

Thanks to an alumnus who had a printing press in his garage, an unusual mailing that needed no outside envelope, and a group of volunteers who folded and stapled the mailing by hand, the alumni association was able to send an attention-getting appeal to 7,500 alumni for less than $600—and they raised $3,400 from the project!

The college has traditionally had trouble raising alumni funds by mail. The year before they tried this "brown bag" program, alumni had contributed $137,000 in cash and $22,000 in gifts-in-kind—yet only $8,100 of that total came in through the mail in response to all the appeals that year!

To break up the monotony of letters and fliers used annually to prod alumni into giving, the alumni association conceived the idea of a brown bag—a plain brown bag imprinted on one side with a message asking recipients to use the bag to carry their lunch during the next week, and give the money they had saved to the college's alumni fund. The interesting lead invited the recipient, "Please join the alumni for lunch next week. This is not the usual sort of luncheon invitation, but it is most sincere."

On the other side of the bag was a bulk rate stamp and the following message where the return address normally goes: "Why would you get a paper bag in the mail? Look inside to find out."

Michael Roorbach, Marion's alumni director, provided the following budget breakdown:

Printing	$ 50.00	(an alumnus did the printing)
Bags	81.60	(from a local supplier)
Handling and mailing	160.36	(a local mailing house did this work)
Mailing labels	26.40	(3-up, cheshire)
Postage	165.68	(bulk rate and overseas postage)
Printing of business reply envelopes	109.71	(8,000 were printed)
Total:	$593.75	

Thus, for less than $600, Marion College was able to reach 7,500 alumni and received $3,400 in contributions.

MARION COLLEGE
1976-77 ALUMNI FUND

BROWN BAG CAMPAIGN

Wherever you are, please join the alumni for lunch next week. This is not the usual sort of luncheon invitation, but it is most sincere. The idea goes like this . . .

NEXT WEEK CARRY YOUR LUNCH instead of buying it. Then give the dollar or two you save each day to the Marion College Alumni Fund. We're providing you with this bag to make your, contribution possible, and really, paper bags are about all we can afford to provide.

SUPPORT THE BROWN BAG CAMPAIGN!

As of March 1, alumni have contributed about $80,000 but that leaves us $50,000 short of the $130,000 campaign goal.

Greater participation is needed, and for the hundreds who have missed in the past, here's a painless way of becoming active alumni. Your participation will enable academic development, debt reduction, campus development, and other exciting steps of progress at Marion College. Thank you for "brown-bagging-it" with us.

The Alumni Finance Committee
Howard B. Castle, Chr.; Harold Bardsley, Phyllis Ihrkey, Sarah Norris, David McKee, Eldine Landis

Figure 1. The other side of this brown bag mailer carried a brief message asking the recipient to read this side, a bulk rate stamp, and room to write the name and address of the prospect. Courtesy Marion College, Marion, Ind.

In addition, nearly three times as many alumni contributed (130 versus 44 the previous year), and one-third of them were new donors. "I realize that 130 responses from 7,500 pieces mailed is less than a two percent response," Roorbach explained, "but I believe that it must be viewed in the light of how well trained (or how poorly trained) one's alumni body is to giving by mail." The previous poor record of Marion's alumni indicate that this project was indeed quite successful in changing their giving habits.

Roorbach offers some final comments about the printing. There were too many thicknesses in the folded bag to print it on an offset press, so the printer used a letterpress. Because of the quality of the paper bag, this was not a high-quality printed piece. Roorbach suggests that development offices having a larger number of prospects (perhaps 20,000 or more) and at least six weeks' lead time go to a paper bag manufacturer and have the bags printed before they are made, yielding a better quality product at a lower price.

"If I had it to do over," he says, "I'd do it exactly the same way. But I can only use this idea once—it's a gimmick, and we just can't overdo it." He adds that his phone kept ringing for weeks, with a number of alumni telling him how impressed they were by this clever idea.[22]

Florida Technological University's Unoccasion

To help raise scholarship money for Florida Technological University in 1971, the FTU Foundation did *not* hold one of the nation's biggest bashes, *without* such stars as Jackie Gleason, Frank Sinatra, Barbra Streisand, The Who, Kiss, Flip Wilson, or Lawrence Welk and His Champagne Music.

The gala that wasn't held was the brainstorm of the university's TAU fraternity. The objective was simple—the students wanted to call attention in a dramatic manner to the need for funds to aid FTU's scholarship program. With that in mind, TAU enlisted the Foundation's help in their cause. The result was a simple invitation and ticket mailed to several hundred prospects throughout the university's service region.

The letter began by noting that the Foundation "proudly announces the first annual Scholarship Dinner-Dance (that will not be held)." It further explained that since "there are so many occasions during the year in which you, as a responsible citizen, must participate, it was decided to plan a gala affair and then not require you to go to the expense of attending. Therefore, on June 1 of this year, the most exciting and glamorous event of the year *will not be held*!"

Also in the letter was a list of "a few of the expenses you will save by not having to attend." These included tuxedo rental ($15), gown ($100), baby-sitter ($3.50), possible traffic ticket ($35), Alka-Seltzer ($.50), and other possible expenses. But then the letter asked:

> Now that we have saved you all that expense, wouldn't you consider donating part of it to the FTU Foundation to assist some worthy student in his educational pursuits?
> Enclosed is a brochure that tells a little about FTU and

the Foundation. Please attach the coupon to your check and mail before June 1. Also enclosed is the program that will not be held, as well as your tickets for the dinner-dance. (Please do not present these at the door!) Each ticket entitles you to the comfort of your own home on the evening of June 1, or any other evening you would so desire to enjoy a good book or your favorite television program.

The letter closed with this message:

> Even though you will not be with us on this unoccasion, we hope you will visit the FTU campus and allow us the privilege of expressing our appreciation for your support in person. You will be as pleased and proud of your University as are we. However, just this once we will be
> LOOKING FORWARD TO NOT HAVING
> YOU WITH US.

The president of the university and the Foundation president signed the letter. How successful was the program? The letter noted that the recipient would save about $473 by not attending the dinner, and about 700 invitations were sent to prospects in the area. By June 1, more than $21,000 had been raised, and the university had received a great deal of publicity and media attention, including coverage from a television station that reported on the unoccasion on the night it was not held.

Expenses were quite low—just the cost of printing and mailing the cover letter, ticket, and program. This idea could be used by an organization seeking an inexpensive way of reaching a large audience with a unique approach. It might just work for *your* organization, and help raise your visibility in the community at the same time.

Oberlin College's Challenge Fund

During the 1976–77 fiscal year, every category—from number of donors and participation rate to the Oberlin Annual Fund gift total and alumni support through all channels—surpassed previous records.

For the first time in several years, the college was not actively engaged in any phase of a capital building campaign. There was, therefore, a perceived shift of priorities in fundraising efforts, with primary attention drawn to the Annual Fund, to provide monies for current operations of the institution. In the fall of 1976, Oberlin launched a two-year Annual Fund effort: In 1976–77 it wanted to increase significantly the number of donors to the Annual Fund. In 1977–78 it aimed to keep these new donors on the rolls and to encourage them to increase their level of giving by use of a dollar-increase challenge funded by the National Endowment for the Humanities. While many of Oberlin's alumni had been very generous in the past, with the average gift high, the percentage of alumni giving had regularly been disappointing.

A convincing case for Oberlin's pressing need for current operations funds was clearly and consistently stated through many techniques. The college wanted to convince the nondonor of the urgency of the situation, that Oberlin's survival as a quality undergraduate liberal arts college depended on increased contributions of unrestricted current operations funds. Simultaneously they sought to demonstrate that the college deserved and warranted alumni support.

The principal technique used to entice new donors was the challenge gift program, whereby an anonymous graduate of the college pledged to give Oberlin $100 for every new donor, defined as an alumnus/alumna who had not contributed in any of the previous three years. A minimum gift of $10 was required. It was an offer that 4,473 new donors could not refuse! Even the number of gifts by previous donors ineligible for the challenge increased by eight percent.

All program efforts within the Annual Fund were coordinated to focus on the challenge. Class agents featured the challenge in their personalized letters and postcards to their classmates. A national spring phonothon was used for the first time, with alumni, students, faculty, and staff calling alumni eligible for the challenge. One class had its own intraclass phonothon, raising its level of participation from 14.5 percent to 43.8 percent. The alumni magazine featured back-cover ads for the challenge in four issues.

The most effective means of communication between the president and alumni in general were: (a) as the speaker at alumni club meetings throughout the country; (b) through institutional mailings; and (c) through the President's Weekend Programs. These were three-day cultivation visits to campus by special gift prospects. During their visits they came into contact with students, faculty, and administrators in formal and informal settings.

Other tested methods for appealing to old and new donors alike were continued. The John Frederick Oberlin Society, whose members each give at least $1,000 annually for current expenses, grew from 111 members and $217,385 in 1975–76 to 120 members giving $293,000. Reunion giving also continued its upward surge, aiding both the Annual Fund and endowment giving.

COMPOUND YOUR INTEREST IN OBERLIN

The interest that alumni and parents and friends have in Oberlin is particularly important in these days when all educational institutions, and especially private colleges, face extreme fiscal problems. People who are not interested in Oberlin cannot be expected to make annual gifts to Oberlin. How could they believe in Oberlin's efforts to provide students with an education that costs nearly twice as much as constantly rising tuition pays for?

If you are interested in Oberlin, however, and if you believe in what Oberlin is trying to do against really overwhelming odds, there are a number of ways between now and next June 30 that your gift to Oberlin can make a big difference.

- If it has been three years or more since you made a gift to the Oberlin Annual Fund, your gift this year, if it is $10 or more, will enable Oberlin to receive a "bounty" of $100 from an anonymous graduate who is concerned because so few Oberlinians have been supporting Oberlin financially.
- If the firm where you work has a "matching grant" program, your employer will match your gift dollar for dollar and your gift will help Oberlin twice as much.
- If your financial situation enables you to give Oberlin $1,000 or more, you can become a member of the John Frederick Oberlin Society whose 111 members in 1975-76 provided $195,000 for Oberlin College's current operations. Your membership in the J.F.O. Society (or any gift to Oberlin) can be anonymous, if you wish.
- If your class is participating in a Reunion Giving Program you can perhaps qualify for *all* of the above-mentioned opportunities to assist Oberlin.
- If you are one of the 1,900 alumni who supported the Oberlin Annual Fund in 1974-75 but did not contribute in 1975-76 you should know that 1,800 Oberlinians who did not contribute in 1974-75 *did* give to Oberlin in 1975-76. If these nearly 4,000 alumni would support Oberlin *annually*, numerous foundations and other potential donors would be more willing to give money to Oberlin because of the higher annual percentage.

Whether your interest in Oberlin is "simple" or can be compounded, it is needed and will be appreciated. Send your check (payable to Oberlin College) to

OBERLIN ANNUAL FUND
Bosworth Hall
Oberlin, Ohio 44074

Figure 2. One of the ads run in Oberlin's alumni magazine pointing out the challenge gift program. Courtesy Oberlin College, Oberlin, Ohio.

Student support, born out of the reality of budget concerns, emerged on campus. Not only did students participate in a phonothon but they contacted local merchants and townspeople for funds needed to meet a special challenge, which required that the students raise at least $10,000 to qualify for an additional $30,000. The students surpassed this goal by raising $13,358.

Oberlin's Ed Tobias notes, "It is interesting to reflect that Oberlin's Annual Fund has grown from very modest beginnings to a powerful budgetary force in only six years by the simple but diligent application of techniques which are classic in concept. If it can be done here, it can be done anywhere!"[23]

Additional Ideas

The number of ways to raise money is endless. New and imaginative ideas appear every day—and their success depends on the skill and energy with which your institution promotes the projects, and the willingness of your constituency to support the project.

Brock University in Canada mails a packet of morning glory seeds to prospects asking them to "help Brock grow." The words on a small poster accompanying the seeds tell the story:

> Few things today grow by accident. In these fragile times, care and support are needed to ensure continued growth and prosperity.
>
> The needs of these Brock seeds, a packet of morning glories, are quite simple. Follow the sowing instructions, provide the right amounts of sunshine and nourishment, and your garden will flourish.
>
> In sharp contrast, the needs of the university are infinitely complex. Brock has reached a critical stage in its development; we have outgrown our "emerging" phase, but require a fresh initiative before we can assert ourselves as an established institution. The "new reality" of the provincial government's budgetary cutbacks could mean that the university will continue to live, but not necessarily thrive. Additional, private support is needed for books, the equipment and the special facilities Brock must have to affirm and eventually surpass its academic goals.
>
> As students during Brock's first decade, you helped the

university to mature and enrich itself. Now, as members of the alumni association, you are being asked to renew your commitment—your faith in Brock's future. Your gift to the alumni fund will help the university to flourish.

Help Brock to grow again. The seeds, this poster, are tokens of appreciation for your generosity and your concern. We hope they will also be a constant, colourful reminder of how important it is that we cultivate our collective garden.[24]

Cardinal Glennon Hospital in St. Louis receives funds from a series of junior football league games held each year.

Lehigh University runs a memorial gift program in which each senior is solicited for twenty years after graduation. The pledge is made when they are still on campus and their interest in Lehigh is at a peak.

Central Methodist College sends alumni a "proof copy" of their honor roll of donors, asking them to check the spelling of names while reminding them of the upcoming fund deadline. In 1980, 300 donors gave more than $22,000 after the mailing was sent.

The Collegiate Schools in Richmond, Virginia, sent donors a bumper sticker reading, "We brake for donors." The message in the brochure accompanying the sticker pointed out that gifts to the school gave tax breaks.

Finally, Old Dominion University promoted early-year gifts by mailing out a New Year's card in January with the message: "Remember when you said, 'I'll give next year'? It's time." Randy Morris of ODU says that the campaign was quite successful in starting off the annual drive.

CASE STUDY

Winter Park Memorial Hospital—Making House Calls

In late 1980, Winter Park Memorial Hospital (Winter Park, Florida) began a campaign to double its association membership within the following twelve months. The theme of the campaign was "We're making house calls . . . through our direct mail program to ask your support for the Hospital Association membership drive. This way you have time to consider carefully all the positive aspects of your participation."

The first phase of the program involved employee solicitation. A handbook containing answers to commonly asked questions about the association was prepared and distributed to all employees along with an application form. Posters, buttons, and other promotional material helped the thirty-day campaign boost membership from 30 to more than 300.

A fictitious character called a "Wapple" was developed as honorary chairman, and two employees on each shift served as co-chairmen (Figure 3).

The second phase of the campaign was the direct mail effort to the nonemployee constituents. A "We're Making House Calls" brochure was mailed to members of the auxiliary, staff physicians, and past patients of the hospital. The unique format of a doctor's bag was used to catch the attention of the 8,600 prospects. The bag was designed as a self-mailer (the handle was folded down and held in place by a small sticker), and it contained a bound-in pledge card/return-address postcard.

The direct mail portion of the campaign began in October 1980. Within the first four months, the campaign had reached more than half of its goal, with more than 5 percent of the prospects responding with donations.

The total cost of the mailer, including postage, was 84 cents. It required special die-cutting, of course, and glue and stapling to make it a self-contained mailing piece.

John N. Reynolds III, the hospital's development director, reports that the black bag approach resulted in many calls and letters of praise, and was a definite public relations asset as well as a successful fundraiser. He adds that the average level of membership has been $19, about 50 percent higher than the employee campaign average contribution.

The Advertising Association of Florida bestowed its first-place ADDY Award on the mailer as the year's best direct mail piece.

The major problems Reynolds encountered were the production time and expense, because of the bag's unique shape, and what he termed a possible "counterproductive" result of the mailer. "Many people told me that the bag was so nice they didn't want to cut it apart," he says, "so they said they saved it." Reynolds has convinced these people that they can contribute anyway, of course. And he's smiling at the great response the piece is bringing so far.[25]

You may not work for a hospital, but the concept of sending the bag to homes can be easily adapted to a wide variety of organiza-

**WINTER PARK
MEMORIAL
HOSPITAL**

200 NORTH LAKEMONT AVENUE
WINTER PARK, FLORIDA 32792
TELEPHONE (305) 646-7000

October 1980

On behalf of the Board of Trustees and members
of the Winter Park Memorial Hospital Association,
Inc. you are cordially invited to carefully
consider all the positive aspects of belonging
to the Hospital Association.

The accompanying booklet contains most of the
information that you might need to make a decision about the Association.

Since we're having a friendly membership competition
with the day shift and evening shift, your participation will put us out in front.

Most Sincerely,

Barbara Houston   Geraldine Johnson
Co-Chairman,   Co-Chairman,
11 to 7 Shift   11 to 7 Shift

P.S. Allow me To invite you To become a member of "my" Association. During October, I will join "your group" as you become a WPMHA "wapple."

"WP" Wapple 1980 Honorary Chairman

*Figure 3. This letter was sent to the workers on various shifts to tell
them of the employee phase of the campaign. Note the effective use
of the "P.S." and the "Wapple" character.* Courtesy Winter Park
Memorial Hospital, Winter Park, Fla.

tions. It has already found commercial use, for example. The First
Georgia Bank used a similar die-cut of a doctor's bag with the
cover wording: "Just what the doctor ordered for your business"
and their logo. The bag unfolded into three spreads that explained
the bank's services. The first spread, for example, showed three IV

Figure 4. The cover of the mailer, showing the words "We're making house calls" printed in reverse on a black bag. The hospital's logo was printed in its colors—a white symbol on a blue background, with a brown border around the outside. When mailed, the bag's handle was folded down and held in place with a small sticker. The back of the bag gave the hospital's return address and the bulk rate imprint, along with the words "address correction requested." Courtesy Winter Park Memorial Hospital, Winter Park, Fla.

bottles filled with money, under the headline "We'll prescribe just the financing you need, in just the right dose." The overall theme of their campaign was "the bank that makes housecalls." Not only does the bank prescribe the right financing, but it also turns "cash management into a smooth operation" and makes "office calls." Because it was printed on a black bag (like the Winter Park piece), the reverse type gave added impact to the message. A follow-up letter from the bank advised prospective customers that it was time for a checkup and that the bank could help improve the circulation of the company's cash flow.

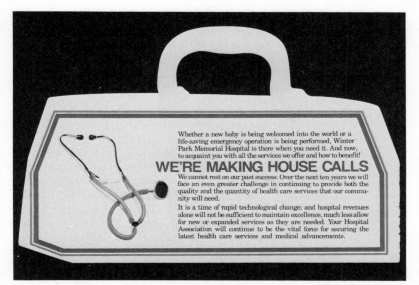

Whether a new baby is being welcomed into the world or a life-saving emergency operation is being performed, Winter Park Memorial Hospital is there when you need it. And now, to acquaint you with all the services we offer and how to benefit!

WE'RE MAKING HOUSE CALLS

We cannot rest on our past success. Over the next ten years we will face an even greater challenge in continuing to provide both the quality and the quantity of health care services that our community will need.

It is a time of rapid technological change; and hospital revenues alone will not be sufficient to maintain excellence, much less allow for new or expanded services as they are needed. Your Hospital Association will continue to be the vital force for securing the latest health care services and medical advancements.

Figure 5. The first page of the brochure gave an introduction to the campaign, explaining the general reasons for supporting the hospital's association. All inside pages, like this one, were framed in blue and brown borders, with headlines printed in blue. Other pages carried photos of people and facilities at the hospital, along with simple, strong reasons for supporting the group. Three levels of gift clubs, involving fees of $10, $25, and $50, were listed. Since former patients were the prime targets of these mailings, the additional benefits of higher-level gift club support—free TV during a hospital stay and rapid admitting procedures, for example—were especially attractive. Courtesy Winter Park Memorial Hospital, Winter Park, Fla.

You could also consider adapting the bag to your particular organization. Why not send a die-cut television set if you're a public TV station? Or a diploma or briefcase for a school? Or a mummy case or songsheet or scout merit badge or whatever it is your group does?

If you can't get your prospects to come to you, this annual fund mail idea may let you go to them.

Gift Clubs

If there be any "magic" in educational fund raising, you can find it in the number and variety of imaginative plans known as associates programs, or gift clubs.[1]

Membership programs—often called gift clubs because contributors receive some form of tangible recognition for their gifts—are not a new idea in the fundraising business. They have been around for a long time and can be considered the "bread and butter" method of building donor involvement. Increased involvement often leads to those funds needed for current operations and special projects.

If you'd like to start a gift club, you won't have to buy a red carpet, but you should prepare to roll one out symbolically the day you contact your first prospective member. Every gift club member, whether the contribution is $25 or $25,000 annually, should receive a bit of royal treatment, with the size of the treatment depending on the size of the gift.

When you are dealing in gift clubs, you are actually dealing in human desires. And, as the psychologists have been telling us for years, we all have many desires, including security, love, and making more money. For gift club members, however, three basic desires will arouse 90 percent of them. Fulfill them, and your market for attracting contributors will be wide open.

The Desire to Feel Important

Ferdinand and Isabella were probably not the least bit interested in proving that the Earth was round. What caused them to open the Spanish treasury and give Columbus his needed funds was a trade route to the East—and the promise of the prestige they would gain by supporting such a worthwhile cause.

You should work hard at selling your prospects on the feeling of importance they will receive by supporting your special cause through club memberships. Consider these three suggestions:

- Start by giving your club a classy name. At Iowa State University, it's the Order of the Knoll; at UCLA, the Chancellor's Associates; at DePaul University, the Society of Fellows; at Miami, the Society of University Founders.
- Work up a simple but elegant-looking invitation to join. It does not have to be expensive, but it should have the sophistication needed to underscore the importance of membership.
- Promote your club with publications and literature that have a quality look.

The Desire to Be Appreciated

Thank your special friends in special ways. After all, they are special people. They have contributed to the success of your organization and they should not have to come begging thanks. Members of Albion College's club, The Briton Round Table, receive lapel pins and lavalieres designed by an authority in British heraldry. They also receive note cards featuring a college scene and The Briton Round Table crest.

Margaret Alsobrook, director of development at Rice University, has this to say: "Save your black-tie dinners for top donors but throw a barbeque for others. The same goes for gifts. Members of Rice's President's Club ($100–$999) get a bronze paperweight; Founding Club members ($1,000+) get a pewter one. . . . Give gifts sparingly, and make them tasteful, unique and expensive in appearance."[2]

At the University of Richmond, annual giving and alumni leaders take part in "Operation Thank You." At the end of the year they call personally on all those who have given $100 or more, and present the donors with a calendar or desk secretary.[3] This helps keep the annual gift coming, and helps build membership in the larger giving clubs by keeping donors happy.

The Desire to Be Liked

Put in even stronger terms, this is the desire to be *loved*. For this commodity there is no seasonal demand. It is wanted every day of the week in every month of the year.

Thousands of books have been written on the "secret of love," yet the real secret is as old as the human race. All you have to do to get people to like you is to tell them how much you like them.

Tell your members that you love them. Tell them as often as possible and in as many ways as possible. Let them know your plans and ideas. Involve them in these activities. Use them on your committees and programs. Herald their accomplishments in your publications. Remember their birthdays and anniversaries. Send them invitations to special programs and events. Show how easily, and at what little cost, the needs to feel important, appreciated, and loved can be satisfied through membership in your institution's gift club, and your contributors should become your best friends.

Remember, though, that a successful gift club requires strategies that continually communicate with, involve, and reward your members. Don't even think about a gift club until you can readily and effectively promote one. The worst thing you can do is to enlist a membership and then neglect your contributors. Whatever goals, activities, and benefits of membership you decide on, be sure to follow through.

THE PURPOSES OF A MEMBERSHIP PROGRAM

The basic purposes of gift clubs are to:
- involve a very special group of institutional friends who will give mainly unrestricted funds, which are the most difficult to get, and the most useful to have
- encourage an increased level of giving by current donors
- attract a high level of annual support
- upgrade donor gifts
- recognize and honor the individuals who have supported the institution financially

- attract new contributors who are influenced by the individual recognition given the more generous donor
- inform and involve the membership in the purposes and plans of the institution
- develop volunteers for their effective use as ambassadors, advisors, and fundraising leaders in support of many important projects of the agency.

QUALIFICATIONS FOR MEMBERSHIP

There is really only one qualification for membership in a gift club: that an individual give to your organization on a regular basis, usually annually. To accomplish this goal, most agencies set an annual gift standard—as low as $10, $25, $50, $100, $250, or $500, or as high as $1,000, $5,000, $10,000, and up. It is not uncommon for some institutions to have a gift standard that reaches $50,000, payable annually. One such institution is the University of Miami. Its gift club, the Society of University Founders, had 140 members in 1966, the year the university's Board of Trustees met to establish a framework by which these large contributors could be recognized.

In announcing the program, university president Henry King Stanford explained that "while 'founder' suggests primarily the early years of the university, we expect the Society to be like the university—a living, growing entity. A vital university develops as new departments, new schools, new centers are founded. As the University of Miami progresses, so too, we trust, will the Society itself flourish as new members join."

The society *has* flourished, with members providing more than $80 million since 1966 in support of Miami's quest for excellence in programs and facilities. Many of the original members have continued making gifts at the $50,000 level, and each year approximately fifty new members are welcomed into the group.

What makes the program especially successful is the annual dinner held each winter to recognize the new members and acknowledge the continuing support of former members. Ed Coll, Miami's vice-president for development affairs, explains that the development office makes all the arrangements for the event.

Though a member of the board of trustees serves as committee chairman, there is no actual committee, and Coll's office handles all the details.

The evening begins with a private reception for new members, held between 6 and 7 P.M. Other selected members who have been extremely active during the year are also invited, along with the chairman, vice-chairman, and members of the trustees. The university president and the chairman of the board of trustees present each new member with a personalized bronze plaque, and photos are taken of the president and the donor. Coll adds that the plaques originally cost around $150, but now are over $300— "and worth every penny," he says.

The wording on the plaques is simple: "In grateful recognition of substantial generosity in providing significant financial support for the University of Miami, the Board of Trustees hereby designates (name of donor) a member of the Society of University Founders with all the rights, privileges, and responsibilities attendant to this office." A color seal of the university and the date also appear along with the president's and the chairman's names.

Following the reception, a larger reception is held for all members of the society. Hors d'oeuvres and drinks are served at this party. Invited are former members, major volunteers, and perhaps most important, key prospects for future solicitation. This informal session allows new members to show off their plaques, talk with former donors, and share their pride with prospective members.

The dinner, a black tie affair, begins at 8 P.M. It is usually held at one of the area's more elegant hotels, such as The Fontainebleau or the Omni International. The university president and board officers sit at the head table. Following the dinner, the president introduces the ceremony and a formal investiture is conducted. The new founders are each called to the stage and the chairman of the board of trustees reads their names. Coll and the president drape founder's medallions over their shoulders.

The president makes appropriate remarks about the recipients —what an honor it is for the university, general comments on the occasion—then reads the plaque and says, "By the powers vested in me as president of the university, I hereby declare that (name of donor) is a member of the Society of University Founders."

Former founders are then recognized, and each stands, wearing his or her medallion. The program concludes with a short talk by the president on the university or higher education in general.

"Because of the large number of elderly people contributing to the society," Coll adds, "the dinner always ends by 10 P.M. We are considering an extended program for our younger members, who wish to stay and dance or socialize, but our policy has been to end at an early hour in deference to the older members."

Invitations to the dinner are sent to all new and former members, of course, but one of the secrets of the affair is to invite the key prospects. "All table seating is assigned," Coll notes, "and we take great pains to have the right people sitting with the right prospects. There is at least one current member of the society at each table."

A formal invitation is sent to members and prospects, and the university pays all expenses for the dinner and reception. The plaques, medallions, and other extras push the total annual cost of the Society of Founders to near $40,000.

The dinner is always held at the height of Miami's winter tourist season, in late February or early March. This helps reach the many winter visitors who support UM and who wish to join the society. Each year, more than 1,000 members and prospects attend the reception and dinner. Those attending the dinner are given a small booklet briefly explaining the program and listing all society members.

It is a simple but elegant way to honor donors at the $50,000 level. And judging by its continued support, Miami has found the key to running a successful gift club.[4]

Most gift clubs are structured so that regardless of the level at which an individual signs up, he or she is encouraged to sign a pledge for a minimum gift each year or for a specific number of years, with the right to cancel or change the pledge should this become necessary.

As a general rule, members carefully selected and enrolled will not hesitate to continue their gifts for several years, provided you and your institution commit to a relationship of time and involvement that is interesting and rewarding to your donors.

As previously stated, the primary purpose of a gift club is to raise the level of unrestricted giving. Many institutions make this a hard and fast rule, and unless the gift is unrestricted, the donor will not qualify. Whether or not you wish to go this far depends upon you and your institution. Certainly, you can consider restricted gifts. If you do so, then it might be to your advantage to limit your restricted giving, as far as a club membership is concerned, to perhaps no more than three carefully chosen areas for which you need funds. Even so, always include the option for a donor to make an unrestricted gift.

FINDING MEMBERS

Before you start your gift club, you should first develop an accurate and up-to-date list of prospects for each giving category. The best place to start is right at home; that is, begin with your current trustees or board members, your own institutional faculty or staff, your own current list of donors. Ask your trustees, your in-house staff, and your current donors to provide you with additional prospects. This referral program is important for building, soliciting, and enrolling new members. This is especially true when you specifically ask present donors to refer you to people who they feel share their interests. Ask them for names of people they feel are the same age group and income level. Ask your current donors for the names and addresses of members at their clubs and organizations. From here, you can move to businesses, to the community, to alumni, to former patrons, and so on. Remember that the necessary number of *qualified* prospects must be available to make the success of each level of giving category of your gift club reasonably assured. You should have 400–500 solid prospects for every 100 members you expect to enroll. And since every prospect should be approached on a one-to-one basis, preferably by a peer volunteer, you will need at least eight to ten volunteers to help you make the contacts for every 100 members.

Oakland University asks each member of its President's Club ($10,000 minimum) to recruit a new member. The university hosts special events during the year to attract and sustain the interest of prospects brought in by current members. With only a small development staff, a modest budget, and a young alumni group, the university recently attracted fifty new members and

$670,000 during a twelve-month effort. The highly successful President's Club at the University of Iowa ($10,000 or more outright or $25,000 deferred gift) uses volunteers in special outreach programs around the country to contact prospective members and accompany development staff members on recruiting visits.[5]

The University of Richmond also uses volunteers heavily in building membership of their Rector's Club ($1,000 per year). Stockbrokers, bankers, and attorneys have played important roles in referring prospects to the campus. Current members are asked to watch their business, church, or social circles for prospective members. Their associate director of development even has his own favorite method of "prospecting." "When I drive through campus," he says, "I note the occasional Mercedes or other expensive cars in the student parking lot. Then I write down the student's parking permit number, and find out who owns the car. It's amazing how many exceptional parent prospects we unearth this way."[6]

SETTING THE NUMBER OF GIVING LEVELS

In deciding how many giving levels are needed, you should:

1. Count your total number of prospects, donors and nondonors. This number could be 1,000, or it could be 25,000.
2. Of the total number of prospects, how many actual contributors do you have? This number could be 500 or it could be 12,000.
3. Once you have the number of contributors, you are ready to determine the current gift stratification of the group. How many contributors do you have who give $10–$99; $100–$249; $250–$499; $500–$999; $1,000 and up?
4. Based on the above answers, you can now establish at what level of giving you could expect the maximum number of people to increase their gifts, with the fewest number of people decreasing their gifts when issued an invitation to join your gift club. For example, Mr. X has been giving you an annual gift of $250. You are considering two gift clubs, one at $100 and another at $500. What might Mr. X do—increase his gift to $500 or drop back to $100? Depending on the number of Mr. X's you have, and your determination of what each might do, should you consider a $250 club?

5. You are now ready to review all of your nondonor prospects. Sit down with a peer committee who knows the prospects and have them rate each person, whether at $50 or $500.

Once all the above is done, you may find that your top level is $5,000, $1,000, $500, or $100. Whatever the top level, the next question is how many lower levels you need, if any. If your top level is $100, you probably want no lower level. If your top level is $500 or $1,000, then you might want to consider some lower levels.

In making this decision, it is best to keep in mind that just as "too many cooks spoil the broth," too many giving levels could spoil your program. You should establish clubs only when they will generate an increase in dollars and participation. Also be sure that there is a distinct dollar difference between levels so as to encourage the donor to go in stages from one club to the next. This will avoid the tendency of your donor to settle in at the minimum level.

Nothing will replace an annual review and evaluation of your current donors and prospects. In so doing, you have the knowledge needed to increase your club membership while at the same time upgrading your current donors. As an individual's level of giving increases, actively cultivate his or her interest in and importance to the program. This will help you elevate the donor to the next level of giving. It is not unusual, for example, that a donor will join a club at, say, $500, then during the course of the year make additional gifts that bring the total within reasonable reach of your $1,000 club. Through adequate record keeping, and annual review of your records, you can solicit such people for those additional dollars that place them in a higher level of giving.

As to staff and budget, the best of all possible worlds is to have a knowledgeable person whose primary assignment—perhaps only assignment—is handling your gift clubs. While it is possible to start and run a program out of your "back pocket," experience dictates that this will be successful only for a time. If you want your program to develop and improve, you must give it major attention. This calls for a person who is imaginative, thorough with details, and capable of direct involvement in the cultivation and solicitation effort.

Give this person an adequate budget. Good people cost money

and need money in order to raise money. You are promoting quality giving—leadership giving—and this requires a quality approach.

ENLISTING MEMBERS

Once you have decided on your level of giving categories and on the goals and programs of the membership, you are ready to begin enlisting your prospects.

Start your enrollment campaign with the following three steps:

1. First, enlist those persons in your highest category. If that category is $500, start there; if $1,000, start there. *Do not start at the bottom and work upward.* A person enrolled at $100 might have been enlisted for $500 had he or she been solicited in the higher category first.

2. Approach your prospects in person. Do not rely on a direct mail invitation except in your lowest categories—up to $100. This does not mean that prospects in the highest categories cannot be solicited by mail. They often are, and they often answer by joining. Nevertheless, the best approach is still a one-to-one personal invitation. More than one visit may be necessary before the gift is secured, but this is to be expected when asking for large gifts.

3. Do not be discouraged by a negative answer. Consider this merely a challenge to try again. Given the right time, with the right person doing the asking, you will be surprised at the success rate.

In making your personal calls, as with direct mail pieces, you must have a "case"—those reasons that will convince your prospects of a need for the funds, and that their involvement with your cause is essential. You will also need a dignified, expensive-looking invitation to join to give each prospect personally, or at least to mail immediately following the call. Your invitation should detail your program of appreciation or benefits of membership. This program is the means of identifying new members with the institution, the way in which you will hold them up before the world, so to speak, as very special friends.

THE PROGRAM OF APPRECIATION

Whatever your program of appreciation, its purpose must always be to maintain a close and informed relationship between your donor and your institution. Keep in mind that the more informed your members are about your organization, the more generous they are likely to be. Remember also that people do not give to an institution simply because it needs support. They give to causes that challenge them when these causes are heralded by other people they like and trust.

What was said earlier should be repeated here: the worst thing you can do is to enlist a membership and then neglect your contributors. If you want your members to give annually, they must be recognized and rewarded *continually*. Clearly, this "thank-you" should be more than a telephone call or a letter. You should consider, in addition to the most common activity of an annual dinner or some other annual observance, such membership benefits as special privileges, publications, events, and awards that are geared to each level of giving categories. Here, a word of caution is in order. Be certain to establish written guidelines for every gratuity your organization is willing to offer. These guidelines will serve you well should questions arise, and they will help assure that Donor A who gives you $10,000 is not treated the same as Donor B who gives you $100.

Spend time in considering just what form your "thank-you" benefit package should take. A gift of $100,000 decidedly deserves more than a desk set and a certificate, whereas these benefits might be in order for a $1,000 gift. As a starting point, you should consider spending no more than 3 percent of the value of your contribution on thank-you gifts. This is certainly not a hard and fast rule, for the occasion may arise when you wish to violate the 3 percent ceiling—particularly if you have reason to believe that a certain donor is a good prospect for a larger gift in the future. Even so, never overdo the "candy and flowers" routine, which could suggest to the donor, as well as to others, that your organization is fiscally irresponsible.

While many donors are uncomfortable in the limelight and prefer simple, very low-key expressions of thanks, others enjoy all the public acclaim they can get. With this knowledge, the wise development officer will get to know the contributors and, within reason, seek to meet their desires. In this regard, Paul Schneiter, director of communications for the Church of Jesus Christ of Latter Day Saints, offers some excellent suggestions for recognizing donors in the higher categories.[7]

$100,000 and Up

Schneiter recognizes that this donor deserves more than a presidential phone call or letter. He or she should be visited by the key executive officer of your organization and thanked in person. The donor should be told that your organization wants to publicly express its thanks and give recognition.

Schneiter offers several ideas for this public expression of thanks: a tribute banquet attended by state and community leaders; a commemorative brochure announcing the contribution and presenting a summary of the donor's life and accomplishments; or a gift that symbolizes the donor's concerns and work. These items should be in addition to any honor the donor may receive by virtue of having made the gift at all, such as having a building or scholarship named after him or her.

He adds that this donor, or any donor at the upper giving levels, should never be given a plaque or a certificate—those off-the-shelf mementos. Instead, a real effort should be made to tailor a gift that is unique to each donor's background, accomplishments, and interest. Schneiter cites a West Coast university that presented a Navajo-made quartz chess set to a donor who had established a scholarship fund for American Indian students. This donor had spent much of his professional life working among Navajos in the Southwest.

A week or so after the thank-you event, send a warm letter that reiterates your appreciation and sets the stage for an ongoing relationship.

$25,000 to $50,000

Schneiter comments that a "personal visit to this donor is entirely appropriate, too, although a letter signed by your organization's key executive officer will suffice." Also in order is a special event honoring the donor; however, he says, "keep the number of participants small. Dinner at a quality restaurant with the leaders of your organization and the donor and his or her family makes sense." So, too, do the gift and follow-up letter described for the $100,000 donor.

$10,000 to $25,000

The donor who gives at this level still merits special thank-you treatment, but on a more modest scale. Lunch or dinner with the president or leaders of your organization and a thoughtfully selected memento of appreciation are appropriate. Schneiter goes on to add that you "may want to invite the donor to spend the day at your organization to see firsthand the work that is being done in his or her interest."

$1 to $10,000

In this range, organizations rarely give special, individual attention to donors because they comprise a much larger group. Here you will find clubs of $100, $500, and $1,000. Nevertheless, an individually typed and signed thank-you letter is appropriate, as well as other avenues of appreciation. Depending on the membership level, you should consider an annual dinner or open house, publications, and an invitation to special events. Cornell University, for example, has the Tower Club for members contributing $2,000 annually. These members attend a dinner each year, a special reception during reunion, and other events.

Members of the Galileo Society at Harvey Mudd College in Claremont, California (they give between $150 and $1,000 annually), are invited to monthly events ranging from tours of scientific facilities to luncheons with faculty speakers. The college's Founding Friends ($2,000 to $10,000 annually) are invited to the same functions, but also go to two dinners each year at which a national speaker is featured. Ohio State's President's Club (one of the country's fastest-growing clubs, it enlisted 1,000 new members—at $1,000 annually—during the first four months of 1981 alone!) lets members join the faculty club, use the campus libraries, and park in campus lots. They also attend pregame football luncheons hosted by the president, and join more than 2,000 other donors at an annual outdoor dinner.[8]

As for tangible gifts or special mementos, they should vary from one level to another. The gift for membership in a $100 club should not be the same as the gift for a $1,000 club. The case study of UCLA's gift clubs at the end of the chapter may give you some more ideas for your program of appreciation. Gifts should also be changed each year for the participants. Remember, these are *annual* giving programs.

The point, of course, is to make your gift club stand out or, for that matter, catch up with many others that may be operating in your own locale. The task is to build a feeling of identity, loyalty, and awareness for your institution. Thus you may want to consider an identifying symbol or logo. Then use this symbol on all your stationery and publications. Each member might also receive a membership pin, car decals, bumper stickers, a keychain, or many other similar items.

All Giving Levels

Regardless of the range of membership levels, whether $10 or $100,000, there are certain benefits that should be available to everyone. Paul Schneiter offers some well-founded comments on what this package should include:

- All donors should get receipts. You need them for your records, and they need them for theirs. Include a printed statement of thanks on the receipt, and personalize it with your chief officer's signature (preprinted or individually signed).
- Always ask donors at the upper giving levels ($10,000 and up) if they want publicity. Many do but are reluctant to initiate it.
- Don't forget to have donors approve all press releases and photographs.
- Send donors cultivational materials to keep them informed about your organization's accomplishments and needs (newsletters, research reports, etc.). Also invite them to activities in which they could have an interest (plays, lectures, athletic contests, symposiums, among others).
- Let donors know that you value them for more than their

money. Individuals who have the means to give large gifts usually also have the means to contribute in other ways—as guest speakers, members of committees, volunteers, etc.[9]

ORGANIZING THE CLUB

In the final analysis, how you organize your gift clubs depends on the programs and goals you have established, and the membership you have enrolled. The members of one club may prefer a simple giving club with only one meeting a year. Another club may want a functioning organization with a committee structure.

Whatever the format, some type of committee structure should be considered and a strong chairman enlisted. You will certainly want a New Donor Committee charged with welcoming new friends to your institution. A Prospect Committee is also in order, to be charged with increasing the visibility of your club and enlisting the cooperation among members in making new prospect recommendations. An Activities Committee can be charged with planning those "timely and interesting events" that need to occur periodically throughout the year. Finally, an Annual Dinner Committee should be charged with the responsibility of arranging your annual affair, whether it be black tie or informal.

You ought to be alert to adapting the gift club format to your group's specific needs. Dartmouth College, for example, boasts of a "gift club that isn't"—their Funding Associates plan. This special deferred giving project, sponsored by the 55th reunion classes, was originally set up to avoid the exclusiveness associated with gift clubs. This "gift club with a difference" emphasizes the perpetuation of annual giving through a deferred giving program. There are membership requirements (life income gifts, endowments, or bequest provisions of minimum amounts), a charter membership category for each class, and a direct mail effort (supplemented by telephone calls and personal visits). The first four classes to participate have each given between $2.3 million and $4.1 million. As Dartmouth's Frank Logan notes, "Dartmouth's Funding Associates plan . . . has capitalized upon the distinctive giving patterns of older donors by providing them with the chance to support annual giving through deferred gifts. And all of it is in the spirit (but not the name) of a reunion gift club."[10]

Start a tradition of your own. An annual giving club will help you identify and enlist hundreds of new donors. Many of those who start out at $25 or $100 will increase their giving to qualify for higher gift levels. This will enable your institution to have a relatively dependable income base, giving you time to concentrate on discovering new sources for gifts.

CASE STUDY

UCLA's Major Gift Clubs

The University of California at Los Angeles (UCLA) has established several gift societies to recognize donors at various levels of giving. These societies include the Chancellor's Associates (gifts of $1,000 or more), the Chancellor's Honor Roll (CHR) Gold ($500–$999), CHR ($250–$499), and the Blue and Gold Circle ($100–$249).[11]

The following case study describes the materials and procedures UCLA uses to promote and retain membership in these clubs.

The Chancellor's Associates group was established in 1967. Then called the Franklin D. Murphy Associates, members gave at least $10,000 to the university. The first thirty-nine members became the board of directors of the UCLA Foundation. Members of the group today are UCLA alumni, faculty, staff, and friends who make an unrestricted contribution of $1,000 or more as a Regular Member or $5,000 or more per year as a Sustaining Member. Last year there were approximately 650 members of this prestigious group.

A small two-color brochure explains the group's purpose:

> Chancellor's Associates are men and women who have a special relationship with UCLA. Supportive of its goals, committed to its excellence, they have joined the University in its work . . . and undertaken a personal responsibility for its future. They are friends of the campus. And their friendship is vital to UCLA.

After some brief copy explaining the university's need for private support and the importance of the gifts ("the Associates contribution is fundamentally at work building UCLA"), the brochure describes the benefits accorded members of the group, along with an explanation of the types of memberships. The brochure ends with this simple statement:

> Chancellor's Associates. Friends of the campus, honored members of the campus community, they make an incomparable contribution to the work of UCLA. Chancellor's Associates. Think about it.

The Chancellor's Associates program is fully described in an exquisite 16-page brochure, featuring a cover photograph of UCLA's Royce Hall and full-color photos of the building's six stained glass windows throughout the brochure. Printed on heavy coated stock, the $8\frac{1}{2}'' \times 11''$ brochure is spiral-bound on the left $8\frac{1}{2}''$ margin. Don Enright and Roy Lee designed and wrote the booklet, while Tom Feldman took the cover photo and Norm Schindler took the inside photos.

The brochure includes extensive white space throughout, with a number of pages containing only very brief copy. The first page, headlined "It is a great enterprise," sets the tone for the publication:

> UCLA.
> The University of California, Los Angeles. One of the ten leading universities in America. And just past fifty years old.
>
> It is an institution inseparable from the community which created it. An institution of impact, world-wide.
>
> UCLA.
> Join us in our work.

Following this introduction is a color picture of a window in Royce Hall. On its facing page is a printed $6\frac{1}{2}'' \times 2\frac{1}{2}''$ card:

> The Chancellor of the University of California, Los Angeles
> nominates and invites
> (handwritten prospect's name)
> to membership in the Chancellor's Associates.

On the following page, under the heading "Chancellor's Associates is an organization of men and women committed to excellence at UCLA," is the following:

It is an association of distinction. From a founding membership of 39, the Associates has, in its second decade, grown to many times its original size. From business, the professions, the arts; from government, and the media; from virtually every area of community leadership, the Associates have come to be a primary resource of the campus.

Certainly, their financial commitment is vitally significant. While the University of California is a "public" school, today *just thirty-seven percent of its operating budget comes from the State.* Never has private support been more directly related to institutional excellence.

And yet the Associates' contribution is not merely financial. While many members must of necessity restrict their volunteer participation, the personal interaction—on the leadership levels—between the University and the community is a primary purpose of the Associates program.

The heading "The financial contribution of Chancellor's Associates provides the University with what it needs most" introduces a page on the specific uses of gifts. The following phrases may suggest appropriate messages for *your* gift clubs:

This flexibility of funding is very significant to a University of great aspirations; carefully spent, these dollars can have power far beyond their size. It is the nature of unrestricted funding to provide the final inches, the refinements, the best. Chancellor's Associates is a rare philanthropic opportunity, a chance to participate in the University's evolution at the cutting edge. Your involvement would be invaluable to UCLA.

The next two pages describe the benefits offered members, under the heading "UCLA welcomes Chancellor's Associates to the campus . . . and to the campus community." They urge the members to take advantage of the many activities offered them, noting that "On campus, members are the guests of the Chancellor; Associates are encouraged to feel at home."

A bound insert, printed on gray paper and measuring 8½" × 5½" carries the names of current members of the Associates. Also included in this booklet are facts and figures about the university, an acceptance form, and the following statement: "UCLA takes pride in proffering this invitation. We hope to see you here."

One reason for the great success of the program has been an effective professional recruitment network composed of the entire membership of Associates, categorized by profession. The most prestigious person in each profession is asked to chair that particular group.

The groups meet once a year to identify and select the prospective donors each member is willing to contact. Members are asked to attend only one meeting; they make their contacts on their own time. The best months for solicitation have been October, November, and December, and the Chancellor's Associates raised one-half of their 1978–79 goal in those months alone. For a more detailed discussion of this effort, see Lynda Boyer's article, "What I Wish They'd Told Me About Personal Solicitation," in the June 1979 issue of *Case Currents.*

The financial responsibility of accepting membership in the Associates can be met in one of these options:

Regular Membership—an unrestricted annual contribution of not less than $1,000 in cash or securities.

Sustaining Membership—an unrestricted annual contribution of not less than $5,000.

Regular Life Membership—an unrestricted one-time gift of not less than $25,000.

The important distinction to note here is that while the majority of donations to UCLA, and to most institutions, are restricted gifts, the Associates program is an *unrestricted* commitment.

The Associates gather about five times a year, with each occasion planned around a university event—athletic or cultural—or featuring an intensive exposure to one aspect of the campus. Recent events have been a special inside tour of UCLA's Brain Research Institute, a black tie dinner dance at the Bel-Air Country Club overlooking the campus, and a trip to the Coliseum for the UCLA-USC football game. More informal regular breakfasts with the Chancellor provide a continuing point of contact. These breakfasts are usually held three times a year and feature a top-notch speaker from the campus.

Among the benefits members receive are:

· preferred seating at most cultural, academic, and athletic events
· use of UCLA's 3.5-million-volume library

- use of UCLA's extensive facilities for recreation and sports
- honorary membership in UCLA's Faculty Center
- virtually unrestricted complimentary parking throughout the UCLA system; reserved parking at the Coliseum is available for Bruin home games
- subscriptions to UCLA's award-winning monthly magazine and the weekly calendar listing of events

The other information piece given to new members is a "Welcome" booklet, a handsome 18-page guide to all the advantages of being a Chancellor's Associate. A plastic membership card is inset into the first page.

Inside the booklet is a detailed description of the various benefits, including descriptions of the major events and presentations, publications, addresses and phone numbers of the libraries, sports facilities, meeting and eating places, and parking facilities.

A variety of brochures is used to promote the smaller gift societies at UCLA that compliment the Chancellor's Associates. Of special interest are the benefits available to donors in each program. For example, members of the Chancellor's Honor Roll Gold ($500–$1000) are invited to selected Chancellor's Associates events, and members of the Chancellor's Honor Roll ($250–$500) can purchase a UCLA Recreation Privilege Card (the card is given free to those in the higher giving categories). Other distinctions can be noted in Figures 6 through 8.

The Chancellor's Honor Roll brochure for donors at the $250 level (Figure 7) carries the simple cover message, "CHR is:". Note that the headlines for each section continue this idea in explaining the details of the organization.

At the bottom of the second page the brochure emphasizes the importance of unrestricted funds so that UCLA can "stay just a little ahead of the future in meeting and anticipating the opportunities and challenges ahead." The next paragraph, headed "CHR is: a share in the future—now," says that the group is unique and means something different to everyone who joins. The final page of the brochure ("CHR is: people") contains names of "some of the many members who help lead CHR today."[12]

Almost every type of organization can use some form of gift club successfully. How you set up your own depends on the pro-

CHR Gold adds a new dimension to CHR at UCLA.

Created by CHR members who felt that an avenue was needed for those who may wish to increase their contribution to UCLA, CHR Gold offers an important opportunity to those who join.

The full complement of programs and activities of CHR membership is available to those who join CHR Gold. However, CHR Gold members are also eligible for several significant additional benefits.

CHR Gold benefits include:

- Year-round parking privileges.
- UCLA Recreation Privilege Card, which opens gym facilities and the Sunset Canyon Recreation Center to CHR Gold members.
- Two tickets to intercollegiate UCLA athletic events subject to availability (basketball and football excepted).
- Library card application.
- Your personal campus representative; a helpful resource.
- Individualized wall plaque.
- Membership credentials.
- Recognition in published reports.
- Invitations to special events for you and your guests.
- Invitations to selected Chancellor's Associates events.
- Complimentary subscriptions to:
The UCLA Weekly,
The UCLA Monthly,
Inside CHR.

Membership in CHR Gold has been established as an annual contribution of $500 or more, payable either in the full amount once per year, or semi-annually ($250 per installment) or quarterly ($125 per installment).

Please contact the CHR office at (213) 825-3901 for further information.

Figure 6. This card, printed on light brown stock with black ink, describes the Chancellor's Honor Roll Gold program for donors at the $500 level. The headline on the card reads: "CHR Gold is: an important opportunity." The word "Gold" is printed in gold ink. Courtesy UCLA, Los Angeles, Calif.

CHR is:
an invitation to
involvement

CHR—Chancellor's Honor Roll—at UCLA is a special group of special people. People who are interested in being a part of all the excitement of a dynamic university. People who want to do something to show they care about the future of a place called UCLA. People like you.

And, the benefits and activities that come with being a member of CHR are designed to serve people like you. Each one is carefully designed to make you a part of what's going on at UCLA now—or to give you a glimpse of the discoveries in science and scholarship that will stamp "made at UCLA" on the future.

Programs

Naturally, athletic events are part of CHR, too. Special football bus parties. A day at the UCLA vs. USC track meet.

But there's more. "Raps with the Regents." Dr. Thelma Moss on ESP and Kirelian photography. A look at alternate energy sources with the School of Engineering. Dr. Barbara Brown on biofeedback. A talk on Tut. A chat with Dr. Anna Fisher, one of NASA's six women astronauts.

That's just a sample of some of the CHR members-only activities offered on campus.

People who join CHR also have a chance to participate in a collection of alumni activities, like the popular "Dinner for Twelve Strangers" program. CHR members can join a UCLA "friends" group, or serve on the CHR Steering Committee, too.

Benefits

CHR members can also take advantage of an array of benefits that make involvement even easier. Some of the many benefits of CHR membership include:

• A chance to buy a UCLA Recreation Privilege Card, which opens up gym facilities and the Sunset Canyon Recreation Center to CHR members.
• A chance to buy a "Night-V" year-round parking permit.
• Library card application.
• Your personal campus representative; a helpful resource.
• Membership credentials.
• Recognition in published reports.
• Invitations to special events for you and your guests.
• Complimentary subscriptions to:
The UCLA Weekly,
The UCLA Monthly,
Inside CHR.

CHR at UCLA. An invitation to involvement.

CHR is:
a partnership for
excellence

UCLA is a public institution. During more than a half-century of service, UCLA has exemplified the ideal of public education by opening its doors to all who qualify.

But, UCLA has accomplished more than fulfilling its unique mission. UCLA has not simply grown; UCLA has grown in excellence as well.

Growth in excellence at UCLA is supported almost exclusively by private gifts. Only about 35% of the current budget at UCLA comes from the State of California. The rest—it's sometimes called "the margin of excellence"—comes from people who care about UCLA.

CHR plays a vital role in insuring the continuation of excellence at UCLA.

Figure 7. The brochure for donors at the $250 level. Courtesy UCLA, Los Angeles, Calif.

grams and goals you have established, and the membership you have enrolled. Some clubs may work best with an involved committee structure and frequent meetings, while the membership of another club may prefer a simple structure and only one meeting per year.

BLUE AND GOLD CIRCLE: AN UNRESTRICTED ANNUAL CONTRIBUTION OF $100 TO UCLA

It may seem unusual to find the above information at the beginning of this brochure. Often in fundraising campaigns, the actual purpose of a solicitation is hidden behind a wall of meaningless words and phrases. Not here. We're proud of UCLA, proud enough to put the bottom line right up front.

BLUE AND GOLD CIRCLE

Blue and Gold Circle is a group of alumni and friends who show their support of UCLA by making an unrestricted annual contribution of $100, (tax-deductible), to UCLA. The contribution can be made in a single payment, or in semi-annual or quarterly installments.

Unrestricted means that the gift is used at the University's discretion. An accounting of how these funds are distributed to donors each year.

Annual means that $100 will give a donor membership in Blue and Gold Circle for one year. After a year, members are asked to renew their membership. There is absolutely no obligation to renew, although as a matter of fact, most do.

There are currently about 850 members in Blue and Gold Circle. Our immediate goal is to grow to 1000 members, with you as one of them.

BENEFITS

As a member of Blue and Gold Circle, you won't receive a lot of costly benefits that will negate the value of your gift to UCLA. What you will receive are:

• Subscriptions to The UCLA Monthly and UCLA Weekly, to help you keep in touch with the campus.
• A UCLA library card upon request: a key to one of the most comprehensive collections of information anywhere.
• Recognition in published reports: a public recognition of your private concern.
• A personal campus representative to assist you in your relationship with UCLA.
• Invitations to special events.
• Membership credentials.

And, of course, your gift is tax-deductible.

WHY PRIVATE SUPPORT FOR A PUBLIC UNIVERSITY?

Indeed, UCLA could exist adequately without private support. But UCLA did not become one of the top universities in the world by striving for adequacy. UCLA actively seeks private support to achieve excellence.

To UCLA, adequacy is a base, not a limit.

R.S.V.P.

Respond, preferably as a new member of Blue and Gold Circle. If not, remember that smaller gifts are also appreciated.

We'll accept any contribution that will make UCLA a better university. And we're proud of that fact.

UCLA
BLUE AND GOLD CIRCLE

Figure 8. The Blue and Gold Circle (gifts of $100–$250) uses a well-written brochure that should give you many ideas for your own printed pieces. Courtesy UCLA, Los Angeles, Calif.

PART TWO

THE
TOOLS
OF FUNDRAISING

The skills and techniques used in directing and participating in fundraising activities are an integral part of the business. Effectively practiced, they strengthen the fundraising potential of the organization.

This section is for people eager to learn but in no mood for frills. It is designed as a reference section for neophyte fundraisers who feel a need for help in getting started, and for experienced fundraisers who desire another look at tested methods and materials. Here you will find practical suggestions about telephone campaigns, direct mail correspondence, special events, and public relations. While only a small percentage of available suggestions can be included in any one presentation, we believe we have selected the most important points. Only material that has been tested by a wide range of professionals and groups has been included.

The Telephone Campaign

What's the next best thing to being there? Your telephone, of course. Use it during annual appeals, capital campaigns, or memorial campaigns, whenever you have too many potential donors to visit.[1]

Call it a phonothon, telethon, phonenite, or whatever you find appropriate. Hold a special one-night intensive program, or run the campaign for several weeks. Let your former patients, alumni, current volunteers, patrons, staff members, or advisory groups make the calls. Contact all former donors, those who have never given before, everyone in certain geographic areas, or your entire mailing list. Accelerate the pace of a total campaign, clean up the year's efforts, create a special fund drive or inaugurate a special program. Restrict the gifts to special accounts or make all contributions for general needs.

Whatever you call it, however you run it, and whatever you do with the money, a telephone campaign can be a very effective tool in your fundraising efforts, adding a personal touch lacking in direct mail and other long-distance efforts. No other fundraising technique comes as close to face-to-face solicitation as do telephone calls. And no matter how well organized your campaign is, or how many volunteer workers you have, you'll usually find it difficult to reach all your prospects in a face-to-face solicitation.

Most successful fundraisers in hospitals, educational institutions, social service agencies, and cultural organizations use some form of telephone campaign during their various giving programs. There are a number of reasons why these campaigns are so effective and popular today. They can be quickly and easily organized, involve relatively few volunteers and not too much of their time, provide the opportunity to answer questions and discuss specific situations, and allow you to reach a large number of your prospects in a short time span. In addition, these campaigns help keep mailing lists current, since wrong phone numbers usually lead to an update in address as well as the correct number.

Though it has been suggested that telephone campaigns should be used to reach the noncontributor, such campaigns have effectively allowed volunteers to kick off special programs, discuss challenge gift campaigns, follow up on direct mail and previous personal visits, reach special groups with appeals from volunteers with similar interests and backgrounds, and clean up a campaign by contacting all those not reached previously.

Telephone campaigns help get alumni, former participants, volunteer workers, and others involved with your institution. Both the callers and the prospects they call get enthusiastic about current developments and programs. The prospects get to ask questions and find out more about the institution.

Another benefit of telephone campaigns is that they help dispel the belief—usually false—that only big gifts are important. Many campaigns are most successful in attracting quantities of relatively small gifts, stressing that gifts of any size help the cause.

Many institutions find that a telephone campaign fits in nicely with their other efforts. Yale, for example, has used a telephone campaign in combination with direct mail in The Campaign for Yale, a capital and endowment fund. Claremont Men's College uses an annual Phonenite as their prime vehicle for all alumni solicitation. Michigan State University used a phone campaign to raise $101,000 in pledges and contributions as part of their $17 Million Enrichment Program capital campaign. This effort used twenty students each night, four nights per week and Saturdays, and contacted alumni in Michigan who had not previously contributed to the campaign. Calls were made six weeks after the direct mail effort (which had brought in $220,000), and prospects were asked to pledge $100 over a three-year period. Contributions ranged from as little as four dollars to $2,000. Callers added personal postscripts on notes sent to all who pledged, a good public relations idea that helps personalize large institutions such as MSU.

The PBS television station in Los Angeles, KCET, turned to a telephone campaign when it decided that its three-times-per-year mailings to lapsed members just weren't doing well enough. The station had an audience of people who had originally responded to on-the-air appeals for membership by phoning in their pledges, and the renewal rates for these members were lower than the average. "I had a gut feeling," the station's development director explained, "that people who responded to an appeal by telephone to become subscribers and who had a lower-than-average response rate to mail campaign promotion renewals would be particularly receptive to a telephone appeal to renew."

Prerecorded messages were shown, featuring Charlton Heston discussing the importance of supporting the station. Three thousand calls were made to former members, generating a 28 percent response, with an average pledge of $19.07. These results were substantially better than originally planned, demonstrating that people have a strong willingness to conduct business by telephone.

There are many other uses and success stories involving telephone campaigns. Many fundraisers report that this technique is more effective than direct mail, allowing for two-way communication between the institution and the prospect. Questions can be answered, case studies explained, and specific gift requests adjusted depending on the solicitor's feelings.

ORGANIZING AND CONDUCTING THE CAMPAIGN

In an April 1979 speech to a CASE regional conference, Donald Lemish of East Carolina University offered a number of guidelines for planning and conducting a telephone campaign. Though his ideas are specifically directed to colleges and universities, they can, of course, be adapted to any type of institution.

1. Secure a good general chairman. When possible, pick a person connected with the local alumni club, a well-known individual who is most interested in helping the university, or an alumnus who is young, energetic, knows a lot of alumni in the area, and will make a gift.

    Never try to obtain this chairman by telephone. Pay a visit, explaining that you came just to see the person and to seek his or her leadership. If your Number 1 prospect declines, ask for a recommendation of another person.

The chairman is responsible for obtaining a phone site that has enough trunk lines to complete the campaign. If possible, the facility should be free of charge. One rule of thumb is to have about seven trunk lines for every 1,000 alumni to be called and to plan to call on three consecutive evenings. This will provide the opportunity to reach persons not at home on the first attempted call.

The general chairman must also secure the captains necessary for the completion of the volunteer structure. Normally this would be one captain for each night of calling; however, this will vary depending on the number of phones to be manned. Attempt to follow the "one hand theory" whenever possible—never ask a captain to be responsible for obtaining more than the number of volunteers you can count on five fingers. The more volunteers one must be responsible for obtaining, the more chance of difficulty, because the average person is limited to the number of persons he or she knows closely enough to ask for favors. The absolute maximum number of volunteers that another leader should ever have to obtain is eight. If the "one hand theory" is used, a major campaign structure utilizing 30 phones on each of the three nights might look like this:

1 general chairman

3 evening chairmen, each having the responsibility of . . .

6 night captains, each having the responsibility of . . .

6 volunteer callers

For a given night this provides a total of 44 persons who should be present to operate 30 telephones. This more than provides for normal attrition, which experience indicates is 2 of every 10 volunteers.

The general chairman should be present at all phone nights and should organize a captains' meeting four or five weeks prior to the campaign. At this meeting a staff member will emphasize the responsibilities of each captain, the scope of the campaign, and deadlines. Again, experience shows that a dinner for the captains usually assures that they will feel obligated to fulfill their responsibilities.

The general chairman should work with the staff person

and local media to obtain good publicity before and after the campaign.

2. Specific responsibilities of the night captains include attending the captains' meeting, obtaining sufficient volunteer callers, notifying the office and chairmen of all workers' names and addresses at least three weeks before the phone night, calling each worker the weekend before as a reminder, and attending the campaign with his or her volunteers.

3. A general mailing should be prepared that will be sent to the area telling alumni of the phone campaign, timed to arrive a week to ten days prior to the calling. If the mailer is a letter, it should be signed by the local chairman, Annual Fund chairman, or some recognizable important volunteer. Do not simply rely on the fact that the prospects are going to get a call as a reason for making a pledge. The mailer *must* state a case for support.

4. Some type of printed pledge form should be used and one form should be processed for every alumnus/alumna in the area. This form should show the volunteer the prospect's telephone number and previous giving record, as well as any other information that might be available and that might benefit the volunteer in obtaining a pledge.

5. A thank-you letter should be sent to all volunteers as soon as they are known by the office.

   The letter should tell the volunteer where and when the campaign will be held. We ask our workers to arrive at 6:20 P.M., briefing begins at 6:30, and telephoning takes place from about 7:00 to 9:30 P.M. The best nights for calling are Mondays through Thursdays.

   Provide the volunteer with all sorts of background such as a sample sales talk, previous statistics reflecting any fund-raising successes your organization has had, and anything else you can provide in advance that will help reassure the volunteer that the job will be simple.

6. Prepare visual materials and background information that will assist in briefing volunteers. Use large charts, special brochures, work sheets, etc.

7. The staff member running the campaign should be at the phoning site at least one-half hour prior to the workers in order to set up shop.

8. Give complete instructions and a "sales pitch" to all workers after the general chairman has expressed thanks to the volunteers. A good briefing will take about 30 minutes and should be presented with great enthusiasm by the staff member.

9. As the volunteers are making their calls, be available to answer questions, keep statistics, and process pledges. It is best if your calling facility is one in which all the workers are close together and not in different rooms.

10. Set a realistic goal for each night, one you know can be reached. A goal that cannot be reached can hurt worker morale.

11. Make sure that some sort of thank-you is sent to each person who pledges, the same night the pledge is received. It is best to have a pledge card that also may be used as a thank-you with a return envelope mailed to the giver.

12. Alumni not reached during the calling should immediately receive a solicitation letter explaining that you were sorry you missed them during the telephoning but hope they will give, etc.

13. In addition to local newspaper publicity, see that the campaign is publicized in the alumni publication and name all volunteers.

14. Various other special tips that may prove effective:

    -   A good phone caller will be able to dial about 100 numbers and talk to about 40 prospects in 2½ hours of calling.
    -   Try to serve some snack/refreshments while volunteers are calling. However, do not serve liquor before the calling.
    -   It is not necessary to have a dinner for workers before calling. We recommend setting goals and buying drinks or food for the volunteers after the calling is completed.
    -   Create special competition between areas and individuals whenever possible. Also, compare yourself with other similar institutions and shoot for being No. 1.
    -   The staff members should always be very enthusiastic—it will rub off onto the workers.
    -   Always arrange pledge cards so that each volunteer has

equal prospects with best prospects on top. Do not hold back best prospects for the second or third nights of calling; simply reorganize cards each night.

- You may wish to exclude major gift club donors from the campaign and have them solicited in person by a staff member.

- Give each volunteer his or her own pledge card and ask him to complete it before making any calls to others.

- Do not expect large gifts to be pledged by telephone. A phone solicitation is best when the intent is to broaden the base of support with $5–$200 gifts.

- Always have one or more staff members running the campaign. Never send materials off to a city and let volunteers run a campaign alone.

As an example of expenses incurred during a phone campaign, Lemish gives these figures from a Ball State University campaign with fifteen regional programs, excluding staff travel:

Food for captains, workers' refreshments, entertaining volunteers	$ 800
Telephone installations, extra lines, special facilities, etc.	$ 1,200
Printing of letters, brochures, worksheets, pledge cards, envelopes	$ 1,000
Miscellaneous	$ 100
Total Expenses	$ 3,100
Amount pledged through campaigns (approximately)	$200,000

Percent of money raised needed to cover campaign costs: 1.55%

Donald Lemish also offers a sample campaign schedule, which the staff member would present to the general chairman for a phonothon with 3,000 prospects in the area.

The pioneering efforts for a number of the most successful telephone programs have come from Ball State University. In the late 1960s, Ball State had 4,100 donors, contributing just over $36,000 to the university. They started their first phonothon and doubled both the number of donors and the amount raised. Each year since then they have had 30 percent or more alumni participa-

Sample Campaign Schedule

Date	Responsibility	Procedure
Jan. 1	Director	General chairman should be confirmed and furnished with list of alumni.
Jan. 9	General Chairman	General chairman should have 16 captains (four for each night) confirmed and names to director.
9 weeks prior (Jan. 14)	Director	Requisition computer list of alumni in telefund area to be run. Include occupations.
	General Chairman	Secure and confirm facility with 20 telephone trunk lines (inform director of facility and person in charge who should receive a thank-you note from the university).
Jan. 19	General Chairman	Arrange and conduct meeting with night captains and director to discuss campaign procedures and to identify potential workers.
3 weeks prior	Night Captains	Must have five volunteer workers for each night captain confirmed and names and addresses to alumni field director. (The campaign cannot be successful unless every telephone is manned.)
	Director	Send thank-you informational letters to all workers. Copies to general chairman and night captains.
2 weeks prior (March 4)	News Bureau	News Bureau should send news release about phone campaign to all local news media and a copy to the general chairman.
	Mail Room	Telefund letter should be mailed to all alumni.

Date	Responsibility	Procedure
Weekend prior to March 15	Night Captains	Telephone each worker to make sure he or she will be at the proper place on the proper date.
Campaign March 18, 19, 20, 21		TELEFUND CAMPAIGN, 6:20 to 9:30 P.M.
After Campaign	Development Office	Send letters to all workers expressing thanks and outlining preliminary campaign pledge results. Send "Sorry We Missed You" notes to persons not contacted by telephone.

tion, and today more than 16,000 donors annually give more than $400,000 to Ball State. Donald Lemish, who helped begin these successful programs, notes that the extensive phonothon network devised by Ball State is the key ingredient in the total giving program. BSU volunteers can now reach nearly all of their alumni through seventeen regional phone campaigns with the broadest telephone program in the country.[2]

The secret is clearly organization—preparing for the campaign, running it smoothly, and evaluating its results for an even better program the next time. Among the details you should carefully consider when planning your own telephone campaign are such matters as the following:

The physical arrangement of the calling area. Phones should be installed in your facility if possible. The phones should be close enough together for the psychological effect of group spirit, and so that callers can learn by listening to each other, but far enough apart so they won't interfere with conversation.

Costs can be reduced by using existing facilities where enough outside lines are available (e.g., banks, insurance companies, investment houses, or even the telephone company offices). Have one service table for every fifteen phones to accommodate the staff workers. Also needed is a refreshment table for coffee, Cokes, etc.

Provide some type of large scoreboard (blackboard, basketball scoreboard if in the gym) for up-to-date reporting of the evening's progress.

Solicitors. Use the same organization as for a personal solicitation campaign: chairman, team captains, and workers. Try to enlist volunteers who are experienced in talking over the phone (e.g., insurance salesmen, stockbrokers, attorneys, PR people, or telephone company employees). Student callers or currently involved group members are sometimes helpful, though normally not as effective as experienced alumni who have a better feeling for raising funds.

Staff personnel (fifteen phones or more). At least one secretary is needed to keep the records and stuff the envelopes to be mailed to the prospects who were contacted. A runner can be used to collect the pledges, serve refreshments, etc. A staff person should make the presentation, answer questions, assist the callers, keep the scoreboard, and generally oversee the operation.

Materials. The callers should have the following supplies:

- Phone forms for each prospect who has not contributed, indicating address, phone number, and recent giving record, and other details such as class year, dates of participation, etc.
- A suggested sales talk, which should gain the prospect's attention, stimulate interest, and create a desire to participate.
- A fact sheet about the institution and answers to possible questions.
- Pen, pencils, note paper, and paper clips.
- Individual scorecards—callers like to know how they are doing, and it will help later in figuring out the statistics of the campaign.
- A cowbell or other noisemaker to help build enthusiasm with each pledge.

The staff member also needs supplies, including an adding machine, envelopes, reply envelopes, stamps, a box to sort cards, pencils, and note paper. A calculator will help to figure percentages quickly.

One of the major items to consider is the support material,

which helps train the callers, keeps the prospects informed of the progress of the campaign, and helps do the selling job. Many institutions even suggest sample conversations, directing the caller in the words and phrases to use. The following conversation, adapted from material used by the University of Central Florida, is typical:

Sample Sales Talk

Introduce yourself.
"Hello. This is ———, University of Central Florida, Class of ———."

Ask for the alumnus/alumna.
"Is ——— home?" It is important that you talk only to alumni!!

Tell why you're calling.
"I'm with a group of alumni and students tonight and we are calling all UCF Alumni in the area asking for their pledges to the 1982 Alumni Annual Fund." ("Your contribution can be earmarked for any program or department you desire. If it is unrestricted, it will be used by the Alumni Association where the need is greatest.")

Suggest a figure.
"I'm happy to have your pledge card, and I would like to put you down for a pledge this year. Ten dollars would be nice, but fifteen, twenty, or twenty-five would be great. Donors of at least ten dollars automatically become members of the UCF Alum-knights, and receive different benefits at various giving levels. All donors will get discount passes to local attractions." If the person says no to the first figure you suggest, suggest a lower figure. Talk turkey—tell the person about the specific programs for which his or her dollars can help. If the person says no, verify address and work location. Mention Annual Spring Banquet. More information will be sent to everyone.

Hint at early payment.
Indicate that we would like the pledge to be paid at the earliest convenience of the alumni. Although the Fund is on the calendar

year basis, pledges paid early give a good indication of the campaign's success. The alumni will receive a thank-you note in the mail this week and a return-address, postage-paid envelope.

Thank the donor and mention the reply procedure.
"Thank you for your $_____ pledge. You will soon receive from UCF a note thanking you and acknowledging your pledge, and a reply envelope in which you can mail your gift to the Alumni Annual Fund."

Ask about matching contributions.
"Did you know some companies match their employees' contributions? If you'll tell me where you work, we can check the file and let you know if yours is a matching gifts employer." ("We also like to know how many graduates have jobs in their major fields.")

Verify the address.
"Let me check your address . . . are you still living at _____?"

And don't forget to say thank you again!!!
Do so whatever the amount of the pledge.

In addition, it is important that you provide each caller with a set of guidelines to cover the basics of calling, points to remember, and procedures to follow in various cases. Central Florida gives the following information to their callers:

Points to Remember

1. Be as brief as possible without distorting your message—if an alumnus says he will give, promptly verify his name, address, amount, say thanks and hang up. Don't bother with needless details.
2. Be sure you close properly by saying, "May I put you down for $_____?"
3. Don't be discouraged by doubting Thomases or stubbornness. Be prepared for anything. Even if you think someone sounds like the "type" who wouldn't make a gift, don't give up.

4. Gifts may be earmarked—a contributor can "earmark" or "designate" a gift to a particular school, college, department, scholarship fund, etc.

5. Deceased alumni—if an alumnus is reported dead, make sure it's the same person you have on your form. Simply say, "Is that the J. Doe who graduated from the University of Central Florida in 1975?"

6. Verify address.

7. Always hang up after the alumnus. This is not only courteous, it's good business. The alumnus may think of something to say at the last minute. If you have already hung up, you'll miss the message, and possibly a pledge.

Have fun and enjoy yourself, but keep your responsibility in mind. You will be raising the dollars that will help provide for scholarships, special projects, alumni activities, and much more. As you can see, the importance of your task cannot be overemphasized.

Procedures

After calling an alum, place the phone card in one of the following piles:

Yes: Person has made a pledge—fill out pledge card and sign your name; fill out phone card and sign your name and organization.

Callbacks: No answer, or alum was not at home. DO NOT write anything on phone card.

Refusals: Write in "refusal" under "comments" and sign your name.

Completed: Wrong numbers, moved, unknown person, alum is out of town. Put reason under "comments" and sign your name. Someone else will try to find correct phone numbers.

Give your YES pile to the captains as they come around.

University of Central Florida callers also receive the following information on good listening, which they keep by their phones during the evening:

Keys to Good Listening

Limit your own talking.
You can't talk and listen at the same time.

Ask questions.
If you don't understand something, or feel you may have missed a point, clear it up now before it embarrasses you later.

Concentrate.
Focus your mind on what the prospect is saying. Practice shutting out outside distractions.

Add interjections.
An occasional "Yes," "I see," etc., shows the alumnus you're still with him or her . . . but don't overdo it or use them as meaningless comments.

Turn off your own worries.
This isn't always easy; but personal fears, worries and problems form a kind of "static" that can blank out the alumnus' message.

Prepare in advance.
Remarks and questions prepared in advance, when possible, free your mind for listening.

React to ideas—not the person.
Don't allow irritation at things the prospect may say, or at his manner, to distract you.

Don't argue mentally.
You may disagree with what the alumnus says, but keep an open mind, or you're likely to unconsciously "close your ears."

Don't jump to conclusions.
Avoid making unwarranted assumptions about what the alumna is going to say, or mentally trying to complete her sentences for her.

At Florida Atlantic University, callers receive a packet of information with an important cover sheet welcoming them to the "Telefund Task Force." This spells out the procedure for the night, including the purpose and format of the briefing period, the flexibility of the suggested conversation, and the importance of the phone campaign to the university's total giving program. One of the most interesting paragraphs puts the program in perspective:

> First, remember that we're not doing any favors by calling alumni and asking them for money. We're not begging, but alumni are doing us and the University a favor by contributing. Do not get upset with anyone. Our biggest job will be to make their giving as painless and justified as possible. All of us know the financial needs of the University. We hope the alumni we call at least suspect these needs. . . .[3]

Most successful phonothons begin by sending advance notice to your prospects that calling will be done on a certain night and for certain needs. This alerts the donor, and helps pave the way for your call during the campaign. The volunteer will not be making a "cold" call; the prospect has received information about the campaign and knows that the call is coming. Figure 9 shows a sample card you might send out to your prospects a week or two before the campaign begins.

Your record keeping is very important, as you must make any necessary corrections on the prospect's name, address, or phone number in your files, and you must accurately record the results of the phone call. A sample pledge card is shown in Figure 10; it combines the record of the call with a card confirming the pledge. The thank-you card should be detached and mailed immediately after the evening's calling. A stamped, return-address envelope should also be sent, of course.

It's interesting to see the different ways organizations use phone campaigns as part of their total annual giving programs. At the University of Texas in El Paso (UTEP), for example, the telephone campaign is part of their Alumni Fund for Excellence, along with three annual direct mail appeals. UTEP uses a mini–phone campaign before the actual calling begins to recruit the class chairmen volunteers, finding that phone calls are very effective in telling the story of the university's needs.

Georgetown University uses a great many promotional materials

"This is NAME OF ORGANIZATION calling!"

Between November 5 and November 19, a volunteer from the ORGANIZATION will be calling to ask for your support of our endowment program.

Before you receive that phone call, I hope that you will think about all that ORGANIZATION has done for your community, and remember how much you benefitted from our programs and services. Your gift in 1982 will help build our endowment to a point where we can increase our service to more than 5,000 people in this area.

When a volunteer calls you next month, I sincerely hope that you will respond with a gift to the 1982 Endowment Drive. Your gift, regardless of the amount, will be needed and appreciated.

Thanks for your support.

John Doe

1982 Volunteer Chairman

Figure 9. Advance notice of a phonothon campaign.

during their phonothons, including pens, stationery, and name tags all bearing a phone receiver and the words "A Call for Georgetown." They mail out the completed pledge cards to donors with a small brochure entitled "So Good to Talk with You." The donors are thanked for their pledge and given a brief statement on the importance of unrestricting giving.

William Jewell College has used a phone campaign as part of a larger capital effort. When they found correspondence slow and personal contact impractical in reaching their 10,000 alumni to describe the five-year, $10-million "William Jewell Tomorrow" capital campaign, development staffers set up a phonothon to raise $200,000 from 6,000 alumni who had never contributed before. Both student and alumni callers participated, competing against each other for a variety of prizes (e.g., most pledges over $1,000, the next pledge after 8:30 P.M., etc.). Streamers, decorations, noisemakers, and balloons were used to create a carnival atmosphere.

Callers asked for five-year pledges—from $1,000 per year for five years to a minimum of $25 per year. When pledges were obtained, callers whistled, rang bells, yelled, and used all available noisemakers.

The effort brought in $270,000 from the 6,000 people contacted. This included 1,680 pledges, 1,900 refusals, and 2,420 alumni who were not at home or who wanted to think about the pledge before making a commitment. The top caller, by the way, obtained a pledge from one of the former noncontributors for $53,000!

One tip you might want to follow is to have desk blotters printed for each caller and placed under the phones. A typical 17″ × 22″ paper might include all the important information for the evening, including instructions, sample conversation, suggested pledge guides, completing the pledge card, and other important information. This helps keep the information before the callers' eyes all evening, and reminds them of the important points (such as to keep saying "thank you" when gifts are made!).

It has also been suggested by several fundraisers that calling the prospect's attention to the amount they gave the previous year often leads to an increased pledge during the current campaign.

XYZ Organization, Inc.

(Prospect's Name) ______

(Address) ______

______

(PLEASE MAKE CORRECTIONS IF ABOVE
INFORMATION IS INCORRECT)

Telephone: ( ) ______

Affiliation with our organization:

______

______

Previous giving record: ______

______

______

Results of Calling

Amount of pledge: ______

Response (circle one):

Already Given   Pledged

Considering   Refusal

If not contacted, why?

(circle one)

No answer   Busy   Moved

Not home   Wrong number

Other: ______

Terms:

______ per month

______ per quarter

Comments: ______

______

______

Caller's name: ______

- -

Dear ______,

Thank you for your generous pledge of $____ to our 1982
Telephone Fund Drive. We appreciate your loyal support.
Please make your check payable to XYZ, Inc., and
return in the enclosed, stamped envelope.

XYZ ORGANIZATION, INC.
Your generous support
is sincerely appreciated.

J. Smith
President

Figure 10. Sample pledge card with thank-you card included at bottom.

These guidelines have worked well for a variety of charitable organizations who have found the telephone an efficient, economical, and enjoyable method of raising money. You'll find that you need to adapt these ideas to the specifics of your own group. For example, if staff time allows, you may want to put one person in charge of keeping phone numbers accurate throughout the year, so that a mad rush doesn't take place every year before the phonothon.

If you have to set up your own phones, it's probably worthwhile to use push-button phones and have direct dialing for all callers. Sometimes this pays for itself, resulting in more funds than would have been raised by accepting free telephones, where you have to dial the numbers or go through an operator for outside lines. The secret of success in a phone effort is to call as many prospects as possible during the campaign, so you'll want to make it as fast-moving as possible.

Many groups find it advantageous to use an overhead projector and large screen to keep important information easily available during the calling. Others use projectors or blackboards to update totals and put special notes in front of everyone (such as a large pledge, an interesting comment, etc.).

Finally, you might contact your local telephone company for booklets on proper telephone procedure and helpful hints for using the phone. Most companies distribute these materials as a public service, and will be glad to provide enough for each of your callers to have. Some advice from the United Telephone Company (Winter Park, Florida) is worth repeating here: "every time you make or receive a telephone call at work, you are representing your company and your company's image is on the line. The impression you create should always be favorable, winning friends for you and your company. When you show interest, speak clearly. . . . When you are courteous and tactful, you shine as someone people will remember."[4]

PHONE TIPS

In addition to the ideas we have suggested, the telephone companies give their own suggestions on ways to utilize the phone better. The following guidelines are compiled from several guides to better phone etiquette:

- Use businesslike phrases instead of slang. Say "Yes," "Certainly," and "Of course" instead of "OK."
- Avoid technical expressions that may confuse the caller.
- Be a good listener; make notes while the caller is speaking.
- Side comments and discussions with others while a person is waiting on the line are inconsiderate and irritating.
- Always acknowledge a request.
- Show that you're interested by using the caller's name.
- Give each caller individual rather than routine consideration.
- Put a smile in your voice by using basic phrases of courtesy such as "Please," "Thank you," and "You're welcome."
- Try to vary your phrases to suit the conditions.
- Show a sincere interest in the caller.
- Save candy, gum, and cigarettes until after your telephone conversation.
- Speak clearly and distinctly. Talk directly into the transmitter, holding it about 1½ inches from your lips.
- Vary your tone but avoid extremes of loudness or softness.
- Talk at a moderate rate, not too fast or too slow.

Perhaps the single best piece of advice, however, comes from Northwestern Telephone Company: "Three or four shouters in a group of telephone solicitors will create bedlam. It isn't necessary to talk loud to be heard or understood over the telephone when you talk *into* the telephone."

The way you use the phone may determine how big a gift your institution will receive. It's worth doing it right!

CASE STUDY

Rutgers University—A Volunteer Involvement Phonothon

Volunteer involvement is essential to the success of most fundraising efforts. The annual phonothon run by the Rutgers University Foundation uses volunteers for thirty sessions in four different segments: a Leadership Phonothon for prior-year donors of $100 or more (held in November), and three general phonothons in Camden, Newark, and New Brunswick, New Jersey (all held in February and March). The general phonothon segments are held on each of Rutgers's three campuses to increase volunteer participation by tapping the pride that faculty, students, and alumni have for their own campuses.

The following case study covers the techniques Rutgers uses to attract help for this campaign. Since the need for volunteers is nearly universal among fundraisers, this study is especially important in all areas of fundraising, not just for phonothons.

For all but the Leadership segment, a two-pronged recruitment process is conducted, relying on a direct mail approach along with various forms of person-to-person recruitment. A number of audiences are contacted for help with the phonothon, including alumni, faculty, staff, students, a select group of parents, and, most important of all, previous phonothon volunteers.

Recruitment for the Leadership segment of the phonothon is simpler than that for the other segments because it builds on past successes. Last year, for example, the Foundation staff reviewed the records of the previous year's phonothon and selected 140 of the very best volunteers. These volunteers were sent a letter, produced on an in-house automatic typewriter, inviting them to participate in the current Leadership effort. No other recruitment activity was deemed necessary, since these volunteers are a very committed group of people. The letter asks the caller to help build on the success of the previous year, and includes a postcard to be returned with the caller's name and dates of availability.

The direct mail recruitment for the February–March phonothon included the following letters:

- A general letter from the annual fund chairman to all alumni who had indicated an interest in assisting in the Foundation's work in an alumni questionnaire they had returned previously.
- Letters from the Camden chairman to prior phonothon volunteers, faculty and staff, prior-year donors, and alumni association dues-payers. Similar letters were also sent to alumni association officers and council members.

  This type of letter included the following:

  A favorite American proverb says that "time is money." Never was that saying more true than for Phonothon '79, when the gift of a few hours of your time can result in increased funding for all the things we need here at Rutgers-Camden: scholarships, research, library resources, improved quality of student life, and more. . . .

  As a Phonothon volunteer, you'll be calling Camden

alumni in New Jersey and throughout the country to ask them for a pledge toward the enhancement of educational opportunities at Rutgers-Camden. You may select an afternoon or evening session. . . .

With your help, I'm confident that we can achieve another banner year in support of Rutgers-Camden. Maybe you can't give as much as you'd like in terms of money, but Phonothon '79 is the opportunity to give generously of your time in an enjoyable way.

- Letters from the Newark chairman to the same groups listed above.
- Letters from the New Brunswick chairman to the same groups listed, and to a select group of parents. An excerpt from the letter to parents:

    With sons and daughters in school, many of us can't give as much as we'd like in terms of money. Phonothon '79 is an excellent opportunity to give generously of your time in an enjoyable way. Moreover, you'll have an unusual opportunity to obtain an "insider's" view of the university as you work alongside Rutgers administrators, faculty, students and alumni.

- Letters from the student chairman of the New Brunswick segment to student dormitory supervisors, financial aid recipients, and officers of student organizations. An excerpt from a sample letter:

    My name is _____, a Rutgers University student. I am also a financial aid recipient grateful for the educational opportunity made possible by considerable financial aid. I'm writing to ask for your help in maintaining and increasing the available funds for financial aid at Rutgers.

    I have always welcomed the funds provided through the financial aid program at Rutgers, but until recently I did not completely understand where the funds come from. I am now aware that a large part of our financial aid comes from private gifts to the University made through the Rutgers University Foundation. The Foundation solicits these gifts from benefactors whose generous contributions are distributed to you, me, and hundreds of other Rutgers financial aid recipients.

After participating in this phonothon, you'll know what it means to be part of a great university; whatever its faults, you'll have helped strengthen this institution.

The direct mail campaign is unified by an emphasis in all letters on the giving of one's time in addition to, or, if necessary, instead of monetary contribution to the university. In particular, several of the appeals use the expression "time is money."

Bruce Newman, chief executive officer of the Rutgers University Foundation, explains that the program of personal contact was conducted largely in December and January to recruit volunteers before the phonothon began on February 6. Staff members made appearances at meetings of various alumni associations, parents' groups, student organizations, and faculty gatherings. In addition, a staffer followed up on the direct mail appeal by contacting dormitory supervisors, who were asked to post sign-up sheets on their dormitory floors or wings. Sign-up sheets were also distributed to those student organizations whose meetings staff members could not attend.

Since four of the nineteen New Brunswick sessions emphasized fundraising for Rutgers athletics, special efforts were made to recruit coaches for those evenings. Working through the coaches, the Foundation staff was also able to recruit captains and members of the various athletic teams.

In further efforts at personal contact, key prior-year volunteers were telephoned by staff and the three chairmen. Agents for five-year reunion classes were enlisted by staff members to recruit three or four class members to phone classmates. Five-year reunion volunteers were encouraged to use the phonothon to urge their classmates to attend the reunion in June. The final step in personal recruitment was a two-day session run by student volunteers; during this period, a sign-up station was set up outside the main student dining hall in New Brunswick and staffed during meal hours.

In addition to this two-pronged approach, Newman says, the Foundation used various media in its recruitment. The *Annual Giving* newsletter, distributed to volunteers and board members in early January, contained an appeal for phonothon workers and a business reply card for sign-up purposes. A news release was issued to media on- and off-campus, announcing dates, dollar goal, and chairmen, and giving details on how to volunteer. A $2' \times 15'$

banner was hung in the major student dining hall on the New Brunswick campus for two weeks, while a seven-foot telephone (the phonothon logo used on all materials), accompanied by sign-up cards, was placed in the foyer of the Faculty-Alumni Club for four weeks.

A follow-up to recruitment was a short acknowledgment letter sent to each person who signed up for one or more sessions. For the Leadership segment, the letter was produced on the automatic typewriter on plain stationery; for all other segments, the letter was typed on a "Sample Conversation" folder, which is actually used at the phonothon. In this way, volunteers could read through some of the information they would be using at the phonothon while being reminded of the session for which they had signed up. Directions and information about parking were included with the acknowledgment letter.

There were a number of audiences for the phonothon recruitment drive, including previous volunteers on all three campuses, faculty on all three campuses, alumni active in their Rutgers organizations, alumni donors and dues-paying alumni living within commuting distance of any of the three phonothon sites, parents living close to the phonothon sites, and students. The student audience could be broken down into the dormitory supervisors, student organizations and service clubs, financial aid recipients, Rutgers College students (students at the central campus of the sprawling New Brunswick complex,) and student athletes.

Bruce Newman adds, "In the estimation of the Foundation staff, last year's recruitment effort was most successful. The Leadership segment, for example, went from 35 to 46 volunteers and the percentage of seats filled compared to total seats available went from 77 percent to 96 percent." There was about a 28 percent increase in volunteers for this effort.

"In last year's February-March New Brunswick segment," Newman continues, "the total number of volunteers increased from 320 to 351, or about 10 percent. Although part of the increase may be attributed to the addition of one session, the role of weather in attendance must be taken into account. The previous year's phonothon benefited from excellent weather conditions, while volunteer attendance during the first week and a half in New Brunswick was lessened by forecast storms."

Phonothon recruitment is primarily the responsibility of Rutgers's associate director of annual giving. Other staff members assist with personal contact and with drafting letters for the direct mail effort. Clerical staff prepare camera-ready copy, which is then printed and mailed by the university's duplicating and mailing facilities. The business reply sign-up card is prepared by an off-campus printer.

The basic costs of the direct mail recruitment are postage for recruitment and acknowledgment ($856), 20,000 return postcards ($240), and printing and processing recruitment and acknowledgment letters ($605), for a total of $1,701.

Newman offers the following comments on the program:

> The Foundation staff feels that the success of the recruitment process determines the success of the phonothon as a whole; hence, a great deal of attention is devoted to acquiring volunteers for the first time and to retaining their interest for succeeding years.
>
> At the phonothon itself, the volunteer is welcomed by a staff member, who chats with the person and shows him or her to the table for a hot dinner. While the volunteers eat, they may read the packet of information on the university and phonothon and telephone techniques. The orientation that follows dinner is calculated to put the volunteer at ease with the myriad details of the phonothon. In addition to a clear explanation of what is to be done, the staff interjects as much humor as time permits. During the session itself, volunteers are given as much autonomy as possible, though staff members are always available to answer questions and do a bit of judicious eavesdropping on new volunteers to make certain that all is going well. A volunteer acquiring his or her first pledge for the evening, or an especially generous gift, is the occasion for attention from a staff member and, if possible without distracting the group, from those volunteers sitting nearest the achiever.
>
> Further, every volunteer is thanked at the end of the evening and told that he or she is directly responsible for the amount shown on the tally sheet. Once the phonothon is over, a thank-you letter is sent to all volunteers, detailing how the phonothon as a whole met its goal and how each segment achieved its totals.

Who is Ken Tjaden?

Ken Tjaden has been active in Rutgers affairs almost from the time of his graduation from University College, Newark, in 1952. While busy pursuing his career, first with Prudential Insurance Company and now with the New Jersey Office of Disability, he has found time for both University College and Rutgers-wide activities. In recognition of his dedication to and interest in the University, he was recently appointed to the Board of Trustees of Rutgers University.

In over twenty-five years of volunteer work, Ken has accumulated a wealth of experience, particularly in the area of fund-raising a winner of the Ashmead Award, he has received the top prize for garnering the greatest number of gifts in the Rutgers University Foundation's Phonothon for three years in a row.

Here in his own words are tips for approaching potential donors.

General Approach

I try to keep four general rules in mind whenever I'm asking for support for Rutgers.

1. **BE POSITIVE.** I try to present all my facts in the best possible light.

2. **BE AGGRESSIVE.** I look at it this way. I'm helping the person I'm calling to exercise his or her charitable prerogative. However, I always guide myself by the individual's response; that keeps me from coming on too strong.

3. **BE LOGICAL.** I know the people I call are intelligent and well-educated—after all, most of them have Rutgers degrees! I find that these people generally respond best to rational, well thought-out arguments.

4. **BE INFORMED.** I've found that knowing the objectives of the annual appeal and the essential facts about Rutgers helps get a good response.

Why Give to Rutgers?

When I ask for gifts to Rutgers, I am always ready to tell why I give to the school. I find that people agree with some or all of my reasons:

1. To help others in the same way that I was helped. Without the millions in land, buildings and dollars that had been given to Rutgers before I enrolled, my costs would have been considerably higher. My support makes it possible for today's students to receive what I received: a fine education at a bargain price.

2. To make Rutgers a better university. I and other New Jerseyans can point with pride to the progress that Rutgers has made in academics, athletics, and community involvement. I know, however, that the school has tremendous needs if it's to maintain its traditional high standards, especially when inflation makes everything more expensive each year.

3. To join with other people in showing my support for Rutgers. In 1954, the year I was first involved in volunteer fund-raising, the Annual Fund raised $69,000. Last year, giving was in the millions, a figure which puts Rutgers in the "big leagues" and shows tremendous support from alumni and friends. People like me not only give the money, but also help raise it by participating in the Phonothon and serving on various campaign committees.

Objections I Hear Most Often—And How I Deal With Them

In my quarter-century or so of volunteering for Rutgers, I've heard the same objections over and over again. I'd like to share the answers I've developed for the most frequently voiced questions.

∽∽∽∽∽∽

• I'm a New Jersey taxpayer, so why should I contribute?

I'm a New Jersey taxpayer, too, and so are all my friends and neighbors, but I'm the one who's reaping the benefits of my Rutgers education. Moreover, the State of New Jersey pays only a little over a third of the costs of running the University.

• I've already given this year. Why are you asking me again?

I've become an expert at explaining that the Foundation runs on a fiscal year which ends on June 15th. Once people understand that that they have given during this calendar year, but not during this fiscal year, they're usually ready to pledge again.

• I've already paid my alumni dues. Isn't that a gift?

Dues support alumni association activities and services such as newsletters, reunions, dinners and meetings. Contributions to the Foundation, however, are tax-deductible; the money supports the university in the form of financial aid, library acquisitions, research, athletic programs, scholarships, and so on. I tell people that they may be supporting their alumni associations with dues, but they haven't answered the University's appeal for support until they contribute to the annual campaign.

• I'd rather wait to pledge because I think I might be able to give more this year.

That's great, but I like to point out that a donor can always increase his or her contribution later on. I pledge as early as possible in a fund year because I want to encourage others to give.

• I don't believe in the school's "open admissions" policy.

I know that Rutgers admits only a small percentage of students who don't have the scores normally necessary for admission. I also know that those who are truly incapable of doing college work flunk out quickly. At Rutgers, open admissions gives a disadvantaged student a second chance, not a free ride. Moreover, some of these open admissions students are refugees trying to start a new life, or older persons seeking a new career; I'm glad to see my University helping them out.

Figure 11. This informative brochure is given to all callers. It answers many of the questions they will have during the calling, and includes general tips on procedures. The most common questions that arise are given, along with the best answers. The cover of this brochure showed a picture of trustee Ken Tjaden, and was head-lined "Tips for Volunteers." Two additional back panels, not shown here, continued commonly asked questions and answers. Courtesy Rutgers University, New Brunswick, N.J.

RUTGERS UNIVERSITY
FOUNDATION

Thank you very much for your generous support of the Rutgers University
Foundation 1978-79 Annual Fund. I want to acknowledge your generous pledge of
$_____ . Like many other loyal alumni and friends, you are making an
investment in Rutgers, its students, its faculty, and its programs.

Many corporations have matching gift programs which can double and sometimes even triple your gift. Please check with your personnel office to see if your
employer has such a program.

Your contribution can do the most good if you will fill out and return the
enclosed envelope right away. Please make your tax deductible gift payable to
Rutgers University Foundation. Our fiscal year ends June 15, 1979.

Sincerely,

*Figure 12. This simple yet effective thank-you letter is sent to donors
making pledges during the phonothon. Note that it points out the
matching gift program, and also encourages donors to mail their
contributions in immediately.* Courtesy Rutgers University, New
Brunswick, N.J.

The concluding paragraph of the thank-you letter from the phonothon chairman is especially interesting: "Thank you for your part in helping me make such an encouraging report. I hope you found the experience gratifying and I hope to see you at Phonothon '80 next year."

Student volunteers are especially important to the phonothon's success. Bruce Newman says that alumni especially enjoy "speaking with those who are actually experiencing a Rutgers education. Student volunteers are, however, the most likely to be timorous about telephone solicitation and at times need special encouragement from the staff before gaining sufficient confidence to be successful volunteers. Staff members agree that one of the joys of working with phonothon volunteers is seeing a timid student 'bloom' into a more confident person—and one who can use his or her new-found confidence and telephone skills in some arduous task, like getting a job."

At Rutgers, the phonothon is the backbone of the Foundation's annual giving effort. The 1979 goal was $300,000, and $321,184 was actually pledged. The previous year's campaign had raised $277,918.

Newman says that he would strongly encourage anyone planning to recruit their own volunteers to start early, develop contingency plans in case participation is short of expectations, and show that you value your callers' times by running as efficient a phonothon as possible.

No matter what type of nonprofit organization you represent, you'll find that a phonothon is an effective, low-cost and highly personal method of reaching your prospects. Rutgers goes a step further than most organizations in the highly developed volunteer recruitment program, and their spectacular results attest to the wisdom of using a large group of volunteers to make the calls.[5]

5 Direct Mail

[In 1978] about 34 million form letters, approximately a third of all mail that passed through the U.S. Postal Service, arrived on American doorsteps. . . . More and more mass mail is selling not products, but causes. The technique is spreading because it works.[1]

At last count, nonprofit organizations were putting seven billion appeal letters into the mail every year.[2]

Ask direct mail specialist Sanky Perlowin why so many organizations are using direct mail. She likes to take causes she believes in (such as Recording for the Blind, Freedom from Hunger Foundation, Planned Parenthood, and a dozen other charities) and put together direct mail programs to help meet their funding needs. She's already raised more than $16 million for her causes with the simple belief that the postal service does a better job than the neighborhood volunteer walking door-to-door. Perlowin also thinks big. "The first big mailing in a 'prospecting' process (yes, as in for gold) is called a test. You send out about 200,000 pieces— 'a modest wave'—and, if the message has weight, you will get gifts (also known as contributions) from 0.8 percent, maybe even one percent. The money they send will just cover the costs of the mailing or perhaps bring in a few extra dollars, say $1.05 for every $1 spent."[3] But it is rare to make money on a first mailing, though you will certainly expand your donor base. Perlowin notes that donors responding to the first appeal are somewhat committed, and about 55 percent of them will mail checks on the second appeal, and 65 percent of that group will respond to a third appeal.

Do all messages have to be fancy? Some of Perlowin's mimeographed messages have brought checks for as much as $50,000, while one letter for Planned Parenthood produced a gift of $100,000.

Richard Viguerie also knows a lot about using the mail. Called the "King Midas of 'The New Right' " by *The Atlantic* magazine, Viguerie specializes in putting together direct mail programs for such groups as the Conservation Caucus, Gun Owners of America, National Conservative Political Action Committee, and a wide variety of other political programs and agencies. In 1978, he raised more than $15 million for his clients, thanks to clever computerized letters with a simulated personal touch. His half dozen direct mail and publishing companies employ 300 people and mail more than 100 million letters each year.[4]

Though charities annually raise more than $10 billion through direct mail efforts, politicians and political causes didn't turn to direct mail in a big way until George McGovern was cut off from the large contributors in 1972. He conducted a mail campaign that brought in $20 million, and others saw the potential of support for political causes through the mail.

Former U.S. Representative John Anderson used the mail in 1980 to make a bid for the Presidency. An unusual direct mail effort, asking former donors to send "any amount you can afford," brought him $1.1 million in less than two months. About 14,000 supporters (6.5 percent of the 208,000 prospects) sent in gifts averaging $80.

St. Mark's School of Texas personalized a direct mail appeal to parents by pasting a picture of their child on the cover of a brochure over the headline "We're planning for his tomorrow." This approach drew support from nearly 89 percent of the parents solicited, versus 73 percent the previous year.

In January 1980, The Fund Raising Institute's *FRI Monthly Portfolio* reported on a letter from The Brethren Home (New Oxford, Pennsylvania), which sent deferred giving prospects a pack of Alka-Seltzer with a message asking if they had "asset indigestion." They then offered their own prescription for this malady—reading the booklet they also enclosed that described their deferred giving program. The letter generated twice the response of their previous appeals. A local pharmacy, by the way, donated the Alka-Seltzer used in the mailing.

And also in 1980, The New York Public Library conducted a mixed-media campaign centered around their direct mail effort to raise operating funds for the library. The campaign stressed the need to "feed the lions" (the famous symbol of the library) and

 **the Lions are Hungry!**

Dear Concerned Friend:

New York's most famous lions are hungry. Keeping those
legendary marble lions on Fifth Avenue well-fed and roaring
is both important and fun. They're the guardians of one of
New York City's prime energy sources, The New York Public
Library.

New York is not like any other city, and its Library is not
like any other library. It is a prime source of knowledge,
stimulation and entertainment that can be mined by anybody
in the world. It is, as well, among the handful of really
great libraries, and one of the irreplaceable attractions
that make New York City a world capital.

The image of a library as a quiet, sparsely-inhabited place
somewhat remote from the real world vanishes the minute you
set foot in this library. Business researchers, scholars,
students and average citizens from all over the world pour in
and out of The New York Public Library's doors, making it
one of the most actively-used places in town.

By feeding the lions now you will help us keep those doors open.

Perhaps you thought the Library was tax-supported. Its neighborhood branches are, but its world-famous Research Libraries--
the Fifth Avenue Central Building and its Annex, the Performing Arts Research Center at Lincoln Center and the Schomburg
Center for Research in Black Culture in Harlem--depend on
private gifts for more than half their support.

The rest comes from state and federal grants. One of the
largest of these is from the National Endowment for the Humanities in Washington. As explained on the enclosed Contribution
Form, your gift to the Library's Central Building or Performing Arts Research Center will be matched by the NEH, fifty
cents on the dollar.

**The New York
Public Library**
Astor, Lenox and Tilden Foundations

*Figure 13. One of
the two letters used
in the direct mail
campaign.* Courtesy
The New York
Public Library,
New York City.

The Research Libraries are the libraries you couldn't duplicate
anywhere else. The libraries that put the distinctive touch of
"New York" in The New York Public Library. They give the world
nothing less than a complete record of human achievement in
almost every field of knowledge and almost every language.

The Research Libraries must buy about 200,000 new books and
journals every year just to keep up with the information explo-
sion, and must microfilm or otherwise preserve books just as
rapidly to keep them from deteriorating and to create shelf
space for the new items.

It all costs money. Lots of money.

That's why we ask you to get involved. Any amount of food for the
lions you can spare will be welcome, but your annual contribution of $25 or more will make you an official Friend of The New
York Public Library.

As a Friend, you are a member of the Library family. You'll
receive Beyond the Lions, an attractive alphabetical guide to all
the libraries of The New York Public Library, and our lively
quarterly Friends' newsletter, Library Lines, which keeps you
abreast of major happenings here.

And there's lots more, too. See the enclosed bookmark for the list
of other Friends benefits (social events, lectures, special tours).
We have begun an exciting new "Working Friends" program that
gives you the chance, if you wish, to help the Library in interesting ways during your spare time!

In any case, please take a moment right now to get involved!
Fill out the enclosed Contribution Form, write a tax-deductible
check to The New York Public Library, and enclose both in the
no-postage envelope.

Thank you!

Sincerely,

Richard W. Couper

Richard W. Couper
President

P.S. Many corporations will match their employees' membership fees
and contributions to The New York Public Library. If you
work for one of them, please take the few extra minutes to
ask your employer to match your gift. Thank you!

"Please feed the lions"

CONTRIBUTION FORM

I understand that if I contribute $25 or more, I will become a Friend of the Library and will receive benefits as shown on the back of this form.

Dear Mr. Couper:

☐ Yes, I would like to be a caretaker for The New York Public Library and help keep it functioning.

Here is my tax-deductible contribution of: ☐ $250 ☐ $100 ☐ $50 ☐ $25 ☐ $10 ☐ $_____

☐ Please send me the guidebook BEYOND THE LIONS.

☐ Please check if receipt is desired. Please use my contributions which will be matched, 50¢ on the dollar by The National Endowment for the Humanities, for:

   ☐ The Central Building, Fifth Avenue at 42nd Street.
   ☐ The Performing Arts Research Center at Lincoln Center.

These will not be matched. Please use my contribution for:
☐ The Branch Libraries ☐ This one particular Branch Library: _____ ☐ Other _____

Figure 14. The library's pledge card. The other side lists the membership privileges and leaves space for the donor to indicate if the gift would be matched by a corporation. This two-color form made it easy for the prospect to respond and to indicate the purpose of the gift. It is interesting to see how the library separated the purposes that would be matched by the NEH grant from the uses for the branch libraries, which would not be matched. Courtesy The New York Public Library, New York City.

used direct mail, advertising, and public relations to create public awareness of the need for giving.

Barbara T. Wells, the library's assistant development officer, tells us that the New York advertising agency Muir, Cornelius and Moore did the creative work on the spots and broadcast scripts (see Chapter 9 for more about some of their advertisements). She researched lists of periodicals, newspapers, and radio stations. Mailings were tied in to a National Endowment for the Humanities challenge grant. During the year, a number of press releases and articles were used by local media, and personalities such as Tony Randall appeared as persuasive spokespeople for their campaign.

Your organization may not be looking for millions of dollars, and your prospect list may not contain several hundred thousand names. But effective use of direct mail can take your case and your needs to many prospects you just can't reach in any other manner. You might be able to raise five times as much from personal solicitation as you would from sending letters, but you can't contact all your prospects in person, no matter how many volunteers you have. Thus direct mail has become an integral part of the fundraising process at most charities today.

THE BASIC RULES OF DIRECT MAIL

There are many rules and guidelines for using direct mail efficiently, and a careful reading of the literature from commercial mailers and nonprofit organizations will show the importance of following the basic steps and using certain essential ingredients in your campaigns.

The late Ed Mayer has probably said it best, and we are indebted to the Direct Mail Marketing Association, to the Creative Direct Mail handbook from the Council for the Advancement and Support of Education, and to Mr. Mayer's appearances at countless fundraising conferences for these seven cardinal rules for direct mail success:

Start with the objectives of your program.
You have to begin by defining your objectives for this particular mailing. Do you want to increase your donor base by 15 percent? Do you want to raise $10,000 for new equipment? Do you want to provide some general information to help pave the way for a detailed brochure and mailing to be sent next spring? In sum, what specifically do you want this program to accomplish? If you can't spell out your objectives in detail, you probably don't need to do this mailing. Too many fundraisers mail for the sake of mailing rather than to accomplish organization objectives.

Reach the right person on the right list.
This becomes the "shotgun vs. rifle" approach to fundraising. Do you send out an appeal to as many people as you can find and hope that a number of them will respond, or do you aim more carefully at your selected target audience and talk specifically to

them? Obviously, the second approach is much more efficient and usually much more productive. Ask yourself who are the best people to support this particular program. Match your need with the type of people who are best prospects. You should begin by studying your prospect list, collecting as much data as possible on the audiences, and then tailoring your appeal to specific people. Advertisers have known for years that commercials aimed at a consumer with a need will sell much better than commercials that first have to create the need, then promote it. The basic advertising strategy today, in fact, is to make your message suitable for as specific an audience as possible. You obviously can't write a national ad for just one person in the country, but if you know the demographics and psychographics of your audience, you can, in effect, tell the benefits of your soap to 45-year-old red-headed John Smith of Main Street in Davenport, Iowa.

Present the case in terms of benefits to the reader.
There are many reasons why people contribute to charitable organizations, but they all center around the idea that the *donor* wants something for making the gift. The donor wants to see some valuable service performed in the community; wants your group's goals to be accomplished; wants a tax deduction; wants his or her name listed in your honor roll to impress friends; or any other of a thousand desires. What is this particular mailing piece offering that prospect? What will his gift do for him, for his family, for his community or for his society? This can be called spelling out the "reason to give." Just because you need money for your group is no reason for someone to contribute. Often this is what separates a successful program from a failure. Many organizations are too "we-oriented" and too little "you-oriented." They talk in terms of *our* needs and *our* wants, and don't really tell why *you* should get involved or why *you* will benefit from supporting us.

Use appropriate copy and layout.
Depending on your audience, you might select a certain approach or paper color or tone of wording or design or artwork. If you're pleading a case of poverty and explaining that your organization can't pay its rent and will fold unless immediate gifts are sent, don't print the message on an expensive brochure with four-color photographs and glossy coated paper. Make the message

appropriate to the mailer. Obviously colleges use different words to talk to alumni than to high school seniors. Respect and understand your audience, and match your mailings to them and their characteristics. Different people want different things from your organization. The people you are now serving, for example, might contribute if it would increase your services to them, while someone in a neighboring town might give if you promised to expand the geographical area you are helping.

Make it easy for the prospect to take action.
Most of the major media require some effort on the part of the consumer for a response: a coupon must be clipped, a phone number called, a letter written. But because you have put the mailing together in the first place, it is easy to add a stamped, return-addressed envelope or card. The prospect can easily respond to your offer. And your offer should ask for action. Many writers today use the "AIDA" formula in their campaigns—arouse the prospect's Attention, create some Interest through your writing, create Desire for whatever you are offering, and urge the prospect to take some form of Action. The action can be sending in the card or making the purchase, but it can also be making a mental commitment to follow a certain course at a later date or to be more receptive to your volunteer when he or she shows up at the prospect's home. What could have been the world's greatest mailing piece must certainly be called a failure if it does not produce a response. Having the respondent say how great the brochure was, how interesting the copy, and how well designed the publication does not pay your bills or provide any services. Unless your prospect takes some type of positive action—or mentally prepares for some future action—the mailing piece has failed.

Tell your story over and over again.
It wasn't too long ago that experts warned fundraisers not to write to the same prospects more than four times each year. Now' some of those same experts are telling us to write every month if we want—maybe even more often. A number of organizations have monthly rather than annual drives, and use the extra mailing dates to promote different forms of giving (e.g., outright gifts one month, deferred another, endowment support in another month). Ed Mayer says that most mailers just don't mail often enough.

Some salespeople will tell you it takes five calls before they make a sale to some prospects. Some advertising people will say that it takes twenty showings of an ad before it makes a positive impression on a consumer. So some professional direct mail writers are now urging that you send the same written piece to your prospects three or four times. Some offer the theory that the "magic number" of mailings is seven. Space your mailings every six weeks during your fund drive and after seven letters you'll have a successful campaign. Sooner or later that prospect will respond, so just be patient and keep telling your story.

Research your direct mail efforts.
Keep testing your mailings. When one is completed you should analyze the results, decide what changes should be made (if any), and use this information for the next mailing. Test the important parts of the piece on portions of your audience. Vary the headline, the photographs, the copy style and tone. Use different colored paper or ink. Have your chairman sign one letter while the head of your advisory board signs another. Then see how the results vary and test a new mailing.[5]

THE MAILING LIST

The S. D. Warren Company, a division of Scott Paper Co., publishes a booklet on direct mail that covers a number of "tricks of the trade" and the uses of direct mail. Mark Myers, who wrote the booklet, notes, "The dimensions of [direct mail] are practically boundless and as changeable as the weather in New England. Direct mail can be a letter, a booklet, a folder, a catalog. . . . The key is to get your message to the right people."[6]

He puts in simple terms the process of choosing a mailing list: "The idea is to maximize the number of hot prospects and minimize the number of cold ones." All of the reference directories discussed in Chapter 2, on annual giving, can be used to build a prospect mailing list. You may also want to consider buying a mailing list (check your Yellow Pages for the names of mailing list companies in your area). You may find that you can buy a list of people who have contributed to organizations similar to yours, or people who have written for information about or bought something similar to the service you provide. Most lists cost between $35 and $50 per thousand names, and many companies have a minimum of 3,000 or 5,000 names at one time.

You can get more information on mailing lists and list brokers (who handle your request on a flat rate basis and are paid their commission by the group supplying the list) from the National Council of Mailing List Brokers, 55 West 42nd Street, New York, New York 10001, or the Mailing List Brokers Professional Association, 663 Fifth Avenue, New York, New York 10022.

But whether you buy a list or use your own, it is essential that you keep it updated and as current as possible. Send out postcards once or twice each year, asking for changes in the information you provide. Or print "Address Correction Requested" on each mailing or certain mailings you send during the year. It will cost you 25 cents for each piece returned, but the post office will give you the current address on Form 3547 for mail other than first class. They will either forward or return first class mail at no cost. This is a small price to pay for an accurate mailing list. Without one, you can't use direct mail; it's as simple as that.

POSTAL REGULATIONS

You also need to be aware of the most up-to-date postal regulations, since a little planning and proper production can help you mail at low rates. The best rates—for third class bulk mailings— are available to holders of a Bulk Rate permit. For a nominal charge (about $40 per year and a one-time fee of about $30), you can mail 200 or more pieces of identical material at the same time at very low rates. Of course, you won't want to send *everything* this way, as there are times when the prestige, timeliness, and impact of a first class letter is the only thing that will work. But for your mass mailings, you'll save the most money by sending materials by the bulk rate.

The standard size of a piece of third class mail is $11\frac{1}{2}$ inches or less in length, $6\frac{1}{8}$ inches or less in height, and $\frac{1}{4}$ of an inch or less in thickness. The piece must also weigh less than 16 ounces.

For further information, contact your local post office about the latest regulations from the Domestic Mail Manual and Postal Bulletins.

WHEN TO MAIL

Research by commercial mailers have found certain months to be most effective for their direct mail sales appeals, while other months yield poor results. This seasonal variation can help you plan your mailings, though the knowledge that other organizations use this same information may guide you toward being "different" and using the poor months as well.

In general, the best month for getting a good response from a commercial message is January, while other above-average months are February, July through September, and November. The poorest time to mail: April through June fall way below average, according to the Direct Mail/Marketing Association.

A 1980 study of fundraising letters, however, found August to be the biggest month for nonprofits to mail their appeals, followed, in order, by March, May, April, June, and July. Though these are not necessarily the best months for returns, they may be the best months for mailing with the least competition from commercial businesses who use the mail.

But just as January is a good month for commercial direct mailers, it is one of the weakest months for those fundraisers whose fiscal years end December 31. Now that the big year-end promotion is over, and all of the reasons for giving before the year ends have been explained, it is often difficult to get the momentum going again in January. As we mentioned earlier, Randy Morris of Old Dominion University found a clever way to raise money early in the year by sending a New Year's card to prospects in January. The mailing went exclusively to donors who had given the previous year but had not given during the calendar year just ended. The cover was a calendar for January with a circle around the first day. The inscription on the inside read: "Remember when you said, 'I'll give next year'? It's time. Happy New Year. Old Dominion University Alumni Fund." A similar card was used by the New England School of Law, which opened with the lines: "Remember when you said, 'I'll give next year'? It's next year."

The Direct Mail/Marketing Association, Inc., at 6 East 43rd Street, New York, New York 10017, can provide a great deal of general information about mailings. They have a number of reprints available at nominal charges on such topics as cutting costs of mailings, writing tips, and how to work with mailing list brokers. They also provide some interesting information on expected responses to mailings. Of course, the response you get on any individual piece depends on many factors, including what you're asking for, how you're asking, when you're asking, etc. Certainly the percentage of response is not always that important. The quality may be so good that it offsets poor quantity.

Thanks to research by the Direct Mail/Marketing Association, we know that you will receive more than three-quarters of your total responses by the end of the third week following your first return. You will probably have all of the responses by the end of the sixth week.

One of the best ways to apply the uses of direct mail to your total fundraising campaign is to utilize Robert and Joan Blum's "donor pyramid." Its base is called "the Universe," and here you find everybody you might consider prospects. The next level up, the "members," consists of those people who have made their first gift, while the third level is the "renewals." Direct mail plays a major role (along with public relations, volunteer involvement and your organization's service) in moving people up to level three.

The "large annual donors" come next—people who have joined your gift clubs and made repeated gifts of substantial amounts (the size of a "substantial" gift varies from organization to organization, of course). They are now prospects for the next two levels— and you should note that each step gets smaller as we move upward—the "capital donors" and the "bequestors." Direct mail is the important educational tool that helps move the donors to the higher levels of support.[7]

So now you know what direct mail can do for you, you know when to do it and why to do it, and you have a pretty good idea of what will happen. The only thing left is to tell you exactly how to do it.

You need to write well. Remember Robert Louis Stevenson's words: "It takes hard writing to make easy reading."

Be dramatic. Be specific. Use metaphors and adjectives and adverbs to make your message come alive. All of the principles that make for good advertising and public relations writing make for good direct mail writing. You are selling, so your job is to write sales material. Have someone important or special or unique sign your letters (such as the chairman of your board, a handicapped child your group helps, or someone who used your services ten years ago). Develop a total concept in which the letters, brochures, return cards, and other mailing pieces all fit together. The best direct mail pieces are part of a complete package. The physical appearance of the materials is important, and you should plan these carefully for the maximum impact on your prospects.

THE MAILING PACKAGE

Every mailing package should include at least four essential items: the outside envelope, some type of reply mechanism, a cover letter, and whatever additional inserts you need for that particular mailing.

The Cover Envelope

There are a number of factors to be considered in planning the cover envelope. You have to take current postal restrictions into account, since envelopes too small or unusual in shape may not be allowed (see page 134). You need to choose the exact size, the color of the paper, the color of the ink, the type of envelope, and other variations in appearance. A good printer can help you make many of these decisions. If you don't have one, find one . . . fast.

Odd-sized or colorful envelopes attract attention. Window envelopes, which can let a provocative piece of artwork show through, have been found to be more successful than standard envelopes, except when you're mailing to a high-status group.

How will you address the envelope? Generally, a typed address is better than that provided by an addressing machine or a mailing label; considerations of time and expense may not make this feasible, however. Be sure the prospect's name is spelled correctly, and use his or her individual title wherever possible.

As far as postage is concerned, experts differ in their opinions, and you will want to test different methods. Virginia Carter of CASE notes that "stamps usually pull better than meter tapes, which usually pull better than an indicia. If you're using stamps, why not request colorful commemoratives to help dress up the mailing?"[8] On certain mailings, it doesn't pay to use first class postage. But if you are mailing to a particularly important group, it's a good idea to send it first class if possible—it makes a greater impact.

What about the return address? Some professionals say not to use one, others say you should identify your organization, and still others stress using the name of the volunteer (though you had better check with the post office since you may not be able to use your organization's bulk rate stamp with a return address different from your own).

Finally, you need to decide if any other type of artwork or "teaser" copy is appropriate for the outside envelope. Is there something that will increase the chances that the envelope will be opened? It has been estimated that 75 percent of the people who receive fundraising mail open it, and more than 60 percent will contribute at some time. You can improve on these figures by improving your outside envelope.

For example, Handgun Control, Inc., ran a campaign in 1979 to limit the sale of handguns and to combat the National Rifle Association's lobbying for fewer controls. Their outside envelope contained no return address—just the bold words, "ENCLOSED: Your first real chance to tell the National Rifle Association to go to hell! . . ." A four-page letter and other material inside explained what the organization was doing and how they had to fight the NRA lobbying efforts. More than three million people active in such causes as the American Civil Liberties Union, Common Cause, and the National Organization for Women received the mailing. The envelope statement certainly helped insure that Handgun Control's message was received.

The Response Mechanism

The best response mechanisms (reply cards, return envelopes) are related somehow to the letters that accompany them. You want to remind the prospect why he is sending in this envelope (especially if he has kept it for a while and has already thrown away the cover letter).

Make it easy for prospects to respond: on the reply card, include spaces where they can simply check the amount they wish to give (and the category they wish to support). You want them to feel they have made the final decision, but the information you include here can help shape their thinking. You might also want to list an "800" toll-free number, if you have one, or suggest the prospect make a collect call to pledge the donation.

The return envelope can be used to collect updated name and address information, to have alumni send in news of their activities, to have donors list questions they want answered or information they want sent to them, or just to allow the respondents to share information of interest with you.

Be sure to follow the current postal requirements. In mid-1979, new rules went into effect regarding the format of business reply mail, specifying the use of a bar-code pattern (called the Facing Identification Mark) and other requirements. New regulations were also put into effect for the size of these reply cards and their thickness ($3\frac{1}{2}'' \times 5''$ is the smallest size; minimum thickness is .007 inch). The Postal Service can impose a substantial surcharge if these requirements are overlooked, so it pays to keep aware of the latest rules and regulations.

What sort of postage should you put on the return envelope? If you use a preprinted business reply box, you will only have to pay the postage on envelopes that are returned. But you will pay more than if you had affixed regular postage stamps to the envelopes (except that you then pay the postage for *all* envelopes, not just those that are returned). You need to estimate the percentage of response expected, and then act accordingly. If you expect a very high rate of return, you may be better off affixing stamps. If you're not sure, the business reply envelope may be most economical.

Many organizations do *not* pay return postage, printing instead in the box for the stamp a phrase such as, "Your stamp adds to your contribution." Direct mail consultant Virgil Angerman suggests that fundraisers might also use this space for "selling" copy: "Campaign closes December 31st," "Keep our Hospital Strong," or something like "Did you meet the challenge?"[9]

Figure 15 shows a sample reply envelope you might adapt for your needs. A reply envelope used by Berkshire Medical Center (Figure 16) illustrates how much information can be provided in one small space.

The Letter

The cover letter is an essential part of the package; without it, the mailing takes on the look of an advertisement. In addition to the style and content of the letter (see page 143 for tips on writing), you will need to decide what size it will be, what type of paper it will go on, whose letterhead will be used, who will sign it, how it will be signed (printed or actual signature), whether the letter will be typed or typeset, and what the salutation and complimentary close will be. Each factor says something a little different and adds to the impact of the letter.

As to the size of the letter, Virginia Carter recommends using the $7\frac{1}{4}'' \times 10\frac{1}{2}''$ monarch size for important donors, and possibly even smaller note paper. The standard $8\frac{1}{2}'' \times 11''$ paper has proved best for mass appeals.[10]

What type and color of paper should you use? In a 1980 test by several direct mail companies, the use of colored paper and textured stock resulted in response rates increasing by as much as 142 percent. The Paramount International Coin Company, for example, sent out two similar mailings—their usual two-color flyer on a white-coated stock, and a one-color mailer on bright yellow, textured cover stock. The first mailing produced 240 responses, while the yellow textured-paper mailer brought in 351—an improvement of more than 46 percent. John Dolibois of Miami University (see the case study at the end of this chapter for some of Dolibois's award-winning letters) also ran a test mailing. He sent a letter and materials to half of Miami's parents' list on a white vellum offset paper, and the same materials on a white textured paper to the other half. The textured stock increased donations by 13.1 percent and the average donation rose by 3.3 percent. Dolibois noted, "The difference was really impressive. While the textured paper cost a bit more, for each additional dollar we spent on it we received $8.74 in donations."[11]

Virginia Carter suggests, "If you can afford it, use a second color to call attention to important paragraphs or lines. If you don't have the extra money, put the important information in all capital letters or underline it."[12]

Opposite:
Figure 16. The front of the envelope carries the return addre
business reply information, and postage-paid imprint. The ba
shows pictures of patients (a newborn, a child, and an elde
woman) with the words "Your gift helps provide the best in li
saving equipment and care for patients at Berkshire Medical Co
ter." Courtesy Berkshire Medical Center, Pittsfield, Mass.

Here's my tax-deductible investment in

The ABC Boy's Club

Please enroll me in the following category:

```
____    $1,000 or more      Patron
____    $500 -- $999        Associate
____    $100  -- $499       Friend
____    $25 -- $99          Honorary Leader
____    _____         Other
```

Figure 15. A sample reply envelope. It is folded down the middle and sealed.

Thank you for your generous contribution.

Your support of The ABC Boy's Club will

help us provide for the needs of Center

City's young men.

John Smith
President

Name: _____

Address: _____

City: _____ State: _____ Zip: _____

Enclosed is my (our) gift of $ _____

To Honor The _____ Of _____
           Occasion   Honoree

To Speed The Recovery Of _____

In Memory Of _____

Please send acknowledgement to:

Name _____

Address _____ Zip _____

Please use this gift in the BMC Fund checked below: (select one)

☐ Building & Equipment Needs Fund
☐ Cancer Fund
☐ Coronary/Intensive Care Fund
☐ Neighborhood Health Center Fund
☐ Renal Dialysis Fund
☐ Challenge Grant Fund
☐ Endowment Fund/Free Patient Care
☐ Endowment Fund/General Purposes
☐ Silvio Conte Perinatal Birth Defects Fund

MAKE CHECKS PAYABLE TO **BERKSHIRE MEDICAL CENTER** — CONTRIBUTIONS ARE TAX DEDUCTIBLE

Your Name _____ Phone _____

Address _____ Zip _____
Please send me _____ HONOR GIFT BOOKLETS.
☐ I would like information about BMC's ESTATE PLANNING SEMINARS.
☐ Send me details about BMC's POOLED INCOME FUND which pays a donor of $1,000 or more an annual income for the rest of his or her life.
As a donor you receive the quarterly publication *HEALTHVIEWS* and all other benefits of membership in BMC's SECOND CENTURY ASSOCIATION for one year. The total contributed during a calendar year determines your membership. Membership categories are:

Friend—Under $25   Sponsor—$25 to $99   Associate—$100 to $249
*Patron—$250 to $999   *Benefactor—$1,000 and above
*receive permanent recognition on the hospital's Donor Recognition Wall

 FOR YOUR GOOD HEALTH

Many institutions have special stationery made up for each mailing program. Why not have your appeal read "Audubon Society 1982 Sponsors Program" instead of using the regular letterhead?

A word needs to be said here about the growing use of the computer in printing fundraising letters. Obviously, the more personal you can make your letter, the stronger impact it will have. This has led to a sophistication in computer letters that lets you print names, addresses, dates, amounts of previous gifts, and other information to make the form letter a little more personal. But does anyone really think that people see such letters as more than form appeals?

It seems to us that the greatest contribution the computer can make in the direct mail field is to help gather the information for your files or return card, and leave you free to write a personal letter that actually looks personal to the recipient.

Finally, you need to consider the possible inserts that can accompany these mailing pieces. They should fit in with the total design of the package, of course, and they should tie in with your theme. But they can cover a variety of areas not included in the letter or return card. For instance, you might enclose special reports, mentions of merchandise for sale, illustrated brochures, extra cover letters from other people in your organization, or other printed pieces. You may also wish to include a disclaimer apologizing if the recipient already received a letter from you.

The "publisher's letter" idea has become popular in recent years in commercial mailings. These are the letters—often sealed or otherwise folded—that carry a cover inscription such as "If you have decided not to respond to our offer, please read this." Why not include an appeal from one of your members or clients or volunteers, asking once again for the donor to respond? This extra message may reach the prospect's emotions at just the right time. And if your other mailing pieces are light enough, you'll find that you can send these extra inserts at no additional postage cost.

The July 1980 issue of the *Januz Direct Marketing Letter* discussed a unique variation of the publisher's letter, used by the Locksmithing Institute (Little Falls, New Jersey). The folded yellow leaflet contained the words "Sorry, I goofed." Inside was the message, "In my hurry to get my first letter to you I forgot to tell you about your subscription to the Locksmithing Institute News." This actually pointed out an additional benefit not mentioned in the original letter, and further copy reinforced the major benefits contained in the letter and materials sent previously. (The Januz letter is a good source of current ideas and examples of direct mail pieces. For subscription information, write to the *Januz Direct Marketing Letter*, P.O. Box 631, Lake Forest, Illinois 60045.)

If you have not printed your return information directly on the envelope, you need also to enclose a return card of some type that can be inserted into the envelope. Some professionals don't like the extra card because it can get lost or mixed in with the other materials, but it may be best for your filing system and records to have a separate card.

Any other materials you think would be helpful should also be included. The National Wildlife Federation, for example, sends a green-on-white leaflet pointing out that donations are tax deductible. Their small leaflet provides a receipt to be retained for tax records. Sometimes mailing pieces like this add that extra incentive needed for the gift to be made.

WRITING TIPS

Virginia Carter's excellent article entitled "The ABCs of Raising Money by Mail" included the following ideas for preparing your mailing piece:

- Remember that you are competing for the reader's time. Readers will take only a few seconds to decide whether or not to read your direct mail piece. It is important that you grab them in those few seconds.
- Your audience is not one big mass, so personalize your appeals. Analyze your prospects for differences so that you do different mailings to subgroups.
- Some type of salutation is better than none at all. If you would rather use a headline than a salutation, consider breaking it up into three or four lines and putting it on the left of the page to make it look like a salutation.
- Write your letter to just one person. Be conversational by using short words, short sentences, and short paragraphs. Restate the important points since your reader may only read parts of your letter. Two groups of motivations should be stressed— altruism, idealism, and the desire to improve conditions; and

ego gratification, obligation, and gratitude. As Carter puts it, "Outline the need to be met. Tell how your institution is meeting the need. Get the reader personally involved. Establish a close link between his or her support and accomplishing the goal. Show what his or her gift can accomplish. Ask for the *contribution*. Suggest an amount if possible. Tell how to make out the check. State a time limit that issues a call for action."

- Make the length of your letter fit your message. The letter should be long enough to tell your story—and no longer.
- Remember the power of the P.S. This is often the most-read part of a letter, and can give the personal touch lacking elsewhere in the message. Carter notes that some experts suggest using the typewriter for P.S. messages longer than 25 words and handwriting them if shorter.

In the June 1980 issue of the *FRI Monthly Portfolio*, Arthur L. Cone, Jr., talked about the important role the P.S. can play in reaching your readers. The P.S. is often read first, he says, and can build some interest for the reader that will lead to the rest of the copy. The postscript can also be used to secure involvement in hopes of getting a gift later, verify or support your case for receiving a gift, convey a personal message, or appeal to a special motivation that may trigger a giving response from the reader. Cone's favorite postscript was for a political mailing: "P.S. Fed up with the mess? Help us get rid of it!"

- If your campaign includes a series of letters, develop a common theme and look for ways to say the same things differently in each message.
- It is important to translate "product features" (your needs) into "donor benefits" (why they should give). Try to keep the letter as personal and emotional as possible, putting facts and details into an accompanying brochure.
- It has been found that carbon copies of letters with a handwritten message printed on them or attached (e.g., "We haven't heard from you yet and there are only three weeks left in this fund year") can be very effective.[13]

Susan Wallgren of Georgia Tech notes that while you can't always *personalize* a letter by putting the donor's name in the copy, you can usually *individualize* it by breaking the list down into groups of people with similar backgrounds. She directs her own appeals at two major groups: prospects (alumni she feels should be giving at a higher level; they are invited to participate in one of three gift clubs), and repeats (previous donors who are thanked, given a case statement for continued support, and asked for a new gift). The volunteer's personal stationery is used, and prospects at the $500 level and above receive personal letters (produced by an automatic typewriter and carrying commemorative stamps).

She adds a number of tips for writers: Since your first sentence counts the most, make it capture the reader's attention. Emphasize the reader, not the writer. Use clever headlines to attract attention and arouse the reader's curiosity. Tell of your group's ability to help people, advance ideas, or achieve new goals.[14]

In a speech to a CASE direct mail conference, Bob Blum offered the following suggestions: Use various types of pauses to change the tone of your copy (commas, dashes, colons, semicolons and periods). Use magic words (e.g., "treasure," "gift," "free"). Use quotation marks—people like to listen in on the conversations of others. Start with a simple theme, add reasoning to convince the reader, and end with an "ah, ha!" After you've written your letter, see what lines or paragraphs can be removed without weakening the letter—then remove them. Remember that you want to help the reader fill needs. Your ideas should explain how he or she will be respected, belong to a prestigious group, win approval, etc. Blum summarizes the direct mail process by explaining that you need to plan your entire campaign in advance, allow sufficient time for error-free production, and improve the image of your direct mail.[15]

You can see all of these tips at work in the letter-writing case study at the end of this chapter. For more than twenty years, John Dolibois has been writing fundraising letters for Miami University, and he has continued to win praise and awards for his creative, interesting, and productive letters. The letters we have included are by both Mr. Dolibois and John Yeck, and they—better than any theories—will show you what fundraising letters can say and do.

Perhaps the best way to conclude a discussion of direct mail is to offer this remark by Francis Andrews, president of American Fund Raising Services, Inc.: "Fund raising by mail is not an isolated annual collection, but a continuous investment process by which donors and members are acquired, cultivated, renewed, and solicited over and over again during a lifetime of charitable support."[16]

Think of direct mail as a planned, organized effort to complement your other fundraising techniques, and you'll be pleasantly surprised at how much it does for you.

CASE STUDY
The Andover Bicentennial Campaign

The Andover Academy Bicentennial Campaign's direct mail appeal was an integral part of a six-month solicitation plan designed to raise $50,610,000 by December 31, 1979. Other elements in the plan included intensive personal solicitation by volunteers, regional "blitz weeks," special regional task forces, and a national phonothon.

In June 1979, the Bicentennial Campaign was at a turning point. They had raised just over $35 million in three years. On June 8, 1979, the campaign chairman announced the offer of a $5 million Challenge Fund. Twenty-six donors had joined together to make this offer and had agreed to give one dollar for every two dollars given until midnight, December 31, 1979. The arithmetic was simple—if they could raise another $10 million, they would earn the $5 million challenge and reach the goal. With the goal in sight and the added incentive of this truly generous offer, the planning for the final six-month period began.

Throughout the campaign, one of the goals had been the personal solicitation of every member of the Andover family. By June 8, 4,123 had made a commitment. With so little time remaining and roughly 18,377 prospects to contact, they realized that direct mail would be a critical element in spreading the campaign message. Nondonors to the campaign were their prime target and they approached them from different perspectives. Donors to the campaign were included in two of the five direct mail appeals and thus were given the opportunity to help earn the Challenge Fund.

The direct mail letters, for many individuals, were the only solicitation they received during the campaign.

Throughout the Bicentennial Campaign, the Andover constituency had been divided into 116 regional areas in accordance with both the density of the Andover population and geographic boundaries. The area volunteer committees had been responsible for personally soliciting all prospective donors who were not designated as Major Gift Prospects ($100,000+). Each area had a chairman coordinating the activity of his or her committee. The first mailing, the August 1979 Area Chairman's Letter, was a personally signed message from the area chairman to all alumni, parents, widows, and friends who had not yet made a commitment to the campaign and who were not rated among the top prospects ($10,000 to $100,000 potential). In all, more than 15,000 of these letters were sent.

This was the most complex of their five mailings, since it required the coordination of 116 separate area chairmen. They had 116 personal letterheads and envelopes printed, along with 116 area report cards. The actual letters were prepared by a mailing house. The Academy provided the mailing house with the text for the letters and the names and addresses of the nondonors (by area). The mailing house took care of matching all the information to insure that an individual in the Boston area, for example, received a letter from the Boston area chairman. When all the letters for one area were prepared, they were packaged along with envelopes, pledge cards, reply envelopes, and area report cards and sent directly to the area chairman. Along with this material went a short set of instructions, urging the chairman to personally sign the letter, change the salutation to an informal one if appropriate, and add any P.S. that he or she felt would strengthen the letter. By early September, all area chairmen had mailed their letters.

For the "Constituency" mailing in early November 1979, the Academy approached its constituency for the first time in the campaign according to their affiliation with Andover, rather than their geographic area. They divided the 17,000 names into five groups: (1) Phillips Academy alumni through the class of 1938; (2) Phillips Academy alumni from 1939 through 1965; (3) Phillips Academy alumni from 1966 through the present; (4) Abbot Academy alumnae (the girls' school with which Andover merged in 1973); and (5) all past and present parents in their active file. One well-known individual from each of these groups was asked to write a letter tailored to his or her particular constituency—outlining Andover's needs and explaining, for example, just why a recent graduate or an Abbot alumna should consider making a pledge. Each of the letter writers reviewed a list of their group members so that personal salutations could be used as the letters were being produced. Personal stationery was designed and a direct mail firm was used for production and mailing of the letters. The signatures were printed in a different color to give the appearance of being hand-signed. Enclosed with each letter was a pledge card and postage-paid reply envelope. In addition, those individuals in the Phillips Academy alumni group through the class of 1938 received a short pamphlet entitled "What Counts," highlighting the advantages of planned giving.

The third mailing, the campaign chairman's letter (sent in late October 1979), was a special message to the 3,000 individuals who had made their campaign commitment prior to the June 1979 announcement of the $5 million Challenge Fund. The campaign chairman reviewed the list of names in this group to indicate proper salutation, and the letters were again produced and mailed by the mailing house. A special pledge card for additional pledges and a postage-paid reply envelope were enclosed.

A "Memorandum from the Headmaster" on December 3, 1979, was the fourth mailing piece used in the campaign. It was a concise message to all 22,500 members of the Andover and Abbot constituency, and it received a very strong response. It was simple and direct, and coincided with the National Phonothon. A window envelope was used for the mailing and a pledge card and postage-paid reply envelope were enclosed.

The final mailing, "The Last Call," was sent on December 18, 1979. It went to all 16,000 nondonors as of December 7, 1979, and this simple one-piece mailer was the final attempt to deliver the campaign message on both the need and the impending deadline. The mailer itself was tabbed shut with a small adhesive stamp and a postage-paid reply envelope was enclosed. The Academy received one pledge for $10,000 as a result of this mailing!

It is difficult to specifically measure the results of the direct mail program because it was only one of several solicitation techniques used in the final months of the campaign; but it played a very important role. The goal of $50,610,000 was exceeded.

A look at the monthly donor and dollar totals (on the next page) demonstrates the swelling tide of support that was evident as the campaign deadline approached.

On December 29, 1979, the campaign goal was reached, and on December 31 Andover received over 400 new gifts and pledges totaling almost $200,000. Many of these pledges were on the

Date	Amount	Donors
July 28, 1979	$36,175,213	4441
August 30, 1979	36,389,833	4733
September 28, 1979	37,167,596	5058
October 26, 1979	39,400,000	5319
November 16, 1979	42,100,000	5556
December 7, 1979	47,910,000	5986
December 28, 1979	50,666,139	7676
January 25, 1980	52,018,532	8051

"Last Call" pledge card. When the books were closed on January 25, 1980, the Academy had raised $52,018,532 in gifts and pledges—$1,408,532 beyond the original goal.

Sandra Thorpe, associate secretary of the Academy, notes, "Perhaps the best thing we did when planning our direct mail campaign was to enlist the services of our printer and their mailing house. Their expertise and professional experience in the field led us through a complex set of decisions and proved invaluable in the production and mailing of the letters. All design work for the five mailings was done at Andover. Throughout the campaign we were truly fortunate to have a full-time graphic designer as a member of our Central Publications Office staff. In addition to the design, all the writing and statistical information was provided from campaign headquarters. Beyond this, our campaign staff effort was supporting the increased volunteer activity that occurred in the final months of the campaign. The mailing service insured that we kept on schedule with our direct mail solicitation plan."

Their costs fell into two categories: computer services for production of lists, labels, and pledge cards; and printing, production, and mailing costs for the five letters.

	Computer	Production/Mailing and Postage	Total
Mailing #1	$1,362.50	$26,345.42	$27,707.92
Mailing #2	1,604.00	13,533.15	15,137.15
Mailing #3	312.50	4,301.00	4,613.50
Mailing #4	1,546.25	10,331.80	11,878.05
Mailing #5	915.00	6,560.00	7,475.00
		Grand Total	$66,811.62

Working with Ms. Thorpe on this campaign, which received an award in CASE's national direct mail competition, were Frederic A. Stott, Ann Caldwell, and Ann Parks.[17]

CASE STUDY

Berkshire Medical Center—A Hospital's Direct Mail Program

In reporting on the outstanding success of the direct mail program at the Berkshire Medical Center in Pittsfield, Massachusetts, *Fund Raising Management* magazine said the key had been the fact that they "make giving meaningful."

C. Edwin Davis, BMC's director of development and public relations, doesn't believe in just an "annual" giving program. Instead, he has set up a comprehensive development office utilizing direct mail to secure gifts on a more regular basis. And it works because their basic philosophy, he says, "is to make it easy for people to give and to make it obvious to them that it is important to give." When Davis arrived at BMC in 1975, the hospital had fewer than 2,000 names on its donor list, including board members, contributors to a 1973 building program, and everyone else. Today there are more than 21,000 names in Davis's file, and they're divided into fifty different constituency codes. He can now selectively identify such individual groups as employees, volunteers, former patients, pooled income prospects, vendors, estate planning seminar prospects, and dozens of other potential audiences.

Every three to four months, selected segments of the mailing list receive BMC's custom-designed Donor Mailer. It doesn't try to act like a personal letter, but it is special enough that people find it hard to resist opening the envelope and reading the material inside. Davis notes, "It is obvious what it is and yet it's unique and people open it." This computer-printed packet has been their best piece for building the donor base. They send it to former patients, previous donors who have not given for several years, and prospects of unknown means.

The envelope features an unusual tear strip for easy opening. A teaser on the front notes that inside is "An Invitation."

Inside the envelope is a message about the hospital's Honor Gift Booklets, as well as a form that provides a great deal of information about BMC's Second Century Association (Figures 17 and 18).

A Special Way Of Caring

At one time or another, you may wish to pay lasting tribute to a loved one, a deceased friend or relative, a special occasion, or an outstanding achievement. When you do, you may have difficulty knowing what to say or do.

The problem is ageless, but many people have found a solution through Berkshire Medical Center's HONOR GIFT PROGRAM. This program enables you to satisfy a personal obligation while arranging for a meaningful tribute.

Acknowledgement Of Your Gift: You receive prompt acknowledgement of your gift. The individual honored or the family of the deceased is notified immediately of your thoughtfulness. The amount of your gift is never mentioned.

How To Make An Honor Gift: Complete the enclosed gift form, enclose your gift in the envelope provided, and mail.

Other Ways Of Caring: Of course, it isn't necessary for your gift to be in honor or in memory of someone. It may simply be restricted for use in the BMC Fund of your choice.

When You Make Your Gift: You become a member of BMC's Second Century Association and receive all benefits of membership during the coming year. This is the hospital's way of showing appreciation for your valued financial support.

For year-round convenience, HONOR GIFT BOOKLETS are available from Berkshire Medical Center. Each contains coupons and postage-paid contribution envelopes. To receive your own Booklet, simply check the appropriate blank on the gift form. When doing so, consider requesting extra ones for friends. They will appreciate your thoughtfulness and the opportunity to give HONOR GIFTS in their own way.

BMC For Your Good Health

Figure 17. This message is actually the cover letter for the rest of the materials. Note that it promotes the Honor Gift Program and invites recipients to send for an Honor Gift Booklet. There is no "hard sell" here, just the explanation that when you make your gift, you become a member of the Second Century Association. Courtesy Berkshire Medical Center, Pittsfield, Mass.

Figure 18. The return card enclosed in the mailing. It allows space for donors to check the purpose of the gift, how they want it used, and what additional information they would like. Though this is obviously a computer-printed form, the wording at the bottom softens the lack of personalization: "Use of this form is the most efficient way to appeal for your support at the least expense to Berkshire Medical Center." Courtesy Berkshire Medical Center, Pittsfield, Mass.

A return envelope is also included. Postage is not paid (the box for the stamp is marked "Your stamp adds to your contribution"), and the envelope is marked "personal" on the front by the hospital's address.

Davis says that first-time gifts from these mailings average more than $21, and it is not uncommon to receive third-time gifts of $250. Everyone who gives to the hospital becomes a member of the Second Century Association, regardless of the amount they give. First-time donors receive an acknowledgment letter, and a thick membership kit is mailed to them later. Davis waits until they have 200 packets to mail out—it takes just a few weeks to accumulate them—and he sends the kits bulk rate to reduce postage costs.

The kit contains a letter from the chairman of the hospital's development council, which begins: "Welcome to Berkshire Medical Center's Second Century Association. As a member you are someone special. You have made a contribution which helps assure that patients at BMC will continue receiving excellent care." Promotional material about the Association is included, as are informative pamphlets on preventive medicine, helping a choking victim, glaucoma, and other medical situations, as well as wallet cards and telephone stickers that carry emergency information and phone numbers.

Donors giving for a second time during the year receive either a personal letter or a preprinted card. Edwin Davis tries to vary each letter or card so that the donor receives a different acknowledgment each time (Figures 19 and 20).

BMC does have a gift club structure, which is designed to promote multiple gifts during the year. All gifts are cumulative, and donors are encouraged to give enough to reach the next club level. Donors giving less than $25 are Friends; $25 to $99, Sponsors; $100 to $249, Associates; $250 to $999, Patrons; and over $1,000 per year, Benefactors. All donors reaching the two highest levels are listed permanently on the Donor Recognition Wall (Figure 21).

In 1979, Davis introduced the Honor Gift program so that donors could make gifts with special meaning. He explains that donors "need to feel that they've done something significant and that what they did was appreciated. They need immediate acknowledgment and they need recognition." His Honor Gift program gives people

Thank you for your recent contribution of   to Berkshire Medical Center. Your gift has been recorded as follows:

As a donor you are automatically a member of BMC's Second Century Association for the current calendar year. Membership is renewable on an annual basis and may change during the year as additional contributions are made.

Your present status is checked below:

BERKSHIRE MEDICAL CENTER
725 North Street
Pittsfield, Massachusetts 01201

☐ Benefactor $1,000 and above
☐ Patron $250 to $999
☐ Associate $100 to $249
☐ Sponsor $25 to $99
☐ Friend   under $25

Benefits of membership are listed on the flap of the membership kit. In addition, Benefactors and Patrons are recognized permanently on BMC's Donor Recognition Wall for each year in which they achieve these levels of giving.

Figures 19 and 20. Examples of the printed acknowledgment forms BMC sends to donors. The BMC logo is blind-stamped for an embossed effect on all of them. **Courtesy Berkshire Medical Center, Pittsfield, Mass.**

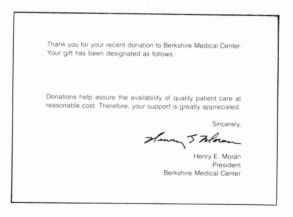

Thank you for your recent donation to Berkshire Medical Center. Your gift has been designated as follows:

Donations help assure the availability of quality patient care at reasonable cost. Therefore, your support is greatly appreciated.

Sincerely,

Henry E. Moran
President
Berkshire Medical Center

the opportunity to donate in memory or in honor of someone. Each booklet contains five perforated coupons on which the donor puts the date, the gift, the purpose (in honor or memory or to speed someone's recovery) and the fund where the gift is designated (Figure 22).

The first four coupons in the book are cream-colored, while the

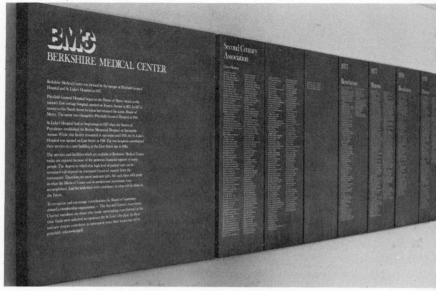

Figure 21. The Donor Recognition Wall lists charter members of the Second Century Association and all donors of $250 or more. Courtesy Berkshire Medical Center, Pittsfield, Mass.

last is orange. When that coupon is received, the development staff sends the donor another booklet. In the first few months of the program, BMC was averaging nearly thirty new memorials each month. The average gift has been $10 to $15, and many of the memorials total $200 or more because of several people giving for the same purpose. Davis also distributes the books to local funeral homes, making it convenient for people to consider BMC for memorials. The family (or the person being honored) receives an acknowledgment of the gift and the total number of donations (no individual gifts are reported to the family).

Davis had seen a similar program at the National Association for Hospital Development conference, and he adapted the idea to his hospital's particular needs. The booklet, coupons, and reply envelopes cost 21 cents each, and most are mailed first class with an acknowledgment letter.

Names of donors are never deleted from their mailing lists, and prospects' names are kept for at least three years.

Local banks have been cooperating in enclosing statement stuffers about the Honor Gift Program to their credit card customers. These mailings have been very successful in boosting the program.

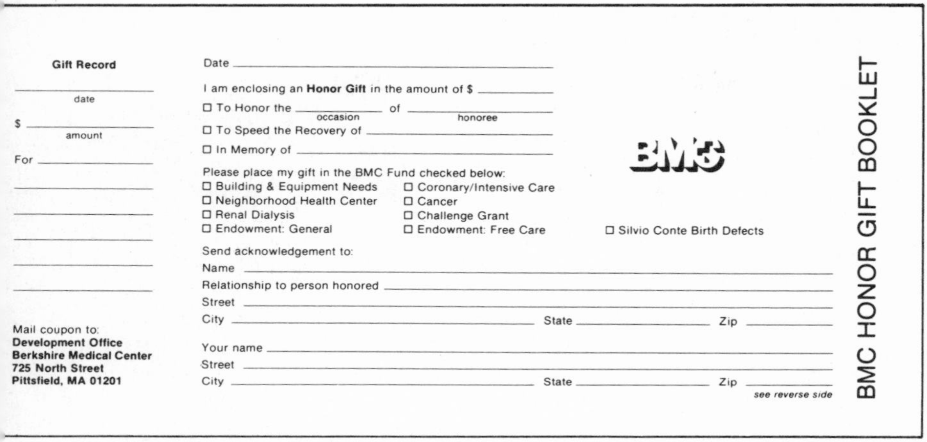

Figure 22. A sample coupon from the Honor Gift booklet. It is perforated so that the gift record section remains in the booklet while the rest of the page is filled out and returned in one of the envelopes enclosed in the booklet. A cover page explains the program and suggests occasions for honor giving (including anniversaries, birthdays, graduations, and other special occasions), along with the memorial gift opportunity. Courtesy Berkshire Medical Center, Pittsfield, Mass.

Berkshire Medical Center has found direct mail to be an efficient way of reaching a wide variety of audiences. They have identified their prospects, and designed materials to motivate regular giving. The program helps the hospital receive hundreds of thousands of dollars each year for their various funds.[18]

CASE STUDY

Miami University—Award-Winning Letters

For more than twenty years, John Dolibois has been writing fundraising letters for Miami University. The following examples (Figures 23–25) should get your creative juices flowing and point you in some directions for fundraising letters of your own.

Dolibois, vice-president for development and alumni affairs at Miami, and John Yeck, partner in Yeck Brothers Group, wrote these letters, many of which have received awards and been cited often for their unique, clever approach (and an approach that has consistently brought in results!).

Office of Alumni Relations | *Oxford, Ohio*

MANY GIFTS IN A COMMON FUND CAN DO GREAT THINGS

April 1961

Dear Miamian:

Back in the early days of prohibition, one little Piggly Wiggly store down South suddenly showed a surprising spurt in sales.

Out dashed the national sales manager, eager to learn the small store's secret of sweet success ... expecting to find a new factory around the corner, a nearby grocery razed by fire or an Irish sweepstakes winner in the neighborhood, but always hopeful that the gain might have come from a new idea.

He found one; a dandy.

Just inside the front door a huge stack of Welch's Grape Juice caught his eye, and near it a small hand-printed sign, reading:

> DANGER! Be careful <u>not</u> to mix the contents of one bottle juice with three pounds sugar and allow to set in a cool place for 10 days, <u>or</u> <u>it</u> <u>may</u> <u>turn</u> <u>to</u> <u>WINE</u>.

That manager learned what the prospects wanted and found a way to give it to them.

Do you think it will work for us? Can I find out what you want for your money by going at it backwards? Is it worth a try? Let's see:

> DANGER! Do <u>not</u> fill out your Loyalty Fund card and enclose in envelope, complete with cash or pledge, <u>or</u> you may find yourself helping higher education in the nicest way possible (through Miami University); bringing back fond memories of your halcyon college days (o.k., look it up); and (because generosity becomes you), <u>just</u> <u>plain</u> <u>feeling</u> <u>FINE</u>.

Now to the card and envelope, please, for time <u>is</u> running out on this Loyalty Fund year. You haven't told us, yet, to take you off the reminder list, so I continue to write ... and, besides, our Directory of Active Alumni is being readied for printing - what would that directory be without your name?

Why not send your contribution now, in spite of the possible "dire" consequences ... appreciation, income-tax-deduction and a real good feeling for Miami?

Sincerely,

John E. Dolibois

John E. Dolibois

JD:gs

Figures 23–25. Three letters by John Dolibois. Courtesy John Dolibois, Miami University, Oxford, Ohio.

"They are fixin'
to hang me Friday ---"

Remember the man in death row who finally made one last, polite,
yet urgent appeal?

"Dear Governor:", he wrote. "They are fixin'
to hang me Friday and here it is Tuesday."

"Hope to hear from you soon."

Miami's potential fate is not nearly so severe. Contributions to
the Miami Fund have been good this year ... many givers showing
substantial increases ... and, for all I know, you are saving your
strength to surprise me with a check twice as large as ever before
(dwell on that for just a moment, won't you?)

Nevertheless, the 1967 Fund year is fixin' to end December 31, and
here it is, late November.

That's all well and good from a strictly calendar point of view
but the thing I need to point out, in polite, yet urgent terms,
is that, giving our records the benefit of the doubt, we haven't
heard from you this whole year long.

Your gift last year, along with those of others, has worked effectively for the good of Miami. Fund money has helped attract outstanding students, encourage faculty, add depth to student life
on the campus and, all in all, enhance Miami's reputation as a fine
university.

But university needs, like Old Man River, keep rolling along ...
and seem to increase each year. Can we count on you to help meet
them again? The size of the gift is not nearly as important as
the gift itself, for it means you still hold Miami in your memory
and support the good work of the fund.

Hope to hear from you soon.

John E. Dolibois

P.S. As in other years, the Fund Honor Roll, listing all donors
will be published soon after the fiscal year ends--December 31--
in the March issue of the Alumnus.

The Miami University Fund of 1967 . . . . *November 30* . . . . *Oxford, Ohio*

Figure 24

The Miami Loyalty Fund—1963

MANY GIFTS IN A COMMON FUND CAN DO GREAT THINGS

September 20, 1963

One of my friends
has a lovely wife;

They are very fond of each other, but they have one problem.
She's afraid of burglars; he likes uninterrupted sleep.

For years after they were married she woke him once or twice
a week to investigate noises downstairs. Then recently, he
had an inspiration. He convinced her that burglars don't make
noise.

Now, whenever she doesn't hear a noise, she thinks there's a
burglar downstairs.

He loses more sleep than before, but in a way, I envy him.

That's because so many Miami alumni and friends think about
our Loyalty Fund only when they're reminded ... when I make
a noise. Each letter I send out is a proof of that, for
contributions pour back every time.

But, of course, more don't answer each letter than do.

Later some tell me they know the Fund is worth while, and
really mean to send a pledge or contribution, but the reminder
came on the wrong day or something interrupted and they put
everything off j-u-s-t long enough to forget about it. Perhaps
that's happened to you.

Wouldn't it be wonderful if everyone thought of the Loyalty
Fund every day they didn't hear from me. We'd reach our goal
quickly each year, I'm sure, because most of Miami's friends
want to share in the great things the fund can do for their
school. They just don't think of it at the right time.

The right time for the 1963 Fund can't be much later than
now, for the books close December 31 and we are still a good
distance from our goal. So won't you send your tax-deductible
contribution today ... or, at least, remind yourself about
it every day during which ...

you don't hear from me?

John Dolibois

John E. Dolibois
Director

JED:kt

Figure 25.

Special Events

Raising money by holding special events is not solely the province of small community organizations concerned with social action. Nowadays, theater openings, auctions, cocktail parties, carnivals, tennis and golf tournaments—any activities that generate donations—are held to benefit almost everything from city improvement projects to educational institutions conducting multimillion dollar campaigns.

Edwin R. Leibert and Bernice E. Sheldon define a special event as "a dramatized effort to promote an idea, a cause, or a program. Its purpose is to improve relationships with an organization's public, develop understanding, and strengthen support through increased effort and contributions."[1] Lee Sinoff ties the holding of an event into an organization's public relations—special events "generate positive attention for the sponsoring organization."[2]

Generally, the functions are planned and staged by volunteers associated with various nonprofit organizations, clubs, and service groups. Some of the events raise thousands of dollars, with very little cash outlay or financial risk. Others, however, barely break even or wind up in the red.

Why do some succeed and others fail?

In most instances, it is simply a matter of ignoring a number of important factors that are essential to success. Chief among these factors is the failure to ask and answer a fairly hard question at the very beginning: "What are the chances that we'll make money if we do this project?" The answer is found in following a few basic principles.

Many an event is started on nothing but impulse. Funds are needed for this or that project and someone says, "Let's have a dinner party, or a bake sale, or something." Because the temptation is there to raise money quickly, the idea is adopted and launched without sufficient thought. What usually follows is frantic activity that leaves everyone worn out at the end, and with little money to show for it.

A better, wiser course is to use a bit of discipline and follow the essential principles behind all successful special event projects: good planning, sufficient preparation time, a sensible budget, enough people to do the work, and an effective publicity program.

GENERAL GUIDELINES

Take Time to Plan

No event should be undertaken without careful thought. Every angle should be considered. This is best done by a planning committee composed of dedicated individuals who understand the organization's needs and objectives. They should know that almost every fundraising event takes a lot of work, many transactions, and a lot of volunteer help. Since volunteers have a limited amount of time to spend on any organization, the goal is to maximize the dollar return per every volunteer hour expended. For example, if the need is for $10,000, it may be a better investment of time to ask ten prospects for $1,000 each than try to sell 400 dinner tickets at $25 each.

If the decision is to hold a special fundraising event, then the type of event to be held is a committee decision. What kinds of charity benefits do people like best? If the event is community-wide, then what are the community-wide preferences? If the event is to reach a special constituency, then what events usually succeed with that constituency? People turn out and support what they like and it is up to the committee to find out.

An excellent first task for any committee is the identification of appropriate fundraising events. Members should be assigned to talk to other successful groups in town, talk to professionals, read books, and even make a trip to other towns to discover *who* did *what* successfully and *how*. A reporting session or sessions should follow to give each member an opportunity to present his or her findings in detail. From this give-and-take the "right" event will emerge.

With the right event selected, the committee can now be creative. Rather than repeating an old idea step by step, a new approach or new theme can be sought for a traditional event that will attract more people, get more publicity, and enable everyone to have more fun.

Kathleen Rydar, associate director of development at the University of Southern California, has noted five stages of the planning process:

1. Identify your audience—have your event appeal to the people you want to reach by tying in the activities with their interests and needs.
2. Define your goals—ask yourself why you are planning the event in the first place, and you will have a better idea of the things you need to include and the types of programs you should be running.
3. Understand your product—decide which aspect of your services or activities relates most to the audience you are trying to reach, and feature this in your event.
4. Break the boredom barrier—to catch your audience's attention, be sure your event is appealing, rewarding and involving.
5. Innovate to stay fresh—because most groups sponsor special events on a regular basis, keep changing, modifying, and revising your events and program. You won't hold the interest of people for very long if all of your events are alike.[3]

In her checklist for special events planning, Rydar includes advance planning, invitations and seating, housing, transportation, general operations, dignitaries, security, reception and meals, and even a rain plan. Your job is to make sure all of these areas are covered, and try to anticipate all of the problems that could possibly occur. If you're lucky, the problems won't all happen at the same time. But it isn't unusual for a sound system to fail, parking spaces to be filled, slides to be upside down, and guests to be forgotten. Try to plan for all contingencies.

Heather Ricker Gilbert of Penn State offers some planning ideas of her own:

1. Use unconventional facilities—receptions in museums, luncheons on a theater stage, or suppers in a library all charm guests.
2. Give events a reason or theme—a clear focus to an event can give it movement and life. State the theme on the invitation and carry it through during the event. Try to tie the reason for the event into your organization's long-range plans.
3. Be organized—invitations should be sent three to six weeks in advance of the event. Be sure to include all of the details your guests will need—host, time, location, date, reason for event, and so on.
4. Invite guests from several constituencies—you can accomplish many long-range objectives by bringing different groups together. Try to have trustees, faculty, alumni, and current students at a university event.
5. Show off—if you have talented staff members, volunteers, students, or workers, have them provide entertainment if appropriate.
6. Name people—it's almost essential that every event include name tags for the guests. They will feel more comfortable knowing everyone else's name (even if they're not thrilled about wearing their own name tags!), and it will help bring the groups together. Place cards at the tables help make people feel more special, too.
7. Print memorabilia—everyone likes souvenirs, so give them programs, menu cards, placemats, and other printed material they can read and save.
8. Appoint hosts—having appropriate people host the occasion lends organization to an event. These hosts and hostesses can help greet people, answer their questions, show them to their seats, and provide many other functions to make the guests feel as special as possible.[4]

Allow Ample Time to Manage the Details

Organizing and staging an event calls for time: to attend to details and to effectively promote the campaign. The amount of time required depends on the size and scope of the event. A charity auction with an ambitious goal takes anywhere from eight months to a year. Something modest, like a plant sale, can usually be put together in three months or less.

Murphy's Law holds that anything that can go wrong, will. Accept the fact that in putting on a special event, Murphy's Law almost always becomes operable with either inadequate planning or short-term planning.

Here is a list of the most commonly overlooked details that cause minor coronaries for the organizers:

- proper insurance
- receipts
- cash boxes and cash in proper denominations for each box
- emergency numbers for police and fire
- first aid kit
- pens, tape, poster board, and markers
- all phone numbers for key participants, including band, speakers, master of ceremonies
- fire extinguisher
- enough bags, if you are selling something
- sound system that works
- runners for emergencies and all things forgotten

Select the Date

It is important that the right date is selected for the event. Beware of holiday times, unless your event is already established as one of *the* holiday affairs that people do not want to miss. Also keep seasons in mind, particularly if you are planning a sale. Don't try to sell hand-knitted sweaters and scarfs during the middle of the summer crafts sale.

Another common problem is that groups seldom think of anything other than the one big event that will raise *all* the money. But what if the biggest rainstorm since the Flood occurs on that day? An alternate date is well worth thinking about.

Establish the Budget

Event expenses should be calculated in advance. Figure the probable profit and the possible loss. If you can't afford the loss, stop at once. There is no sense wasting your time and that of others involved in the project.

Look for financial support from individuals, businesses, and corporations in the form of expense underwriting. It is not unusual, with this type of backing, to have the entire proceeds from an event free and clear. Many firms support such activities because it gives them exposure and recognition in the community.

Canvassing firms for donations of materials and merchandise is another way to keep down costs. Do the asking in person. If this is not feasible, a letter should be sent to the individual who has full authority to make the decision. The letter should include a full description of the event, and how the funds you raise will benefit the community.

If your organization has *never* planned and held a special event, have the first event be one with relatively high profit and low overhead. Try flea markets, garage sales, bazaars, bake sales, plant sales, and card parties. In these instances, the things to be sold are usually given free by the donors. This enables an organization to build up its special event fund to conduct more costly events such as dinners, auctions, balls, and concerts.

Get Enough Volunteers

The first priority is a topnotch chairman. Qualifications to look for are high motivation, the ability to work with individuals and groups, a good sense of humor, and the ability to remain calm under pressure.

The second priority is enough volunteers to do the job. Recruit as many as possible and give each one a specific part of the event to work on. Be certain that every volunteer understands the event, why it is important, why it must succeed, and that he or she is an integral part of the entire program.

Getting volunteers involved in a special event should help keep them more involved in all of your organization's activities, even after the event is over.

Promote the Event

Promotion and publicity create momentum and a spirit that keeps enthusiasm and support high. No event promotes itself. No cause is so just or so worthy of support that it can succeed without a well-planned, well-coordinated publicity campaign.

Press, radio, and TV coverage will give you credibility and legitimacy. Most radio stations and many TV stations are willing to broadcast public service announcements of community events. Ordinarily, these announcements are 15-, 30-, or 60-second spots resembling commercials; therefore, the announcement must be brief. When writing the announcement for the station, include only the who, what, why, where, and when. State the price of the tickets and where they can be purchased. (See Chapter 7 for complete information on obtaining publicity.)

In addition to media coverage, other ways to publicize an event include posters, flyers, handbills, buttons, balloons, marquee messages, and store counter displays in banks, cafés, and other viable outlets. Excellent publicity can also be obtained by getting banks, utility companies, and department stores to let you include a "statement stuffer" in their monthly statements. Also, do not overlook any business that offers "time and temperature" announcements over the telephone. Almost without exception the time and temperature is preceded by a public service announcement. Why not one about your organization's special event?

Thank All Concerned

When the event is over, write a thank-you letter to everyone who contributed to the success of the event. Do this promptly, and make it personal. Send an expression of gratitude to all committee members and volunteers, all donors of services and materials, and all news media people and others who helped publicize the affair.

IDEAS FOR SPECIAL EVENTS

There are literally hundreds of possible events, including kickoff dinners, anniversaries, fairs, art shows, dances, fashion shows, bridge parties, theater benefits, grand openings, trips and tours, sporting events, work programs, guest speakers, and special types of festivals and shows. And within each type of event are possibilities for variety. The *Ayer Fund-Raising Dinner Guide*, for example, offers more than fifty ideas for dinner themes, including

Celebrity Supper, Polynesian Pizazz, Pink Tie Ball, Dutch Treat Supper, Oriental Gardens Bash, and a South of the Border Fiesta.[5] Many organizations have taken these ideas and further adapted them to their own needs.

The following examples illustrate several types of money-making events that bring volunteers together to work on a common cause, focus the community's attention on your organization and its programs, and alert people to your needs and gift-giving opportunities.

Restaurant Meals Auction

The Jewish Community Center of Central Florida sponsors an annual auction of restaurant meals and attractions that raises more than $5,000 for their programs and services. Marvin Friedman, the Center's executive director, points out that planning for the fall event starts in June, when form letters are sent to restaurants throughout the state of Florida and to a selected group of restaurants and resorts in other parts of the country. Names and addresses are obtained from books and materials used by local travel agents and from telephone books. The letters tell about the organization and its activities, that many members travel and dine out through the year, and that the donation of meals often amounts to free word-of-mouth advertising.

Similar letters are sent to local restaurants, requesting two or more meals for the auction. All letters ask for the donor to set an approximate price to help value the items for auctioning.

In late August and early September, follow-up letters are sent to all resorts, attractions, and restaurants not responding to the original mailing. A committee of volunteers visits local establishments and personally asks for donations. It has been found that letters often bring in dinners for two, while personal visits often lead to several sets of dinners for more than one weekend or group.

During the 1981 program, more than 115 restaurants gave meals for two or more. More than two dozen restaurants, including six of the area's finest, gave multiple dinners for three or more couples, to be auctioned separately.

During the last week in September, a committee takes over the local arrangements and plans for members to bake cakes and cookies, provide salads and other food, and contribute beverages for the auction. A cash bar is also planned, staffed by volunteer members.

A member of the organization serves as auctioneer, dispensing with the traditional "professional" techniques and instead bringing a friendly, personal tone to the evening's events.

The auction itself, held in late October or early November in the group's assembly room, usually attracts more than two hundred members planning to spend their money. Items typically go for 40 to 50 percent of retail value, though many of the more popular items go for full value—and often even higher, adding a tax deduction to the buyer. An additional bonus—a lunch or dessert at a local restaurant—is usually given to buyers paying more than the retail amount.

The event has been so successful, and so much fun for the volunteers and guests alike, that the Center is now starting to hold two separate auctions each year. One is for trips and special items (members offer meals, haircuts, car washes, etc.), while the other offers just restaurant meals and other food items.

Movie Premiere

St. Joseph Mercy Hospital in Ann Arbor, Michigan, raised more than $104,500 in one night—with a cocktail party, dinner, and "premiere" showing of the 1933 Clark Gable/Joan Crawford film, *Dancing Lady.* The 150 top donors (including 34 couples who paid $1,000 or more each) attended a pre-theater cocktail party at a local hotel, then joined the other 850 guests in the Michigan Theatre lobby for a champagne reception before the film and stage show. Donors of $100 or more were invited to an after-theater buffet supper and a dance contest. The $1,000 donors were driven to the theater in vintage automobiles. It took more than one hundred volunteers to organize the event, sell tickets, contact sponsors (most of the expenses were underwritten by donors), and see that all events ran smoothly.[6]

Golden Anniversary Celebration

In 1977, Edgewood College (Madison, Wisconsin) celebrated its 50th year with a concentrated series of events focusing upon the various elements of the college. These events not only generated a great deal of attention toward the college among the various publics it serves, but they also provided a single focus that brought the campus community closer together while helping the university begin long-range plans for the 1980s.

John C. Butler, director of planning and development at Edgewood, explained that an appropriate "kick-off" date was decided upon for early in the year, and a joint resolution was written and passed by the State Senate and Assembly. A reception was held in the state capitol with the governor presenting the resolution to the Edgewood president. Guests attending included alumni, friends and the Golden Anniversary Committee, whose chairman presented the governor with a special plaque commemorating the Golden Anniversary Celebration.

The guests then returned to the campus where the president held a party to cut a huge Golden Anniversary cake, which was shared with the crowd. A brief ceremony followed where the president discussed the significance of the day and related several upcoming anniversary events.

The following thirteen projects show the scope of the special promotions planned during the year to highlight the college and its 50th anniversary:

Newspaper supplement. The college's Office of Development and Public Relations produced a tabloid supplement that was inserted in daily and weekly newspapers throughout the area. The supplement contained pictures of the fifty years on campus along with historical copy on the college's development. Several of the newspapers agreed to insert it without cost. A number of additional copies were printed and used at various events throughout the year. Other copies were mailed to members of the alumni association.

Student newspaper. A special edition was published featuring the anniversary story and the college's history.

Radio and television. In addition to special programs on the history and development of the college, local radio and TV stations interviewed faculty, alumni, trustees, and others about the college and its role in the community.

50-Year Report. This beautifully produced publication, commemorating the anniversary, was distributed to contributors and a select group of friends.

Golden Anniversary Emblem. A campus-wide contest open to faculty and students focused on the design of an emblem appropriate to the celebration. The chosen design was used on all literature during the year-long activities.

Artifacts. A campaign was conducted, focused primarily on alumni in the area, asking friends and alumni to donate pictures, documents, books, letters, and other artifacts to be placed in the college library and archives. These memorabilia were displayed in campus locations, the city library, and at various locations throughout the area, including the State Historical Society.

Career Education Conference. This unique program brought educators, business leaders, and industrialists from throughout the region to the campus to hear several outstanding speakers and to participate in roundtable discussions about career possibilities. Students attended as well.

Picnic and reunion. Held on the campus, this celebration brought parents, alumni, students, and friends together for a picnic and a chance to talk about the college and share their memories.

Religious Emphasis Week. The campus ministry and religious studies department joined together to sponsor programs conducted by various denominational groups and several campus-wide programs.

Performing Arts Symposium. This program brought to the campus a number of drama instructors and students from high schools throughout the Midwest.

High School Guest Days. Hundreds of youngsters were attracted to the campus for a series of planned events, including athletic events such as intercollegiate basketball games.

Banquet and Ball. This major fundraising function, held at a local hotel, was designed to help underwrite costs of the entire Golden Anniversary celebration. Approximately six hundred people attended, enjoying an orchestra playing music from various periods during the past fifty years. A small program was presented to each guest. Included inside was an overview of the college and a statement of its role, a brief history and discussion of highlights and major events, and a listing of the college's trustees and benefit ball committee. The evening's program began with a poolside cocktail hour from 6 to 7:30 P.M., dinner from 7:30 to 9, and then the Golden Jubilee Awards Presentation. Dancing and entertainment followed until midnight.

Madison Salutes Edgewood College. This was the final event of the year-long celebration, and featured a tribute from the mayor and city council, board of education and others, bringing together townspeople and Edgewood faculty and staff in a show of community support for the college. The highlight of the evening was the presentation of a gift to the college.

At the beginning of the year, the college had set a goal of $50,000 in extra funds to be raised during the celebration. The various events brought all aspects of the community, media, alumni, and college together, and more than $57,000 was raised directly from Golden Jubilee events. In addition, nearly $7,000 extra was raised during the annual fund drives, resulting in a total of $64,000 raised as a result of the campaign. The added impact of the closer ties with all constituents should help the college even more in the coming years.[7]

Swim-A-Thon

This event is a variation on the fundraising technique of having volunteers walk, march or run on a per-mile-donation basis. Participants swim as many lengths as they want (or can) to help raise money for the project. Sponsors pledge the amount designated (e.g., 10 cents and up per length).

Recruit as many participants as you can find and don't forget to ask well-known community people—those who can command prime per-length rates. These high-rate swimmers are doctors, lawyers, educators, clergy, bankers, and anyone else who can make the event a success by getting sponsors to put up dollars instead of dimes for every length completed. Each participant recruits his or her own sponsors.

There are many variations of this event, and all seem to involve people who otherwise would not be interested in fundraising projects.

Such a swimming event is typical of the many "A-Thons" held by organizations to raise money. An Illinois League of Women Voters chapter, for example, held a Diet-A-Thon, with sponsors paying $1 for each pound lost during the time period. They raised $1,000 for passage of the Equal Rights Amendment.

The Boston United Cerebral Palsy chapter held a Slim-A-Thon, with health club members paying for each sit-up. The theme was "Let's Do Sit-Ups for Those Who Can't."

In Hingham, Massachusetts, a church group held a Rock-A-Thon and raised $1,400 by sitting in rocking chairs for twenty-four hours. The money was used to make the church more accessible to handicapped people.

A Colorado chapter of the March of Dimes sponsored a Sleep-A-Thon, with their local Jaycee president and a disc jockey staying on a waterbed in a store window for forty-two hours.

And a library in North Attleboro, Massachusetts, held a Read-A-Thon to raise money for a new circulation desk. Sponsors paid for every library book read during one month.[8]

Card Parties

Don't schedule one or two. Schedule fifty or more—as many as you can find volunteers for. Bridge, gin rummy, and poker are generally the favorite games. Participants pay $5, $10, or $25 for a morning or afternoon or evening. Your volunteer host and hostess invite the players to their home, serve light refreshments, and award prizes to the winners.

Other Ideas

Your events can be as specific and as tied to your group as you'd like. The Knoxville, Tennessee, Boys Club, for example, sponsored a "Tom Sawyer" contest where boys climbed greased poles, whitewashed fences, raced on stilts, and spit watermelon seeds. A cake and ice cream party is used by the St. Louis Tuberculosis and Health Society to introduce its slide program to neighborhoods. Roger Williams Hospital in Providence, Rhode Island, puts on exhibits and demonstrations in shopping centers. And the Pontiac, Michigan, United Fund sent Playboy bunnies (dressed in sweaters and skirts) to greet volunteers at their advance gifts kickoff breakfast.[9] All of these programs offered tremendous publicity value and the opportunity to tie in fundraising by showing off their programs and needs.

Berkshire Medical Center has found special events to be highly successful, so it conducts a wide variety of programs during the year. Recent events have included Donor Appreciation Night (held at a local country club, with donors invited "at cost"), Night at the Symphony (nearly five hundred people attended in 1981, raising $8,000), and a Night at the Races (at a local race track, netting the hospital more than $4,000).

A final word on the growing use of television for auctions, telethons, and other special events. Joe Little, vice president of direct marketing at Russ Reid Company, notes that the growing "electronic church" uses talk shows, variety programs, and other formats to bring messages and needs to television viewers. If your group is considering using television—and many charities have successfully staged telethons in the past few years—Little suggests that you consider the following questions:

- Why do you wish to use television? Ask yourself what your motivation really is and why television is to be used.
- What financial goals will you set? Are there certain needs you can meet if the program is successful?
- How much can you afford to lose in risk capital? You may jeopardize other programs if you lose money on this one.
- How much are new donors worth to you? Do you mail to them enough during the year to make the expense of getting them worthwhile?
- What would be the staff implications if you received thousands of new donations and members?[10]

Most groups find that television programs broaden their constituency, but you have to be willing (and able) to use these new donors and prospects after you obtain them.

Jim LaMont of Chilton Memorial Hospital (Pompton Plains, New Jersey) runs a successful annual telethon on a local cable TV station. He holds talent auditions for local performers, and invites well-known sports stars and celebrities to perform. Winnie the Pooh (from Sears), Ronald McDonald, and other characters are usually available to entertain the children. Between three and four hundred volunteers are needed to take care of all the details, and more than five months of planning and publicity precede the event. LaMont says that the 1979 telethon raised $18,000, but he adds that the tremendous publicity is worth another $50,000 or more.[11]

Remember that a special event must be "special," and you need to make yours different and attractive to your prospects. Michigan Tech did this some years ago when they staged a "hammerfest" to kick off construction of a new high-rise on campus.

The opportunities for staging open houses, wine-tasting parties, parades, exhibits, and other events are unlimited. Not all your events will be successes. But neither will they all be failures, especially if you are willing to plan and implement the program carefully. No matter what size group you represent, it can be done.

CASE STUDY

Florida Public Relations Association, Orlando Chapter— a Roast and Toast

In September 1980, the Orlando chapter (then called the Orange Blossom Chapter) of the Florida Public Relations Association "roasted" well-known golfer Arnold Palmer, a resident of Orlando. The event provided a great deal of publicity for the group, was an enjoyable dinner and show for more than 550 guests, and raised more than $14,000, which was used to establish a scholarship in Mr. Palmer's name at the University of Central Florida.

This was the third successive year that the organization had staged a roast as a major fundraiser, and each year the results were similar. More than five hundred guests attended each of the events, with at least $14,000 raised each year.

The idea for the annual event began in 1978, when the group's members decided to raise funds for a journalism scholarship at the University of Central Florida (then called Florida Technological University). That year they roasted Charlie Wadsworth, a well-known newspaper columnist, and followed that a year later with a dinner honoring Dick Pope, Sr., founder of Florida's Cypress Gardens.

The following case study shows the step-by-step development of their original program—a format that has been modified only slightly each year to achieve the same success. You should find it easy to use their ideas and their materials to honor your own local civic and business leaders. You'll have an evening of fun and great public relations, as well as raise funds for your own needs.

In addition to wanting to establish a scholarship, the group had several other reasons for creating this annual program—they wanted to involve their chapter members in a common cause to aid chapter unity and membership development; reinforce the image of the group as a community-minded organization; honor someone from journalism to strengthen their ties to the media community; and involve local business and political leaders in a public service effort with the chapter to show what could be done with proper planning and hard work.

To fulfill their objectives, the group decided that a "roast and toast" of a prominent community leader would be the proper method, especially since several of the group's members had had prior experience with this type of project.

They chose a columnist for the Orlando *Sentinel Star*, Charlie Wadsworth, to be the "roastee" at their first event. Wadsworth writes a daily column for the newspaper, and after forty years in the business is widely recognized as a beloved, nonpolitical, non-controversial member of the community. He was also willing to be the subject of the roast, and he assisted during the five months of planning for the program.

The group decided that they wished to endow the scholarship in Wadsworth's name with at least $10,000, and they used this figure as the base to determine prices, costs, and expenses. They set up two price levels for tickets—regular seating at $25 per person and "Founding Sponsorships" at $250. These sponsors received two V.I.P. dinner seats, special recognition in the souvenir program, a commemorative plaque and a private cocktail party with the roastee. The prices were set to provide a $10 profit from regular tickets and a $200 profit from each sponsor.

A general chairman was selected and a date for the event researched so that it would not conflict with other major events in the area. Ten subcommittees were established to work with the general chairman on the planning and details—ticket reservations

Florida Public Relations Association
Orange Blossom Chapter
PRESENTS

THE
CHARLIE WADSWORTH
ROAST & TOAST

Saturday, September 9
Marriott Inn
Sand Lake Road
Founder's "Cocktails With Charlie" Party
6:30 P.M. The Palm Room
8:00 P.M. Dinner The Ballroom

$250 FOUNDER SPONSOR
PROCEEDS TO ESTABLISH
THE FPRA/CHARLIE WADSWORTH SCHOLARSHIP FUND
- -
Detach & present when served dinner

ADMIT 2
FOUNDER SPONSOR'S
V.I.P. SEATING AREA

Figure 26. This distinctive ticket featured original artwork and a souvenir ticket stub. Courtesy F.P.R.A., Orlando Chapter, Orlando, Fla.

and banquet arrangements; roaster selection and scripting; program and audiovisual; program coordination; ticket/program graphics and design; publicity and public relations; greeting, seating, and decorating; founding sponsors; university assistance; and student assistance.

Once these committees were established and their objectives defined, plans were set for the implementation of the project. It soon became apparent, however, that the scope of this function would require two cochairmen, and they were named to coordinate all activities of the committees, reporting to the general chairman.

One of the first steps was to compile a mailing list of major community leaders and organizations. More than two thousand names were obtained from committee members and local civic groups, and invitations with return-order cards were hand-addressed and mailed.

Two hundred letters were personally typed and sent to the area's top community/business leaders, soliciting founding sponsorships. If no response was received within two weeks, follow-up phone calls were made to each individual. Between the mailing of this first letter and the roast—two months later—fifty-one firms and individuals bought sponsorships, bringing in $10,200 in profit for the scholarship. This first letter was sent from the former president of Florida Tech, who served as honorary chairman of the founder's committee.

Several different target audiences were identified, and all were sent general letters as "Hush Puppies Fans" (Wadsworth's column is called "Hush Puppies"). In each mailing, the body content of the letter was modified to parallel interests of that particular audience. Letters to political figures, for example, named the participating roasters who were also politicians.

A letter was also sent to FTU communication graduates living in the area, explaining that the roast was to establish a scholarship in their area of study and including an invitation to a cocktail party for them to be held prior to the actual program. A number of the graduates attended the event.

The publicity campaign began concurrently with the mailings. It used press releases, public service and radio announcements, and television appearances by committee members.

Since the subject of this roast was in the newspaper business and was widely known locally, the releases attracted a great deal of

Florida Public Relations Association
Orange Blossom Chapter

August 7, 1978

Dear Hushpuppies Fan:

Perhaps you've already heard that on September 9 our friend Charlie Wadsworth will be "on the skewer" at a gala Roast & Toast Banquet being sponsored by the local chapter of the Florida Public Relations Association.

It's all in fun and for a good purpose... to establish the Charlie Wadsworth/FPRA Scholarship in Communication at Florida Technological University. Each year, a full tuition scholarship will be awarded to a worthy student.

This letter is an invitation to you to participate. Roasting Charlie will be some of his longtime friends...Mayor Carl Langford, Judge Richard Cooper, Jean Yothers, Robert Eagan, Jim York, Howard McClain, General Felices, Grace Chewing, Gene Burns, Charlie Reese, Wayne Densch, Avie Abramowitz, Jim Squires...and many more.

Two avenues of ticket purchase are available. Regular tickets are priced at $25 per person. Or you might wish to be a "Founding Sponsor" at $250 which entitles you to two VIP seats with other sponsors, plus special recognition in the souvenier program, a special commemorative plaque and admission to a private pre-dinner cocktail party with Charlie.

Response to this scholarship program has already been fantastic. We suggest that if you wish to attend, your tax deductible check to the F.T.U. Foundation be sent with the enclosed reservation card immediately. We truly anticipate a sellout crowd, and seating assignment is on a first-come, first-serve basis. All seating is reserved and your tickets will be returned by mail.

In an effort to reach as many of Charlie's friends in the community as possible, we are making several mailings. Since you are involved in politics, this may also interest you; the roast is scheduled for the weekend immediately preceding the primary which is Tuesday the 11th of September.

Please, send checks and reservations to: Truman M. Myers, c/o Stars Hall of Fame, 6825 Starway Drive, Orlando, FL 32809. It is important that checks be made out to the F.T.U. Foundation.

See you at the Marriott Inn, Sandlake Road at I-4, September 9.

Roger Pynn
President

Joseph Curley
Chairman

For further information, contact:
Truman Myers, Ticket Chairman
Phone: 305/351-1120

Figure 27. One of the invitation letters (this one was sent to a group of political figures). Courtesy F.P.R.A., Orlando Chapter, Orlando, Fla.

media interest. Most of the local weekly and daily newspapers and area magazines carried the releases and related information. The chairman and cochairman also appeared on local radio and TV talk shows and public service programs to promote the activities.

Public service radio announcements were another important part of the media relations aspect of the program. The keen interest and support the community was showing for the project prompted many local AM and FM stations to air the spots frequently, generating a great deal of extra publicity for the program. A sample script follows:

> Long-time Sentinel Star columnist Charlie Wadsworth will be honored at a Roast & Toast, Saturday, September 9th, at the Marriott Hotel to raise funds for a scholarship in communications at FTU. Sponsored by the local chapter of the Florida Public Relations Association, the event will provide funds for an annual scholarship to a worthy student. Information on tax-deductible ticket contributions is available by calling Truman Myers at Stars Hall of Fame 351-1120. That's Truman Myers at 351-1120. Refreshments undoubtedly will be served.

The publicity generated many calls from firms and individuals who pledged their help in support of the program. As a result, many overhead costs were eliminated—wine for the dinner, tuxedos for head table guests, floral centerpieces, and printing services were all donated, thus increasing the net profit for the scholarship fund.

On Saturday evening, September 9, 1978, 558 of Central Florida's most prominent citizens enjoyed dinner and "scorched" Charlie Wadsworth in an hour-and-a-half Roast and Toast that included two songs with original lyrics, eight roasters and fourteen "Mini-Roasters" at floor mikes. The mini-roaster concept was used to accommodate many more speakers without taking the full time allotted to the longer speeches. The local public broadcasting station videotaped the entire event and broadcast excerpts as an hour-long special a few weeks later.

An eight-page program listing the founding sponsors, program and menu, roasters and mini-roasters, contributing organizations, committee members, and chapter officers, was given out the night of the roast. It also contained a humorous mock Hush Puppies

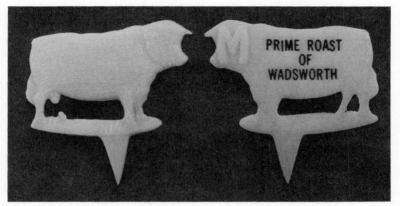

Figure 28. Special yellow plastic meat spears were stuck in the center of each prime rib served. Courtesy F.P.R.A., Orlando Chapter, Orlando, Fla.

column and an announcement regarding the TV broadcast.

To follow through with the "roast" theme, the entree was listed as "Prime Roast of Wadsworth Au Jus." A local specialty company produced plastic meat spears which were stuck in the center of each prime rib served the guests (Figure 28).

The evening's program opened with an eight-minute audiovisual presentation that humorously traced Wadsworth's life from boyhood to the present. The show was presented by twin synchronized three-projector computerized rear-screen slide units, with one unit on each side of the head table to assure excellent viewing by the audience. Committee members wrote Wadsworth's friends and family for photographs, film, and anecdotes to use in the presentations. A local media company produced the program at no cost to the public relations organization.

A local husband and wife team, nationally known for their writing, volunteered to write the scripts and related material. Included in their work were opening and closing songs for the evening, with original lyrics sung by a chapter member. Original artwork was transferred to an iron-on decal and was given to everyone attending the program.

Since Wadsworth's daily column is entitled "Hush Puppies," it was only natural that hush puppies be served at the event. Red Lobster Inns of America agreed to provide fresh hush puppies. Student members of the F.P.R.A. Orlando chapter served the hush puppies. Their costumes included shirts with the original artwork and clothing reminiscent of the Louisiana Cajuns, who reportedly invented hush puppies.

A poster company was contacted, and they prepared a large photo of Wadsworth to be displayed at the roast.

To keep the roast as professional as possible, the planners scheduled it minute-by-minute and wrote the script in a TV format. The actual program ran only a few minutes longer than planned.

Total ticket sales enabled the chapter to present the University with net proceeds in excess of $14,000. The event also brought a great deal of newspaper and broadcast coverage to the group and their activities.

This type of fundraising event, and its organization and implementation, can be easily adaptable by any type of organization.[12]

7 Public Relations

Philanthropy is big business in the United States, one of the biggest. To raise the money required takes a lot of publicity, promotion, organization, committee hours, and door-to-door canvassing. John Price Jones taught us, "Fund-raising is public relations, for without sound public relations no philanthropy can live long. . . . It takes better public relations to get a man to give a dollar than it does to convince him to spend a dollar. Favorable public opinion is the basis upon which American philanthropy has been built."[1]

Perhaps no major aspect of business today is as misunderstood as is the area of public relations. The words have come to stand for everything from propaganda to publicity, from lobbying to press-agentry, from consumer relations to advertising.

In effect, public relations is all of these things and more. It might be simply defined as "everything a company does to inform and influence the groups with which it interacts." Such a broad definition would include the many functions often ascribed to PR, and goes beyond the traditional one, which labels it a business designed simply to influence public opinion.

Public relations is more than just a concerted effort to change people's attitudes. It includes the way your receptionist answers the phone, the way you handle complaint letters, the way your speakers' bureau responds to the needs of civic groups seeking programs, and other ways your organization interacts with its audiences.

How important is PR to the fundraiser? James Murphy, Notre Dame's associate vice-president, has noted that public relations can get along without fundraising, but the opposite is not true—fundraising needs considerable PR support. The role of public relations is to create the most favorable possible context for your fundraising efforts.[2]

No matter how it is defined or what examples are used to explain the process, PR has three major component parts that must be understood by every fundraiser:

1. PR is more than just publicity, though the media relations function is an important part of the entire process. Since public relations is most often visible in the form of the press release, many people think that this *is* the business. In reality, this is only a part of the total business, and fits in with all of the organization's efforts to deal with its constituents. Much of this chapter will be devoted to the publicity function, since this is an important area for fundraisers and one that can be easily understood by knowing the basic techniques and tools of the trade.

2. PR should probably stand for *publics* relations, since an essential part of any organization's PR involves communication with a wide variety of people and institutions.

   The typical nonprofit group, for example, has a need to communicate on occasion with volunteer workers, professional staff, current donors, prospective donors, board members, other community organizations, government leaders, and, of course, the clientele the organization serves. A basic tenet of PR is that communications directed to each group be written in terms that will interest and inform that particular group. An increase in membership fees, for example, has one effect on users of the service, another effect on the professional staff, and another effect on the donors' attitudes toward your needs.

3. PR is a planned, organized effort to tell your story to your audience. You can't wake up in the morning and say that today would be a good day to have public relations. Every day is a good day for PR, because not having a public relations program automatically gives you one—a poor public relations program. It has been said that you cannot *not* communicate to your audiences.

You need to maintain continuing communication with your volunteers to keep them motivated and informed. You need regular reports to your donors and prospects, so they will know of your progress and problems. Your board of directors and staff members need information to do their jobs better. And the many other audiences in your community also need information from you.

The founders of this country realized that only an informed public could be a wise public. Your continuing program of communication will make a major difference in your fundraising success, for public relations can be used to help tell your story, to motivate workers, to build your case for support, and to provide avenues for your audiences to get involved with your group.

During the highly successful "Campaign for Notre Dame," for example, PR played a major part in the effort to raise $130 million. Public relations people produced a campaign prospectus that included a 24-page statement by the university's president on the future of the institution, and a description of thirty-four specific campaign goals. A campaign handbook was also prepared, setting forth in detail how the campaign was to be organized and conducted, and specifying deadlines for each stage of the project.

A unique PR activity, a "fly-in," was developed for this effort. During a fifteen-month period, five or six "pivotal" couples—selected from the 5 percent of the prospect list that could give 85 percent of the money—were flown to the campus for a weekend as guests of the president. They toured the campus, met the top administrators, attended special events, and were told that someone from the university would be calling them soon to discuss their commitment to the campaign. Did it help? The average commitment from the "fly-in" guests was $600,000!

PR also played a role in the campaign literature, special events, and celebrations during the course of the campaign. As Notre Dame's chief development officer explained, "PR has an important, even indispensable, role to play in fundraising. . . . If politics are too important to be left to politicians, then fundraising is too important to be left to development officers."[3]

At Occidental College in Los Angeles, public relations played a major role in their New Capital Program to raise $42 million. The purpose of their program was "to create a higher profile for the college, increase the awareness of its educational program, and develop a knowledge of its needs."[4] All of this is essential to running a fundraising program, especially the large capital campaigns.

You will do a better PR job—and write better PR materials—if you keep in mind that PR's greatest benefit will be to create understanding among your audiences. Many things you do can help create awareness, and people will know more about—or *think* they know more about—your organization and your work. Properly conducted public relations campaigns, however, will help them better *understand* what you are doing. There is a business axiom that what people don't know about your organization can be harmful, but what they don't understand about it can be fatal. Public relations can help bridge that gap between knowledge and understanding. Furthermore, the best time for an organization to make friends is before it needs them. Otherwise you might be too late.

One of the best ways to insure understanding is to work with the media in a professional manner, as the media are the most important liaison between you and your audiences. By understanding what media want, what they can use, and the form they need it in, you will make their job easier and it is more likely that your story will be presented accurately.

We must caution you at this point not to lose sight of the fact that publicity alone will not do the public relations job. You have to get involved in a regular program of research, planning a total PR effort, carrying out your campaign, and then evaluating the results.

A good public relations program is also one that is put together and planned *before* problems arise. Too many organizations feel they don't need PR until a crisis strikes, and then they turn to a last-ditch effort to stem negative attitudes. Few remedial efforts work as effectively as do well-planned, constructive campaigns.

The rest of this chapter is devoted to the principles and techniques of media relations. You may find that your own situation requires some modification, but these guidelines should help you get started. If you're in a small town, for example, you'll have better luck developing personal contacts with reporters than will someone in New York or Los Angeles. If there are a number of weekly newspapers and "shoppers" in your area, you'll find a more receptive market for your releases then you will in an area served only by one major paper.

You'll also find that there are no magical rules for obtaining publicity. The following guidelines, partially adapted from a publicity handbook published by the Council of Arts and Sciences in Orlando, Florida, are a good starting point for learning the basics of media relations.[5] But you'll learn best by doing—by making mistakes and correcting them, by asking questions and finding out the answers.

PUBLICITY

You might begin by considering publicity to be information with news value that your group issues to gain attention or support. Publicity can be conveyed through both written and spoken words, as well as through visual materials. You will want to use publicity to support a particular fundraising effort, to keep your audiences involved with day-to-day activities, and to promote special events and programs.

Among the terms you need to understand are:

- *Publicity*—information with news value
- *Public Service Announcements*—free messages that the media carry for nonprofit organizations. The Federal Communications Commission has long required broadcast media to air a specified number of PSAs on their stations, and most print media feel that such announcements are of benefit to their readers, so they attempt to include as many as possible.
- *Advertising*—paid notices that you might use to create interest or to sell an event, service, or program. An advantage of these paid messages is that you control the content, and can plan exactly what you want said and how it is to be said.
- *Promotion*—covers a wide range of activities, including news, advertising, and other attempts to promote your organization's activities.
- *Public Relations*—usually including all of the above as well as the regular contacts with the people and activities you serve; PR also can be thought of as a general attempt to build sound and productive relations between your organization and your community. PR uses the above techniques to accomplish this.

You may find yourself raising funds for a small organization with few paid staff members. You might be the *only* professional staff member, in fact, or you may be part of a much larger team. Regardless of the organization's structure, some thought has to be given to the choice of a publicity person. What special skills are needed? What qualities make for the best type of publicist?

First, formal educational training is not essential. While many publicity people have degrees in journalism or communications, many others have had little or no training. Instead, they use common sense, a positive attitude, and the basic skills of the profession. To do the job properly, a publicist ought to be able to write and talk clearly, organize information, keep informed about the policies, programs, and projects of your organization, and enjoy working with people.

Other traits essential for success include the ability to discriminate between routine happenings and newsworthy events, keeping informed of the local media resources and contact people, and willingness to work hard at meeting deadlines and function under pressure.

The publicist will work closely with the fundraisers, seeing that the facts are available, the contact people know the answers to questions, and material is timely, newsworthy, and well written.

Very few formal tools are needed to get the job done. You ought to have a well-outlined program on the current campaign or projects, the names and addresses of key staff members and volunteers, and probably a notebook with lots of room to make plans and write notes.

The basic job of the publicist is to place information about the organization's events and programs in front of the public. To do this, we recommend these basic steps:

1. Establish personal contacts at the newspapers, magazines, and radio and television stations in your area. Find out when their deadlines are and how they prefer to have copy submitted. You should coordinate this effort with other staff members at your organization so that only one person is the media contact. It can be very awkward if several people from the same organization contact the media for coverage.

2. Get in the habit of writing everything down—don't trust important facts and information to your memory.

3. Plan your publicity efforts in advance, just as you plan your fundraising campaigns. Many groups plan for the entire year; others start planning the next event when they begin the current one.

4. Don't ask for publicity for bingo, lotteries, rummage sales, and other "business-type" events. Editors get annoyed with requests for free publicity that actually belong in the advertising

department as paid ads. When you've got events that call for admission costs, gambling, large giveaways and other money-raising ideas, let your ads promote them. Save the editors for the major fund drives and the "news" of your organization.

5. Coordinate all efforts with the fundraising staff. Your publicity effort is to make their work easier and smoother, so you need to release information to coincide with their important dates. It is essential that publicity people and fundraisers work together.

6. Be honest and factual. Editors have the right to assume your information is candid, accurate, and complete.

THE PRINT MEDIA

One of the best ways to reach a large number of people is through the print media—your daily and weekly newspapers, and local magazines. People can study print messages for as long as they'd like; they can clip the messages and read them later; they can easily share this information with others.

Though the major big-city dailies have been declining around the country in recent years, there has been a steady increase in the number of weekly newspapers, suburban editions, "shoppers," and other specialized publications. Many of these papers depend on press releases to provide the bulk of their news content, while their own staffs concentrate on advertising and specialized beats. They not only *welcome* your news, they often seek it. These papers include the many tabloid television guides and real estate show-pieces. Often their readers are in relaxed moods when they read these publications, and are most susceptible to persuasive messages regarding your fundraising program.

There are a number of ways to get your story into print. You might try writing to a popular columnist. Many newspapers have specialized columnists who like to include bits of information with news about people (e.g., your key volunteers or board members), unique programs, or activities of widespread interest to their readers. You may be sponsoring a symphony performance as a special event, for example, so the society columnist might be interested in the names of prominent invited guests. The same program would be of interest to the music and drama columnist, as well as to the editor or columnist who writes the information on special events in the community.

You should also consider using the editorial page. Appeals involving the entire community often warrant editorials. The best approach is to send one or two of your prominent board members or volunteers to meet with the editorial staffs of the local newspapers and explain the fund drive to them. Outline the program and what it means to the community as well as to your group, and let the newspaper staff write their own editorial. You can also use the letters to the editor space, which is often reserved for calling attention to a worthy cause, enlisting support for a special program, or expressing an organization's appreciation for community support.

Most publications also have a community calendar that lists upcoming special events. Again, they depend on publicity releases for the information to fill their column space.

A word of advice here. Don't count on your release appearing in the newspaper exactly as you wrote it—or even appearing at all! In most publications, the news comes first, and then the special features and stories of general interest. An editor may drastically rewrite your story to fit more closely with the newspaper's style or format (though you can avoid much of this by learning their style in the first place) or just to fit better in the available space. Or they may have so much advertising or news that day that they can't use your material at all. Don't be discouraged. Just keep sending releases on future programs and you'll be surprised at how many actually do see print. If the release is that important, or if it's the only source of information about an event, you should consider taking paid ads as well to insure that some message does get into the newspaper.

PREPARING A PRESS RELEASE

You can help make it easier for the editor—and thus make it more likely that your story will be printed—if you write your release in proper news style. This style is, by design, simple writing that conveys a basic message. There are several fundamental rules that you should follow.

Be factual, and put the important facts first. Write in the third person (never "I" or "we"). Use a straightforward method of explaining your news or information, writing the way you would talk to the editor. Don't use "fine" writing or flowery language. You are writing a news story for a general audience, not a proposal to a foundation.

Use simple, short words and sentences. Editors are busy people, and if they can rely on you to provide accurate, easy-to-read copy, you'll have a better chance of having your materials used.

Remember that you are writing news and not just bragging about your organization. Avoid too many adjectives (the wonderful organization, spectacular special event, fabulous campaign).

You should also use quotes in your materials whenever possible. People enjoy hearing or seeing their names; you'll find that giving credit to volunteers keeps them excited and motivated. Many charitable groups give credit whenever they can to their volunteers, even though much of the background work is done by the professional staff.

Most important of all, make sure you are accurate. Check and double-check quotations, numbers, important facts, and other information.

Whenever editors are questioned about their likes and dislikes, one theme is always mentioned: their surprise at how many news releases are not used—or cannot be used—because they are incomplete or otherwise improperly put together. Don't let this happen to you, since the publicity your fundraising campaign gets may make the difference between meeting the goal and failure.

The standard method for writing a news release is the "inverted pyramid" (see page 190). Begin the release with the most important information, usually by putting the 5 "W's" (and sometimes the "H") into the very first paragraph—Who, What, Where, When, Why (and How). Less important information follows, with the least important material at the end. There is a simple reason for doing this. Editors usually cut stories from the bottom when they need to be shortened, and putting the most important information in the beginning insures that it won't be accidentally deleted.

This first paragraph, called the lead, is designed to capture the interest of the readers. Put the most important information there and you'll get the attention of people interested in your project.

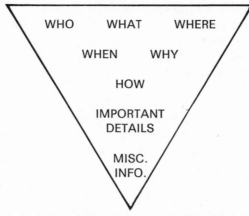

The first page of a press release from the Muscular Dystrophy Association (Figure 29) is an example of the basic writing style. The lead contains the essential information needed by the reader.

Who: the Muscular Dystrophy Association
What: opening of an outpatient clinic at Crippled Children's Hospital
Where: Richmond, Virginia
When: recently (specific date not important here)
Why: offering free diagnosis and follow-up care to children and adults with muscular dystrophy and related diseases
How: Muscular Dystrophy Association now supports 220 such facilities (a bit of related information)

Also of interest in this release prepared by the national headquarters is the opportunity provided for chapters to fill in their own local information. The chapters complete the last line of the first paragraph and then send out the release with all the details.

The first page of a release from The National Council on the Aging, Inc., also shows how the important information is put in the lead, with the rest of the material coming later in the release. If edited, the main facts are still available in the beginning of the story (Figure 30).

Once the lead is written, the rest of the release covers other information relating to the event. When a specific date is involved, give it in full—"Tuesday, February 23, 1982," not just "Tuesday."

MUSCULAR DYSTROPHY ASSOCIATION, INC.
Greater Washington Chapter

1800 MASS. AVE., N.W. WASHINGTON, D.C. 20036
SUITE 100

NEWS RELEASE

(202) 466-7450

FOR IMMEDIATE RELEASE

MUSCULAR DYSTROPHY ASSOCIATION OPENS NEW CLINIC

AT CRIPPLED CHILDREN'S HOSPITAL IN RICHMOND

With the recent opening of an outpatient clinic at Crippled
Children's Hospital in Richmond, Virginia, the Muscular Dystrophy
Association now supports 220 such facilities offering free diagnosis
and follow-up care to children and adults with muscular dystrophy
and related diseases. Located throughout the United States, Puerto
Rico and Guam, this patient care network includes clinic(s) at
(NAME(S) OF INSTITUTION(S)) in the (CITY/STATE) area.

Patients attending MDA clinic sessions receive diagnosis and
follow-up treatment; physical and occupational therapy; genetic
counseling; orthopedic aids such as wheelchairs, braces, and hydraulic
lifts; and flu shots, all completely free of charge. The Muscular
Dystrophy Association is unique in the health agency field, because it
offers all medical services free to patients and their families, with
no means test required.

In addition to its extensive patient care program, MDA sponsors
a worldwide research effort, including over 700 individual projects
and 10 university-based research/clinical centers in the U.S. and England.
The Association's programs cover 40 neuromuscular disorders, among them

MDA sponsors basic and applied research into neuromuscular disorders, including the muscular dystrophies, the myosites, amyotrophic lateral sclerosis (ALS) and other spinal muscular atrophies, and provides services to those afflicted by these diseases.

*Figure 29. This first page of a press release illustrates the basic
writing style and shows ways releases can be localized to particular
situations.* Courtesy Muscular Dystrophy Association, Greater
Washington Chapter, Washington, D.C.

NEWS
From

The National Council On The Aging, Inc.

1828 L Street, N.W., Washington, D.C. 20036   (202) 223-6250

FOR IMMEDIATE RELEASE   CONTACT: PATRICIA WARDEN

NATIONAL COUNCIL ON THE AGING TO ADDRESS
CRITICAL ISSUES AT 1981 CONFERENCE

Washington, D.C., September 10. "The Aging Today and Tomorrow"

will be the theme of the 1981 Annual Conference of the National

Council on the Aging to be held in Nashville, Tennessee, March

29 - April 1.

The Conference will focus on current and impending issues facing

older Americans, the fastest growing segment of the nation's

population.

Among critical issues to be highlighted are the economics of aging,

health and social services, community and family support systems and

advocacy efforts on behalf of older persons. Conferees also will

explore the question of integrating older people into society

and utilizing them as resources in the community.

Prominent speakers from the fields of economics, gerontology,

politics and social work have been invited to speak at the

conference, expected to draw more than 2,000 practitioners in

aging and related fields.

(more)

Figure 30. The basic information is in the lead and in the other introductory paragraphs in this first page of a press release. Courtesy The National Council on the Aging, Inc., Washington, D.C.

Doublecheck to make sure that the day and date are accurate. Also be sure to give the address as well as the name of the location of an event—readers may want to know this, especially in areas some distance away, and the editor may also use it to send a reporter out to cover the event.

It is usually a good idea to keep your release to only one page, about two hundred words. Of course, the more important the event, and the more details involved, the longer the release must be. It is not uncommon for projects calling for extensive explanation to be announced in releases of three, four, or five pages. If the material is timely, interesting, and relevant, put it in the release. If not, keep the release as brief as possible. And yes, all releases should be typed!

You should consider yourself fortunate if more than two paragraphs of your release get into print. Unless a release is of interest to the readers, it will not be used.

The following elements are also important in preparing a press release:

Paper. Most editors prefer plain white stock, 20 lb. bond, standard 8½″ × 11″ paper. Odd colors and sizes may stand out but most editors prefer the traditional appearance.

Format. Type on only one side of the paper. Double space the copy, using upper and lower case letters. Use wide margins, 1″ to 1½″ on all sides—it lets the editor make changes right on your copy. Indent each paragraph five spaces. Leave some room at the top of the release for the editor to write in a headline or change a headline if you provide one.

Upper left corner. If your organization does not have stationery or other paper suitable for sending press releases, put your name and phone number, and your organization's name, address, and phone number in the upper left corner. The editor can then contact you or someone at the organization if there are any questions about your release.

Release instructions. Except in extreme circumstances (such as sending a release of a *major* event far in advance so the editor can make travel plans), information should be available "for immediate release." If you have to submit copy early, indicate the appropriate release time (e.g., for release after 11 A.M. on March 15, 1982). Editors do not like being asked to file releases far in advance for their use at a later date.

Date. Use the date that the release was written.

Headline. If you can come up with a catchy, succinct phrase that could serve as a headline, put it above the copy. If not, leave the space blank and let the editor write the headline for your story.

Most public relations writers do not include a headline, leaving it up to the editor. But some others argue that a carefully worded headline will help the editor better grasp the idea of the story and thus better determine how to use it.

Length. If there is more than one page, write "more" at the bottom of each page except the last one. Don't end a page in the middle of a sentence or paragraph. Pages should also be "slugged" for the page number (e.g., "Concert, page 2."). Slugs are short words or phrases at the top of each page that let the editor quickly refer to a specific story (Fundraiser, Campaign Speaker, President Names, Hospital Opens). End the release with some type of end mark (most often used are "# # #," "-0-," "-30-").

Don't staple pages together, because they have to be separated in the news room and may be torn. Use paper clips instead. Save a copy for your files and mail the release before the newspaper's deadline. Make sure you proofread carefully to avoid typographical errors—they often suggest to the editor that you are careless with the facts as well.

The following first page of a Smithsonian Institution press release (Figure 31) contains a wealth of information. At the top right are listed the names of the contact people, release dates, and special information on a press preview. The lead gives all the important information. Quotations are used to make the story more interesting.

Note the code at the bottom of this first page. It would be clear to editors that this is a numbering system for releases, along with the date the release was written.

This release contains mostly feature material and general infor-

NEWS
from the Office of Public Affairs
Smithsonian Institution
Washington, D.C. 20560
Telephone: (202) 357-2627

FOR IMMEDIATE RELEASE

Contacts: Sidney Lawrence
           (202) 357-1618

           Alvin Rosenfeld
           (202) 357-2816
* * * * * * * * * * * * * * * * * *
Press preview: Wednesday, Feb. 11,
                10 a.m.-noon
Special Exhibition Gallery, Lower
level.

"DIRECTIONS 1981" AT HIRSHHORN MUSEUM

"Directions 1981," an exhibition of more than 50 recent works by 16 contemporary artists, will open Thursday, Feb. 12, at the Smithsonian's Hirshhorn Museum and Sculpture Garden and continue through May 3. This will be the second exhibition in the "Directions" series inaugurated by the Museum two years ago.

Included will be paintings, sculptures, drawings, photographs, constructions, video and mixed-media installations reflecting the diversity of current art. Twelve Americans, three Europeans and one Canadian will be represented.

The exhibition, organized by Museum curator Miranda McClintic, will be presented in three sections, or directions--"Artistry," "Myth and Metaphor" and "Social Observation"--each suggesting a focus shared by many artists today.

"Neither trends nor movements, these three directions indicate fundamental ways of seeing and making art," McClintic says. "No single school has dominated art in recent years: Artists have been re-evaluating their work in relation to the art of the recent and distant past and in relation to contemporary culture. This show indicates the range of current work, from 'art for art's sake' to art directed toward interpreting experience or changing the world."

SI-22-81 1-16-81

-more-

Figure 31. This release (of which only the first page is shown) provides a great deal of information on an art exhibition, including the works represented, quotes, and special sections in the exhibit.
Courtesy Smithsonian Institution, Washington, D.C.

mation after the first page. If the newspaper has space, they can use it all. If not, this material can be cut, as the first paragraph or two gives the main part of the story. It concludes with information of general interest, including the location of the museum, operating hours, admission charge, and even the name of the nearest subway station.

There are also some press releases that are feature-oriented rather than news-oriented (Figure 32). If you have an interesting story to tell, a feature release may help reach many readers of newspapers and magazines.

Even if there are no magazines produced in your area, you'll find that many Sunday editions of newspapers now contain magazinelike sections. There are many opportunities in these sections for calendar listings, feature stories, editorials, and letters. A major difference between magazines and newspapers is the longer lead time needed in magazine preparation. Many plan their issues and produce them weeks and even months in advance of the issue date. Magazines are also more likely to use photographs since their paper and printing are usually better, so try to include pictures when appropriate.

You should also consider sending your press release to the many specialized publications in your area—publications by fraternal, social, and political groups and automobile, health, hobby, church, sports, conservation, farming, fashion, homemaking, art, dance, and professional magazines all have large readerships. They need your news to help fill their space, too.

You can help the chances of your release getting into print by timing its distribution properly. Because most important government, business, and education offices are closed over the weekend, Monday morning newspapers are especially receptive to news ideas. There are light and heavy news days (for example, Sunday is a very heavy day for feature and in-depth material), so you should try to schedule your releases to coincide with editors' needs. One caution: even though editors need news on certain days, you shouldn't send all your releases then. Saturday is very weak news day, but it is also a typically low readership day.

Find out when your local media deadlines are. If you're aiming for a morning newspaper or broadcast, you'll find that editors need the information by 6 P.M. the previous day, though spot news can often be handled as late as 11 P.M. For afternoon media, last-

GEORGETOWN NEWS

GEORGETOWN UNIVERSITY • 37th & O STREETS, N.W. • WASHINGTON, D.C. 20057

FOR IMMEDIATE RELEASE

CONTACT:
DAVE FULGHUM
(202) 625-3722 (O)

GEORGETOWN SETTING INTERNATIONAL EXAMPLE
IN DRIVE TO MAKE UNIVERSITY ENERGY SELF-SUFFICIENT

WASHINGTON, D.C.---Out of growing economic necessity, Washington's
senior university is marshalling its expertise and energy savvy to make
it---possibly in as few as five to ten years---one of America's few energy
self-sufficient university and hospital complexes.

Georgetown University is, in reality, tightening its belt, going
underground, clearing the air, reaching for the sky, and taking a leap into
the future, all in the context of a new energy plan that is designed to
serve as an international example for institutions of higher education here
and abroad that are being badly hurt by high fuel costs.

For many colleges and universities, the 1974 oil shortage was nearly
a fatal blow. Even conventional energy conservation could not stop the growing
drain on their budgets. Now Georgetown is becoming, for them, an institutional
model of energy efficiency wedded to "beyond" state-of-the-art technology.

Georgetown, founded in 1789 as the first university in what is now the
Nation's Capital, is "tightening its belt" with an energy conservation program
that has already saved the University more than $4.4 million and reduced annual
energy consumption by 20 percent since 1973. Reduced lighting, better pipe
insulation and replacement, and lower hot water temperatures have played

-more-

*Figure 32. Note how this first page of a feature press release from
Georgetown University reads like a magazine story. It is not as
timely as a news story, but can instead be used when the publication
has room and need for longer feature material.* Courtesy Georgetown University, Washington, D.C.

minute deadlines are typically 9 A.M. for general information and close to 11 A.M. for late-breaking stories.

If you want your information in the heavily read (though very crowded) Sunday newspaper, you should be certain to have all material to the editor by Friday noon at the latest.

PHOTOS

Coverage of any activity or event can be enhanced by using photographs. If you have a good photographer—amateur or professional—helping your organization, you can supply the media with your own photos. Otherwise you should contact editors in advance to give them the details and date of the event, so they can plan to have pictures taken by their own photographers if they want coverage.

Newspapers and magazines need crisp black-and-white photos, either 5″ × 7″ or 8″ × 10″. Try to provide a vertical scene or a close-fitting horizontal (have people stand close together) that can be cropped into a newspaper's narrow columns.

Action pictures are best, though you'll find some photographers who like to line groups up against a wall "firing-squad style" and take the old-fashioned "left to right" type of photo. You should keep the background simple, and try to have the people in the picture doing something—looking at a book, studying a painting, or some other active scene. Just staring at the camera makes for a pretty dull photo. Don't crowd your pictures with too many people—many papers won't use photos with more than four people in them. They get too cluttered otherwise.

When you submit your pictures, make sure everyone is identified clearly. It's also a good idea to get publication releases from people in the picture.

Do not use staples or paper clips on your photos—they usually leave marks no matter how careful you are. Also make sure you do not write on the back of the picture with a ball point pen—it will show through and mar the photo. The best way to handle identifications is to type the information on the middle of an 8″ × 5″ piece of paper and tape the end of the sheet to the back of the photo, folding the paper to cover the picture. This lets the editor and others handle the photo while it is protected by the paper cover, and gives ready access to the photo information.

Captions (also called cutlines) should be as well written as the text of the release. You can write them in either the present tense (John Fundraiser receives $1 million gift) or the past tense (John Fundraiser received a $1 million gift yesterday). The length of the caption depends on the picture itself (how much must be said about it?) and whether or not a press release is sent with it (some pictures stand alone and actually *are* the release—captions for these must necessarily be longer). We once heard that the best caption will make the reader look at the picture again.

It is standard to identify people from left to right. You can write out these words, use "l to r," or use something similar. And if the identifications are obvious (a man and a woman, for example), you don't need the left-to-right designation.

When you are sending releases to more than one medium, it is a good idea to have several photos taken and send each paper or magazine a different photo or two.

If you need the photos returned, enclose a stamped, self-addressed envelope.

THE BROADCAST MEDIA

The immediacy and dynamism of the broadcast medium make it an invaluable source for publicity, especially when the audience is asked to support something, do something, or take some other form of action. Broadcast media are also particularly receptive to public service material, and thus are good vehicles for your messages.

The major problem is the time limitation—competition for air time is keen, and there are only so many minutes in an hour. While a newspaper can add extra pages or even extra sections, the broadcast media cannot lengthen their hours.

The procedure in establishing good media relations is the same as for the print media. Contact the news directors and/or public service directors at your local stations. Give them the background on your organization, and the details of your current fundraising efforts or general projects and activities. You'll find that this initial visit will establish the personal contact that is often vital in having your publicity used. From this point on, you can mail releases to the stations, saving personal calls for the really big stories. Many people think that they should hand-deliver releases to all editors and broadcast representatives, but the media usually prefer mailed materials.

There are four major types of broadcast coverage available on radio and television stations that can publicize your group's activities. These are:

- *News*—regular newscasts report on national and local "newsworthy" stories.
- *Spot announcements*—these are brief announcements ranging in length from 10 seconds to one minute, available as either paid advertising or as free public service announcements.
- *Editorial*—although broadcast media do not take the editorial support that many print media do for major issues, it is growing more common for broadcast officials to air "minute memos" and editorials on key issues in their communities.
- *Public affairs programs*—many opportunities exist for members of your organization on talk shows, interview programs, panel discussions, and other station-sponsored programming. Many stations also include filler material about community organizations and events between breaks in their daytime movies and local news programs.

Writing for broadcast media is considerably different from print media preparation. If you have a story that is newsworthy and which you feel merits considerable attention, we recommend sending a fact sheet to the stations' news directors, who can decide whether or not they want to cover the story, and will contact you for additional information. Fact sheets can be sent to both print editors and broadcast news directors to alert them to an upcoming story.

If your material is more appropriate for a public service announcement, you can write it yourself.

For radio, we recommend following the basic print media format of covering the 5 W's. The difference is in the style—radio is more conversational, informal, and filled with short words, short sentences, and lots of contractions. Since most stations adhere to a "no-gimmick" policy for their public service announcements, you should be factual and direct, and keep the message simple. Important information (phone numbers, dates, etc.) should be repeated.

For a 10-second spot, you should write between 15 and 25 words. Use 40 to 50 words for a 20-second spot, 60 to 70 for a 30-second spot, and between 120 and 150 words for a minute-long message. Even though the public service director may wish to rewrite your message, it should be written as close to "air ready" as possible.

Following is a sample message written for radio.

10-second spot   *State University Youth Ensemble*

ANNOUNCER   PLAN TO ATTEND THE FREE

PERFORMANCE OF THE STATE

UNIVERSITY YOUTH ENSEMBLE

. . . SUNDAY AFTERNOON . . .

APRIL FIFTH . . . AT THE

UNIVERSITY . . . FEATURING

MORE THAN FIFTY TOP MUSI-

CIANS . . . THREE P. M. . . .

SUNDAY . . . APRIL FIFTH.

You should follow the mechanics of releases for the print media for your radio spots, using white paper, typing, leaving large margins, and writing on only one side of the page. Double- or triple-space all copy, making it easier to read. Some radio stations prefer that the copy be typed in all capital letters as well. Find out what your local stations prefer.

These rules are especially important for radio, because of the nature of the medium today. Radio reaches people while they are doing something (other than just listening to the radio). It has become a major background force, providing "noise" while people drive, iron, read, talk, or whatever else they are doing. You have to write for people who really are not listening that closely, so you need as interesting a message as possible.

Writing for television is even more challenging. You are combining the use of words with action, and often have an audience concentrating far more closely on the message (though not always on the commercials).

You sometimes have the best chance of media coverage by contacting TV stations far in advance (even four to six weeks ahead) so that they can tape interviews and short features, to be used when their news runs short.

As with radio, the basic suggestions hold true: send fact sheets to the news directors, provide general information for their planning, and keep them on your mailing list for press releases. But if you're going to write your own television spots, you need to know some of the specifics of the medium.

Television writers use a special copy format. Draw a line down the center of an $8\frac{1}{2}'' \times 11''$ piece of paper, and use the right side for a description of the visuals, the left side for the copy to accompany them. If you set your typewriter margins at 35 and 85, you can type approximately 21 full lines of copy for a 60-second spot, and 11 full lines for a 30-second message. You can also indicate any special camera techniques, such as dissolves and fades. Many publicists send different length spots to television stations so that the station can choose the appropriate one for their time frame.

A sample television script for a public service announcement begins on the next page.

You also need to prepare the visuals for television spots. Keep in mind that the image on the screen should reinforce the spoken word. A good rule of thumb to follow is that for every 10 seconds of audio, there needs to be a different visual. This visual can be a photograph, artwork, or a 35mm slide. Whatever format you provide, remember that the visual needs to be clear, uncluttered, and horizontally composed ($10'' \times 8''$ rather than $8'' \times 10''$).

If you're providing photos, try to send a dull (matte) finish rather than a glossy. The intense TV lights pick up reflections from

TV spot   *30-seconds*

AUDIO	*VIDEO*
PLAN NOW TO ATTEND THE FREE PERFORMANCE OF THE STATE UNIVERSITY YOUTH ENSEMBLE.	Slide 1—ensemble in concert
SUNDAY AFTERNOON . . . APRIL FIFTH . . . AT THE UNIVERSITY.	Slide 2—exterior of university theater
MORE THAN FIFTY TOP MUSICIANS FROM THE AREA WILL PERFORM.	Slide 3—musicians in rehearsal
SPEND AN ENJOYABLE AFTERNOON ON SUNDAY . . . APRIL FIFTH . . . BEGINNING AT THREE P.M.	Slide 4—different shot of ensemble in concert

FOR FURTHER INFORMA- TION ON THIS MUSIC SPECIAL, CALL THE UNI- VERSITY BOX OFFICE AT 275-2727 . . . THAT'S 275-2727.	Slide 5—phone number and name of University Box Office
ENJOY THE POPULAR STATE UNIVERSITY YOUTH ENSEMBLE.	Slide 6—another shot of ensemble in concert

slick photo finishes. Art and photography stores usually carry a spray that converts glossy photos to matte.

For slides, color is essential, of course, and the slides must be of excellent quality. The easiest way to make a slide is to prepare a 14″ × 11″ (horizontal) poster with all the vital information inside a 9″ × 7″ horizontal area. Use bold, bright colors and take a picture of the poster for a slide.

Stations will usually return your materials if you request it. You will find that slides and other visuals can be used in many different situations, so you will probably want to ask for them back.

OTHER MEDIA

In addition to the news and public service coverage you may get through the media, there are many other sources that will carry your message at no cost to the organization. Consider using any of the following for your campaign:

Shopping news. Free handouts concentrating on food stores and other retail outlets are often distributed through the mail, door-to-door, or at shopping malls. Many of these publications carry community announcements along with their ads.

Marquees. You'll find dozens of marquees in your area, at banks, churches, retail stores, and other locations. Many firms and institutions allow this space to be used by charitable organizations.

House organs and industry publications. Local industries often print news of their company or organization for their members or employees. Call the editors and ask what types of general information they use, and when their deadlines are.

"Piggy-back publicity." Every community affords many opportunities for this type of public relations message. Some organizations will use mail slugs from charitable groups for their metered mail for a certain time period (e.g., "Support the Health Fund"). Banks and department stores will often include a message about your program on the backs of their statements and bills, or in the envelope sent to their customers. Phone companies and power companies also are often receptive to using statement stuffers. Ask your local restaurants about including messages on their menus or ask other advertisers to mention your campaign in their ads as a public service.

Community bulletin boards. Many service and retail outlets, from laundries to restaurants, from beauty shops to grocery stores, have community bulletin boards with news of interest to the area. Similar boards are often found in apartment complexes, churches, schools, and community centers. Sometimes you need prior approval for the notices, while other times anyone can place messages on the boards. Stop by the locations yourself and see what their requirements are. You may get a better space on the board if you post the notice yourself rather than mail it out.

Visitors' information. Hotels often print a daily or weekly list of local activities for their guests. Your special event or activity may be of interest to visitors to your area. You might also be able to leave your brochures on hotel desks.

Telephone time and temperature recordings. Even though these are usually sponsored by a local commercial organization, many of them include information from charitable organizations on a periodic basis.

Public previews. Set up a display at a local shopping mall or downtown area and give a sample of the special event your group is holding, using pictures, performances, or whatever is appropriate. Let the public have a preview of the event, along with general information on your fundraising drive.

THE PUBLICITY KIT

To announce major campaigns or give in-depth information, we suggest putting together a publicity kit. This usually involves a folder with fact sheets, background information, black-and-white photos, logos from your group, information on individuals associated with the project (sometimes using quotes from these people), and other general information and materials.

THE PUBLICITY SCHEDULE

Since the best public relations comes from advance planning, you can use the following guidelines to help publicize your events and programs. You will have to make adjustments and additions as each specific campaign progresses, but these time frames are good starting points. While this has been designed for a special event, you can easily adapt the schedule to a general fundraising campaign.

Two to Six Months Before an Event

- Begin collecting facts about the event and set up a publicity calendar.
- Establish deadlines for magazines, including relevant trade publications.

- Prepare a list of radio and television feature possibilities that have long-range planning needs.
- Prepare a basic news release on the event or fund drive with as many known details as possible.
- Contact editors, writers, and producers about interview and feature possibilities, with suggested dates.
- Establish a photographic file relating to the event. Begin to create visual materials to be used in the publicity—logo, graphics, etc.
- Establish a background file of materials relating to the event—previous features of a similar nature, biographical data, credits, human interest stories.
- Check schedules of celebrities or VIPs for interview appointments well before and at the time of the event.
- Determine the extent of your miscellaneous publicity devices—buttons to billboards—and begin planning, scheduling, ordering.

Four to Six Weeks Before an Event

- Double-check media deadlines.
- Send out initial news release to all daily and weekly newspapers, all radio and television stations, and local magazines.
- Send initial spot announcements to radio stations, spot announcements with visuals to television stations.
- Call radio and television talk show producers (a few days after the release is sent) to try to arrange interviews, particularly with shows that are taped in advance. (Certain dates and times have already been cleared with celebrities and VIPs.)
- Begin to contact editors (particularly those at weekly publications) about feature possibilities.
- Issue miscellaneous publicity materials to a committee (if possible) who will distribute them throughout the community.
- Make sure you have enough glossy photographs. Caption each one.
- Prepare publicity kits to send to editors and producers.
- Check with editors and radio and television producers who expressed an interest in feature stories and interviews.
- Send invitations.
- Send photographs to weeklies.

- Mobilize the best prospects from your speakers' bureau. Contact other potentially interested organizations, as well as your own membership.
- Set aside tickets for media.

One Week Before the Event

- Send out a second news release with more specific information on the event.
- Send photographs to daily newspapers.
- Secure reviewers, if required, for the event.
- Send tickets to media personnel.
- Try to arrange for a photograph if there are any set-up operations or rehearsals that might be of public interest.
- Clip all articles from newspapers and magazines as they appear.

A Day Before the Event

- Call television producers to verify coverage.
- Keep a supply of publicity kits handy for reporters, reviewers, etc.

A Day or So After the Event

- Put together all releases, miscellaneous publicity materials, and clippings of the event.
- Pick up any posters, photographs, etc.
- Write notes to media contacts thanking them for their coverage of the event.

ADVERTISING

In addition to the free publicity you are seeking, your organization may decide to use some paid advertising throughout the campaign. You may be fortunate enough to find a corporate sponsor to pay the cost of your ads, or your group may have to pay the bill.

In any event, it is often essential that some paid advertising be used to insure that your message reaches your public. This is particularly important if you are having a special event and want a

Figure 33. This ad for The New York Public Library was prepared in various sizes and sent to local and national newspapers and magazines. Many were used by the publications as a public service and at no cost to the library. Note how "Uncle Sam" was used to point out the matching gift grant from the National Endowment for the Humanities. Courtesy The New York Public Library, New York City.

Heart attack or stroke could knock you down on your way up.

You're working for the challenge, the satisfaction, the success. The last thing you want is a heart attack or stroke. Yet nearly one million Americans die of heart disease and stroke every year. And 200,000 of them die before retirement age.

The American Heart Association is fighting to reduce early death and disability from heart disease and stroke with research, professional and public education, and community service programs.

But more needs to be done.

You can help us find the answers by sending your dollars today to your local Heart Association, listed in your telephone directory.

Put your money where your Heart is.

American Heart Association
WE'RE FIGHTING FOR YOUR LIFE

MWO-4 (6½" w. x 9" d.)

Heart Healthy Recipe

BEEF BOURGUIGNON

5	medium onions, sliced
4	tablespoons oil
2	pounds lean beef, cut into 1-inch cubes
1½	tablespoons flour
¼	teaspoon marjoram
¼	teaspoon thyme
	freshly ground black pepper
½	cup beef broth
1	cup dry red wine
½	pound fresh mushrooms, sliced

In a heavy skillet, cook the onions in the oil until tender. Remove them to another dish. In the same pan, saute the beef cubes until browned. Sprinkle with flour and seasonings. Add broth and wine. Stir well and simmer slowly for 1½ to 2 hours. Add more broth and wine (1 part stock to 2 parts wine) as necessary to keep beef barely covered. Return onions to the stew, add mushrooms and cook stirring 30 minutes longer, adding more broth and wine if necessary. Sauce should be thick and dark brown.

Yield: 8 servings
Approx. cal/serv.: 375

Heart Healthy Recipes are from the Third Edition of the American Heart Association Cookbook. Copyright © 1973, 1975, 1979 by the American Heart Association, Inc.

American Heart Association

Heart Healthy Recipe

BEEF BOURGUIGNON

5	medium onions, sliced	¼	teaspoon thyme
4	tablespoons oil		freshly ground black pepper
2	pounds lean beef, cut into 1-inch cubes	½	cup beef broth
1½	tablespoons flour	1	cup dry red wine
¼	teaspoon marjoram	½	pound fresh mushrooms, sliced

In a heavy skillet, cook the onions in the oil until tender. Remove them to another dish. In the same pan, saute the beef cubes until browned. Sprinkle with flour and seasonings. Add broth and wine. Stir well and simmer slowly for 1½ to 2 hours. Add more broth and wine (1 part stock to 2 parts wine) as necessary to keep beef barely covered. Return onions to the stew, add mushrooms and cook stirring 30 minutes longer, adding more broth and wine if necessary. Sauce should be thick and dark brown.

Yield: 8 servings   Approx. cal/serv.: 375

Heart Healthy Recipes are from the Third Edition of the American Heart Association Cookbook. Copyright © 1973, 1975, 1979 by the American Heart Association, Inc.

American Heart Association

minimum number of participants. Sometimes free publicity just isn't enough.

You can keep your advertising costs low by writing a simple and direct message. The media sales staffs at your local newspapers and broadcast stations will suggest the best way to prepare your ad and the best space or time to run it.

There are also other paid opportunities for messages in most areas, including street banners, skywriting, searchlights, and other forms of promotion. The Yellow Pages will provide a number of advertising and promotion firms that can help you with these.

Good public relations will make your fundraising efforts more efficient. You'll find that this form of "friend raising" helps make the "fundraising" a smoother process. Let public relations tell your story, build your case, and create awareness. Then ask for the gift.

CASE STUDY

The American Red Cross—Editor's Kit

An editor's kit was developed by the American Red Cross to assist editors in providing stories and feature material. Robert D. Walhay of the organization's Office of Public Affairs sent the kit to small daily newspapers, weekly newspapers, and company publications. Note that the cover letter gave a reason for using the material, and offered the assistance of the Red Cross in further developing the stories.

These materials are samples of the kit's enclosures, which consisted of ads, photographs, fillers, and releases with feature material. Various copies and sizes of the ads and releases were included.[6]

Opposite:
Figures 34 and 35. Ads and public service messages from the American Heart Association were also sent out in different sizes to publications. They're striking and provide interesting filler material for the media to use. Courtesy American Heart Association, Central Florida Chapter, Orlando, Fla.

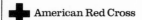 **American Red Cross**   National Headquarters
Washington, D.C. 20006

November 1, 1980

Dear Editor:

Somewhere within the enclosed copy is the admonition of that great
baseball pitcher and philosopher, Satchel Paige: "Don't look back
because somebody may be catching up with you." While this counsel
may be good at times, there comes a milestone in every marriage or
organizational existence when the best thing to do is to look back,
take stock, and attempt to see what the future prospects are. It's
called an anniversary.

The one hundredth anniversary of the American Red Cross is 1981.
This Editor's Kit is devoted to the Red Cross Centennial. Since
the Red Cross has an impact on the lives of Americans in many ways,
there is interest about where it has been, what it is doing, and
where it is going.

We hope that you will enjoy the stories and other enclosures and
be able to use them or that they may perk your interest in developing
a feature on the Red Cross. Be assured that the Red Cross Public
Affairs staff stands ready to help with story angles, researching of
photos and other material, and arrangements for interviews.

The American Red Cross appreciates your support and looks forward
to working with you in the years ahead.

Sincerely,

Robert W Wallan

Office of Public Affairs

Figure 36. The kit's cover letter. Courtesy
American Red Cross, Washington, D.C.

*Figures 37 and 38. Also included in the kit were prescreened pic-
tures and posters, and camera-ready public service ads.* Courtesy
American Red Cross, Washington, D.C.

**Red Cross:
Ready for a new century.**

**Ready for
Mt. St. Helens,
Hurricane Allen,
Love Canal.**

Red Cross: Ready for a new century.

**Ready to teach
home nursing, first aid,
parenting, child care,
water safety, CPR.**

Red Cross: Ready for a new century.

THE RED CROSS: WHAT IS IT DOING NOW?

It has taken 100 years, but the small society that Clara Barton founded in 1881 has become the largest humanitarian organization in the country.

Despite this fact, however, most Americans admit they have a fuzzy image of the American Red Cross. Most are familiar with some parts, but grasping the full impact on society eludes them. And remember, the Red Cross probably affects the lives of more Americans than any other nongovernmental organization.

The source of the problem seems to be the diversity of the Red Cross, its involvement in so many services -- disaster preparedness and relief, blood services, services to members of the armed forces and veterans, work with youth, community health, and international relations. In the public's mind, the parts never make a single picture.

Opinion surveys tested the public's knowledge of the Red Cross. The results were dismaying. For instance, the organization has been teaching lifesaving for decades and most lifeguards are certified by the Red Cross, but the general public was dismally uninformed about this aspect.

However, even if the public's image of the present Red Cross improved, the image would be likely to become rapidly outdated. To meet the challenges of its second century, the Red Cross is moving in new directions. Until recently, it seldom heeded Satchel Paige's admonition, "Don't look back because somebody may be catching up."

FILLERS

A self-expanding bloodmobile has been designed and developed by the American Red Cross and currently is in use in New York State. The vehicle, the first of its kind in the United States, expands its sides by eight feet to make room to accommodate as many as six donors at one time plus space to serve refreshments to those who have already donated.

****

The first foreign disaster relief operation by the American Red Cross occurred during a Russian famine in 1892.

****

Whenever an urgent need arises, the American Red Cross sends blood, its derivatives, or other medical assistance unobtainable to Red Cross societies around the world.

****

More than $2 million in unsolicited contributions were sent to the American Red Cross last year to help support International Red Cross operations for Cambodian relief and refugee support in Thailand.

****

Since the San Francisco earthquake and fires of 1906, American Red Cross disaster relief operations have topped a million dollars on 73 occasions.

****

During the past 10 years, the American Red Cross has responded to an average of 31,000 disasters annually to bring relief to victims.

Figures 39 and 40. Fact sheets, feature items, and short "filler" pieces such as these completed the Editor's Kit materials. Courtesy American Red Cross, Washington, D.C.

PART THREE

SPECIAL
TYPES
OF FUNDRAISING

The last three chapters cover specialized forms of fund-raising—deferred giving (bequests and life income programs), capital campaigns (three- to five-year efforts to raise money for buildings or equipment), and foundation grants (writing proposals to private foundations and corporations).

It is possible to conduct ongoing fundraising efforts and never get involved in these three specialized areas. But the long-term growth plans and large gifts made possible by deferred efforts, the special funds provided for construction by the capital campaign, and the major gifts for specialized projects funded by foundations all make these forms of giving attractive to charitable organizations.

They require specialized knowledge and additional efforts in your overall fundraising plans, but the results of successful campaigns and proposals are well worth it. Even the smallest organization will find appropriate times to implement these programs.

Deferred Giving

Conrad Teitell, the noted tax attorney, tells the story of the book-store in Massachusetts that put the first edition of An Estate Planner's Handbook *on its shelves with works on landscaping of estates and gardening.*[1]

Most fundraisers can appreciate the irony of this situation, as those who find more and more of their time taken up with estate planning and other areas of deferred giving know that this field is still widely misunderstood and a source of confusion for many people.

The deferred giving business as we know it today was born in 1969, when a major tax reform act added the popular unitrust and annuity trust to the various plans by which individuals could make "deferred gifts" to nonprofit organizations. These new plans helped make a misnomer of the term deferred giving, for rather than being gifts that were put off until a later time, they were actually current gifts, with immediate tax benefits for the donor and an irrevocable contribution for the organization. Though the institution might not receive the bulk of the gift until a later date, the donation had already been made and could not be changed.

Bequest programs have long been a part of the fundraising efforts of many institutions. Harvard University, in fact, was made possible because of a bequest from John Harvard. In 1951, Dartmouth College created a formal bequest program, helping guide other colleges and universities into this area. Religious groups have been issuing gift annuities, another form of deferred giving, for many years. And in 1946, Pomona College started advertising the opportunity for people to pool their funds with the college endowment.[2]

Deferred gifts are attractive sources of revenue for many organizations, but a word of warning is called for. Fundraising consultant Leonard Bucklin cautions that just because the cost per dollar raised is the lowest of any form of fundraising, a deferred giving program still requires adequate funds for successful operation.[3] Indeed, while these gifts may provide the bulk of your endowment or operating fund, they are often the costliest in terms of the time invested in identifying and cultivating prospects and in the amount of explanatory literature needed to describe the various types of gift plans.

Those involved in deferred giving stress that advice from the professionals—bankers, trust officers, insurance agents, attorneys, and others—is essential in keeping up with the changing tax laws. Good deferred giving officers need to blend this specialized knowledge with the general skills of the business to make effective presentations, state the complex material as clearly as possible, know when to advise prospects to get further advice, and have the commitment to follow through and see that all details are completed. Even though they have become knowledgeable about their profession, they still need the experts. If your board includes attorneys, accountants, and others in this field, you already have taken a step toward setting up your own program.

In this chapter, we will introduce you to the various forms of deferred giving popular today. We are not trying to make you experts in the field, nor do we intend to qualify you to practice law. We do hope, though, to acquaint you with some generalities of a specialized business, in the hope that you will become interested enough in the field and what it can do for you and your donor to pursue knowledge in more depth.

THE DEFERRED GIVING PROGRAM

Obviously, your first job as a fundraiser is to get money your organization can use *now*. But those donors who can't make a gift now, or who might make larger or additional gifts later, are ideal prospects for deferred giving efforts. William B. Dunseth of

Pomona College has pointed out that the deferred annuity and life income plans offer donors several important benefits, including an opportunity to make a gift during their lifetime when they cannot give up income from the asset; to make larger gifts now than they could otherwise make; to give to your organization and also assure income for life for a spouse or their children; to have their wishes best met by good estate planning and preparation of a will; to create a memorial or honor during their lifetime, and to gratify the basic human need for recognition.[4]

These sophisticated plans have helped many organizations meet capital campaign goals, increase endowment, establish scholarship funds, or take care of expenses that they might not be able to fund otherwise.

The basic procedure for conducting a deferred gifts program is similar in many respects to the operation of an annual campaign. It is essential that you have the support of your board and other interested volunteers. You need to identify key prospects, and cultivate these people carefully, listening to them and their needs. You must provide informative literature that the prospects can share with their own advisers. You have to keep careful records, and accurately record all transactions and developments. But most of all, in a deferred giving program, you must be willing to make an initial investment that may not begin to pay off for three, four, or five years—or maybe even longer.

Edwin E. Steward, a noted deferred giving consultant who is known to many as "a whiz of a wills-and-bequests man," told *Forbes* magazine, "In this business you work your heart out for three years before you begin to see things happen."[5] For many groups it takes even longer for results to show, and your organization has to be willing to set up a deferred giving program, train the staff and budget for the office, and then continue finding prospects and converting the prospects into donors, while waiting for the gifts to be realized.

C. Ray Clements of Brigham Young University has noted that it is difficult to evaluate the work of the deferred giving officer during these first few years. He suggests that instead of putting down dollar goals, you use other quantitative measures such as the number of contacts made with prospective donors, the number of deferred contracts drawn up, and the projected dollar volume of these gifts.[6] Because you are investing "present dollars for future benefits," Clements advises setting up an adequate budget to see that the job is done right.

So how do you begin your deferred giving efforts? Most experts advise that you start by calling on the top prospects first—your oldest constituents (people over sixty are considered the best prospects), widows, unmarried older women, people who have recently retired or sold extensive business holdings, couples without children or with wealthy children, and others who may be especially concerned with preserving their assets for their lifetime but who may also be interested in seeing that your organization is helped after their death.

It is a basic tenet of most other fundraising efforts that you begin your work with the belief that the prospective donor is interested in doing something for your organization. You then tailor a gift program to meet that donor's needs. But in deferred giving efforts, you will find that many good prospects have no prior interest in helping your group. The deferred giving program you set up for them is the reason they wish to contribute. By your help in planning their estate, in arranging a trust that will give them tax deductions and other benefits, and in keeping them informed of current laws and programs to increase their assets, you are creating the reason for the gift. They may never have attended your college, used your services, been a patient in your hospital, or watched your public television station, but because you can set up a plan by which they will benefit financially, you have "earned" the right to receive this gift from them.

Of course, those people most closely identified with your organization are still the best prospects, as they can combine their interest in tax savings with their desire to help your group. But beyond them, there are many people with special tax problems (or potential tax problems), and quite often even basic direct mail efforts can locate and motivate these people to explore gift opportunities. Though your unitrust may pay the same interest as do other unitrusts in your community, you may have won their favor by courting and informing them first. They are getting income and money management, and they are also doing something worthwhile with their money.

Contrary to what many people believe, direct mail *can* work in a deferred giving program. You certainly can't give many technical details this way, but you can stimulate interest and urge the recipient to seek out further information. John Dolibois has effectively used direct mail in his deferred giving efforts at Miami University. In the following letter, he combines a number of basic appeals into one strong push for setting up a trust:

"I'VE TAKEN MIAMI OUT OF MY WILL."

"I've taken Miami *out* of my Will," a *very* good friend of the University said the other day. My mouth dropped—until she told me the whole story. "Well, you know," she said, "if I give property in trust to Miami now but keep the income for life, I get the same income from the property every year and get a deduction from my income tax, too. For Miami, it's the same as a Will, but I'm much better off. And I guess the government likes it, too, because they passed this new law." (The one that lets you spread gifts of more than 30 percent of current income over five years, so one can give a reasonable amount of income-producing property at a time.)

Another friend recently *sold* the Loyalty Fund some General Motors stock at the same price he paid for it a few years ago—51. We resold it at the market and the Loyalty Fund gained over $50 a share, which he deducted as an educational gift. Because he saved the capital gains tax, too, it actually cost him less this year than he normally gives—but Alumni scholarships got a lot *more*.

These are two of the ways Congress has used to make it easier to give to Miami . . . and, while everybody realizes that Miami's friends don't give for tax-savings reasons alone, those who are going to give might just as well get the best deal out of it.

Miami University has several capital gifts projects on the drawing board. The proposed Alumni Center and Dramatic Arts and Music buildings provide an excellent opportunity for naming a wing or a room or other item as a permanent memorial. Let us tell you more about it. Write or call me today.

Sincerely,
John E. Dolibois[7]

Greg Olberding of Glenmary Home Missioners conducts a successful planned giving program through personalized mailings. He explains that direct mail makes it possible to get donors to respond to inquiries and to tell them how their money is being used. It is also possible to feature individuals in the organization who have a story to tell and whose story will get people involved, rationally and emotionally, with your organization.[8]

Trusts

A trust is an arrangement whereby one person owns property but holds and manages it for the use of someone else. There are thousands and thousands of trusts for the benefit of employees, for the benefit of charities, for the benefit of stockholders, and for other business purposes. There are also personal trusts—those created by individuals for individual beneficiaries.[9]

A personal trust may be testamentary (created by will) or it may be a living trust (created by lifetime transfer). The latter is also known as an *intervivos* trust.

A living trust may be revocable or irrevocable. The power to revoke may exist under an infinite variety of limitations, and it may be made subject to an infinite variety of conditions. In fact, the character and the purposes of trusts are as unlimited as the imagination of persons with property and their legal advisors.

Gilbert Stephenson, a leading trust authority, says that personal trusts are created in order to supply one or more missing elements of ability, or those aptitudes essential to the proper care, management, and use of property. He lists their essential elements: physical capacity, mental competence, providence or prudence, maturity, experience, interest in the management of property.

On this level, trusts are provided either to supply management of the trust property for the benefit of the beneficiary, or to conserve the trust property for the beneficiaries and to protect them against their own tendency to mismanage, misuse, or waste the property that is made the corpus of the trust.

Other common purposes in the establishment of trusts are the prospect of saving income and estate taxes, and the desire to take advantage of the ease and privacy of property transfer that is available under the trust arrangement.

A person may create a trust, having in mind himself as the primary beneficiary, for reasons and purposes like these:

1. One may want to obtain investment management and build up an estate by the steady and systematic transfer of savings to a trust year by year.
2. One may merely want to be free from the burden of managing the property. Thus a trustee may be utilized as a management agent by a person owning property whose only interest is in getting the income from the property.
3. A businessperson may create a trust for the purpose of building up assets entirely apart and separate from the business.
4. A person going into a risky venture may decide to cushion personal and family fortunes by transferring enough property to provide a living income before making the speculative plunge.

A person may create a trust for the benefit of family members or others for such reasons as these:

1. To assure the spouse an independent income.
2. To provide children with independent incomes in order to permit them to pursue a career or line of activity that is either not particularly remunerative, or that would entail excessive financial risk.
3. To provide for parents, or brothers and sisters, by gift in trust for a variety of reasons, including these:
   a. One might lack confidence in his or her own prudence and ability to manage money.
   b. There are tax advantages in transferring income-producing property to discharge such a responsibility, rather than transferring annual chunks of income, which would come first to the transferor to whom it would be taxed in higher income tax brackets.
   c. One might want to assure that the income will continue after one's death.
   d. One might want the fund to be supplied by a trustee rather than by personal gift for reasons of morale and psychological effect on the beneficiary.
4. Finally, property may be transferred in trust for the purpose of establishing a working relationship between the trustee and the grantor's ultimate beneficiaries; the person transferring the

property gets the opportunity to train and educate both the trustee and the beneficiaries, to see how property would be managed in his or her absence, and to guide the development of a satisfactory working relationship between the beneficiaries and those who would manage the property after the grantor's death.

In setting up a trust, an individual may do any of the following:

1. Clearly make it revocable (terminable at the will of the grantor).
2. Clearly specify that the trust is irrevocable (the grantor cannot terminate it).
3. Say nothing about revocability, in which case the applicable state law will indicate whether it is to be construed as revocable or irrevocable. There are states in which a trust is presumed to be revocable unless the instrument expressly declares it to be irrevocable. In most states, however, a trust is presumed to be irrevocable unless expressly declared to be revocable.
4. Rely on the termination of an irrevocable trust by the consent of the beneficiaries. Here again the law varies. In some states it is not possible to terminate a trust even though the grantor is the sole beneficiary and both grantor and trustee agree to terminate.
5. Rely on a power to change the terms of the trust without revocation. The power to amend a revocable trust is of little importance because the grantor can achieve the same purpose by revoking one trust and establishing another one. The power to amend an irrevocable trust, however, may have far-reaching consequences. Flexibility to deal with unknown future conditions can be imparted to an irrevocable trust by the reservation of a power to change the ultimate beneficiaries and the terms of income distribution.

One of the problems to be considered is whether to have the trust instrument provide for termination by distribution of the corpus to the beneficiaries when they reach a certain age, or give the beneficiaries the option to decide themselves when they want their trust principal. The trustor has full flexibility in this matter, as long as the rule against perpetuities is not violated. Usually this limits duration of the trust to lives in being at the creation of the trust; these laws vary, however, and the applicable state law should be checked.

There are advantages in giving the beneficiary a choice as to whether to take the principal or continue it in trust. This doesn't mean the beneficiary has the right to take the principal at any time. But if you have decided to provide for the end of the trust when the beneficiary reaches twenty-five, consider instead merely giving him or her the right at age twenty-five to draw the principal and end the trust. Thus a beneficiary who is ill, or who would prefer not to hold property in his or her name for financial or other reasons, won't be burdened with unwanted property because of a provision in a trust made before the difficulty arose.

It is true the beneficiary can accomplish the same result by putting the principal into a new revocable trust at the distribution date. But he or she may be out of the country, or incapable or unwilling to act for some other reason. Normal human inertia can play a part here too. It is much simpler to provide flexibility for beneficiaries in the original trust instrument than to make them create it themselves.

Policies

To help insure that you and your donor follow the proper details of deferred giving, most experts recommend putting your policies into writing—and then sticking by them. Ray Clements argues that written policies are most helpful because of their objectivity, time savings, education value, and continuity. His institution, Brigham Young University, has developed operating policies for accepting deferred gifts. Among these policies are the following:

1. No gift will be accepted from any individuals from whom there is not obvious charitable intent.
2. The development committee must approve all gifts that will or may require expenditure of funds.
3. Expenses connected with gifts should be payable from the gift and not from institutional funds.

4. Proposed charitable remainder trusts should have assets of at least $50,000.
5. All donors need competent legal counsel, and we will always recommend that they obtain such.
6. Complicated involvements should be avoided because the time requirements often involve more expenses than the potential gift.[10]

Other policies cover the valuation of gifts, setting of interest rates, and investment procedures.

Pomona College has a simple policy statement covering its deferred giving program: "It is the policy of the Board of Trustees of Pomona College to offer through the estate planning program an opportunity for donors to make gifts reserving income for life to themselves and other beneficiaries, to make such gifts by will and to make outright gifts by bequest; to aggressively seek out such gifts; and to provide adequate staff and resources for a full and effective program."[11]

An interesting part of the Pomona statement is that the college will provide an adequate staff for the program. The donor will certainly be interested in this before he or she commits large amounts of assets to your organization.

Staff training is essential, because work of this nature is very specialized. A number of firms offer seminars throughout the year on deferred giving, and fundraisers interested in pursuing these gifts are urged to keep themselves informed of tax law changes and other developments in the field.

There is no doubt that the handling of these gifts will change dramatically in the coming years. It has only been since 1969 that the Tax Reform Act made it possible for donors to receive tax incentives while retaining a life income and avoiding such tax liabilities as capital gains taxes. Now fundraisers are turning toward the computer as a tool to facilitate the development of estate plans. Several colleges and universities in the northwest have already formed a consortium to develop and share a computer service that will provide a tool by which development officers can determine the best type of planned gift for the prospective donors.

If you're interested in beginning a program for your organization, heed the message of Norman Fink of the University of Pennsylvania. For success in the deferred or planned giving field, he says that programs must incorporate the following considerations: the institution must gain rather than lose from contributions in the form of charitable remainder life income gifts or annuities; the institution should evaluate periodically its life income gift and annuity program to assure that the advantages to the institution outweigh the disadvantages; the institutional development program should include a range of methods of giving, encouraged by tax incentives, so that its donors have options; the institution and its staff must be alert to changing laws and circumstances, and responsibilities and authority must be defined and delineated.[12]

You also need to work out formal arrangements between the fundraisers, the business office, and the investment office or committee. As the fundraiser, you are expected to make contacts with prospects and cultivate this relationship; prepare written material to explain the planned gifts your organization can offer; compute the tax benefits and other details of the gift for the donor; see that all information is available for the agreements to be prepared, and, in general, maintain contact with the donor (and the beneficiaries) through the life of the trust.

The rest of this chapter will deal briefly with the five major forms of deferred giving—bequests, living trusts, charitable gift annuities, charitable remainder trusts, and pooled income fund trusts. Obviously, there are many other types of deferred gifts, including real estate and other property, life insurance, and various other types of donations, but the six to be discussed are the most common ones handled by deferred giving officers.

If you find this material interesting and of benefit to your organization, you may wish to contact some of the firms and consultants offering training in deferred giving. The Conrad Teitell seminars are probably the best known (Teitell's address is Philanthropy Tax Institute, 12 Arcadia Road, Old Greenwich, Connecticut 06870), though a number of other firms and consultants offer their own training programs. In addition, the Council for the Advancement and Support of Education sponsors many seminars during the year that cover all aspects of deferred giving. You can contact CASE at Suite 400, 11 Dupont Circle, Washington, D.C. 20036.

BEQUESTS

Donors who give to organizations through their wills are often the first step for a charity in obtaining other types of deferred gifts. While these gifts are valuable themselves, they can be even more beneficial because once you know that someone has provided for

JOIN **HEART O' GOLD** TODAY

By naming the **American Heart Association, Central Florida Chapter,** as a beneficiary in your will, you become a member of the Association's **HEART O'GOLD.** Just notify us that HEART is in your will. You'll become a Life Member of the American Heart Association, Central Florida Chapter, with full voting rights and privileges. Your name will be engraved on a permanent plaque located at the Heart Office. You will receive a gold-tone lapel pin at a future meeting of the Board of Directors.

HEART O'GOLD is a program designed to continue the American Heart Association's vital programs of cardiovascular research, education and community services. By participating, many individuals can reduce their estate tax liability via a charitable tax allowance granted on a total estate.

_____ I have Heart in my Will now; please enroll me in the **HEART O'GOLD** program.

_____ I plan to put Heart in my Will; I will notify the Heart office when I do.

_____ I do not have Heart in my Will, but please send me more information about **HEART O'GOLD.**

_____ I do not have Heart in my Will, but I would be interested in attending a Will and Planned Giving Seminar.

Name _____

Street_____ Phone_____

City_____ State_____ Zip_____

AMERICAN HEART ASSOCIATION - CENTRAL FLORIDA CHAPTER
237 East Mark Street • P.O. Box 6665
Orlando, Florida 32853
(305) 843-1330

Figure 41. The Heart O' Gold club allows the American Heart Association to recognize donors who have put the association in their wills. When notified that it is part of a will, the association enrolls the donor in this club, and grants certain benefits including a lapel pin and recognition on a plaque. Courtesy American Heart Association, Central Florida Chapter, Orlando, Fla.

your organization in his or her will, you can present the advantages of life income trusts, which offer both you and the donor immediate benefits.

Don't assume that all of your prospects have already drawn up their wills. It has been estimated that 85 percent of the adults in this country die without having made valid wills. And every single week, nearly $100 million—left by people who died without valid wills—is tied up in probate courts around the United States.[13]

It's strange that so few people actually make wills, since a will allows them to determine how their property will be distributed, who will be guardian of their children, who will manage their estate, and many other decisions that must be made after an individual's death. A will also provides certain estate and income tax savings and reduced administration costs.

If you have potential donors who feel they can't afford to make gifts to your organization during their lifetime, a gift by will still allows them to help you. Many organizations send out information brochures explaining the importance of having an updated will, and mention that the will can provide gifts for the organization if the individual so desires. Again, these brochures can be bought from the various companies specializing in deferred giving material, or your organization can write its own brochures.

You may wish to consider establishing a bequest committee to help plan your programs. Have experts from your board or from the community advise on the printed materials and policies to be established.

Asbury Theological Seminary in Wilmore, Kentucky, uses such brochures to keep their constituents informed of various aspects of deferred giving. Figure 42 illustrates pages from a brochure entitled "A Will . . . simply good stewardship." They provide an interesting "case study" of someone who had a will, and give reasons why potential donors need wills of their own.

LIVING TRUSTS

In addition to providing for an organization through a will or codicil (a supplement to a will), donors may make gifts during their lifetime, giving instructions as to the retention and disposition

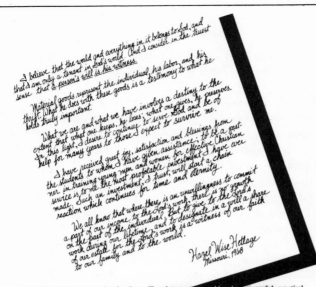

Hazel Wise Hetlage knew that her last will and testament could make a powerful, practical statement about her faith. Her will became not simply a legal document, but a witness of her Christian lifestyle to the people closest to her. She had discovered that all she owned came from the hand of God, and that she could enjoy her possessions most by using them to glorify Him.

Asbury Theological Seminary and the world have benefited from the insight of Hazel Wise Hetlage and others like her. Today, the Seminary's 3,000 graduates minister to the world serving as pastors, missionaries, teachers, counselors, administrators, education directors, and music directors.

Many of the Seminary's buildings, academic chairs, endowed scholarships, and other projects essential to the training of these Christian leaders have resulted from the bequests of wise and thoughtful Christian people.

WHY A WILL?

A will is usually written for one or more of the following reasons:

(1) To distribute your estate as you desire. If you die without a will, the state will dispose of your assets through the laws of intestacy.

(2) To designate a person or corporation as executor to administer all the final details of your estate.

(3) To appoint a guardian for minor children and avoid court proceedings.

(4) To create a trust for the benefit of children or other family members. *This act will carry out your desires, and avoid court proceedings in many cases.*

(5) To designate part of your estate for your church, for Asbury Theological Seminary, or for other favored causes.

(6) To avoid unnecessary payment of estate and inheritance taxes.

Writing a will is simply good stewardship. The Office of Deferred Giving at Asbury Theological Seminary can assist you in gathering information to plan your estate. Through wills, trusts, and annuities, you can save probate costs and minimize taxes. Return the enclosed card if the Seminary can be of further help to you. All information will be held in strictest confidence, and there is no obligation on your part.

Figure 42. This brochure calls attention to the need for a will, and at the same time points out how a bequest could benefit the seminary. Courtesy Asbury Theological Seminary, Wilmore, Ky.

of the property at death. There are a number of advantages to the living trust method of transfer. It

- entails trustee fees during life, if someone other than the grantor or a family member acts as trustee. But the grantor gets investment management during life.
- minimizes administration costs at death.
- avoids the interruption of an ongoing business on death. More important, the owner has the opportunity to provide the trustee with guidance and experience in the conduct of the business.
- permits the estate owner to see his plans in operation, to test and appraise the experience and the management skill of the institution selected to manage the property for the benefit of his or her family after death. The estate owner can judge the

adequacy of the instrument of instructions that is to guide the management of property after death, and to make any necessary revisions.

- avoids and minimizes the interruption of family support, which may occur at death during the time necessary to locate witnesses to a will, qualify the executor, get appraisers appointed, etc.
- avoids publicity with respect to the transfer of property, whereas a testamentary transfer makes all the details as to assets, property disposition, and value a matter of public record.
- avoids ancillary administration, where the estate owner has property in more than one state.
- avoids the filling of periodic accountings, which may divulge business details, facts, and figures to competitors.
- can be the recipient of life insurance proceeds without exposing these proceeds to the claims of creditors, which occurs when life insurance is made payable to the estate.

Certain elements are essential to creating a living trust. The four basic requirements are: a designated beneficiary; a designated trustee who is not the sole beneficiary; funds or other property sufficiently identified so that title can pass to the trustee; and actual delivery of the fund or property or assignment thereof to the trustee, with intent to pass title to him or her as trustee.

The creation of a trust, by lifetime or testamentary transfer, can save taxes and accelerate the accumulation of capital in a variety of ways, including estate tax savings that can be achieved by transfer of income-producing property to a trust in which the income is taxed either to the trust or to the trust beneficiary. In this way income is transferred from the top brackets of the grantor to lower brackets of a trust or beneficiary. A trust arrangement may also use the additional exemptions of the trust and the beneficiary to provide tax-free income, and income tax savings can be achieved by the so-called sprinkling trust, which give the trustee discretion to distribute trust income among beneficiaries in varying proportions from year to year, depending on their needs. Trust income can be kept out of the higher income tax brackets by giving it to the beneficiaries in lower income brackets, who presumably need it more.

CHARITABLE GIFT ANNUITIES

Charitable gift annuities are contracts between a donor and a charitable organization in which the donor gives an irrevocable gift (money or property) to the organization, and the charity in turn promises to pay a fixed dollar amount annually to one or two annuitants for life.

These annuities are part gift and part purchase, with the amount paid determined by the age of the annuitants according to an actuarial rate table. The Committee on Gift Annuities (1865 Broadway, New York, New York 10023), which is composed of many of the charitable organizations that issue gift annuities, studies mortality tables and projected investment earnings, and publishes recommended rates every three years.

These annuities are among the most widely used forms of life income contracts, and are easier to write than are most other plans. They have been in use for many years, and were amended in 1969 when the Tax Reform Act limited an annuity of this type to be written on a maximum of two lives.

The amount of payment is constant for life and does not vary, and a large portion of each payment is tax-free. A major difference between the charitable gift annuity and the charitable remainder annuity trust (page 237) is that the gift annuity is backed by all of the organization's assets, not just the donor's gift. Also, the amount of the gift annuity's annual payment depends on the annuitant's age at the time the annuity is established.

If you are interested in starting this program for your group, contact the Committee on Gift Annuities and ask for their workbook, which includes worksheets, tables, and actuarial rates for determining the amount of payment and tax deduction for each donor.

Rate tables for charitable gift annuities are detailed in Revenue Ruling 72-438 of the Internal Revenue Code. In addition, some states require that charities report on these annuities, so be sure to check the law in your state.

In sum, then, a charitable gift annuity is a contract between a donor and an organization. In exchange for cash or another form of gift, the charity agrees to pay a guaranteed income for life, and only upon the death of the donor or a specific survivor does the full amount of the gift become available for the charity's purpose. Lifetime income for the donor is guaranteed since the charity's entire assets stand behind payment of the annuity benefits. Also, the allowable rates are competitive with those that could be obtained from other investments.

CHARITABLE REMAINDER TRUSTS

Donors with highly appreciated property who are "locked up" by a capital gain liability but would like to diversify their risk, gain more spendable cash, take a charitable deduction on their income tax return, and make a commitment to your organization, might wish to explore the advantages of a charitable remainder trust.

The charitable remainder trust has been an important aid to many people in financial planning. The advantages of such a vehicle include:

- Unlocking "locked in" assets. Highly appreciated stock with a large capital gain liability may be transferred to a trust and sold, and the entire proceeds, with minimum or no depletion by capital gains taxes, may then be reinvested for the use of whomever is designated beneficiary, including the donor.
- An income tax deduction. They are entitled to take a tax deduction on the property contributed to the remainder trust in the year in which the gift is made. Where the contribution is in appreciated property, the allowable charitable deduction may be up to 30 percent of adjusted gross income (or in certain instances, up to 50 percent of adjusted gross income), with the balance of any unused portion of the deduction available to carry forward in the next five taxable years.
- Increased cash flow. Donors can provide themselves with a monetary payment for life—or a stated term of years—possibly in excess of the amount that they currently receive from the property transferred.
- Benefits for the donor's favorite charity. Donors act as benefactors to the charities of their choice and receive recognition during their lifetime.

A charitable remainder trust permits an individual to retain an income interest in property transferred to the trust, with the remainder of the principal eventually to pass to the charity. There are two types of trusts from which to choose. The unitrust provides for a fixed percentage of the net fair market value of the transferred property, valued annually, to be paid to the income beneficiary, with 5 percent the required minimum. This means that the return paid by a unitrust will vary depending on the underlying value of the trust property. As the value of the trust assets grow, so will the dollar amount of income payable; the converse would also be true. For example, a trust with assets worth $200,000 providing for a 5 percent payout rate would return $10,000 for the first annual payment. If the trust depreciated to $180,000 in the second year, the payout would drop to $9,000; but, if the trust appreciated in value to $240,000, the payout would increase to $12,000.

The second type of trust, the annuity trust, provides for a fixed sum to be paid, at least annually, to the income beneficiary in an amount not less than 5 percent of the fair market value of the property when transferred. For example, if property worth $200,-000 is transferred, the fixed annual payment must be at least $10,000. The amount of this payment does not vary.

In order to establish a valid charitable remainder trust, the following requirements have to be met:

1. The trust is irrevocable once established.
2. Payments must be made for a specified number of years or the lifespan of the beneficiary.
3. Principal cannot be invaded except to meet the fixed percentage or fixed sum payout.
4. Payment of the entire remainder interest to, or for the use of, the charity must be made at the end of the term of noncharitable distributions.
5. For income tax purposes, payments of trust income to the beneficiary are treated as coming, first, from ordinary income to the extent of the sum of the trust's ordinary income for the taxable year of the trust and its undistributed capital gains including both prior and current capital gains, with short-term gains paid before long-term gains; then, from other income; and, finally, from return of principal.

6. A unitrust may provide that only trust income be distributed. If income from the trust is less than the percentage amount specified, such deficiency could be made up in any later year.

7. The trust is tax-exempt provided it does not realize any unrelated business income.

Charitable Remainder Unitrusts

Sections 664(d)(2) and (3) of the Internal Revenue Code provide for three variations of the charitable remainder unitrust:

1. The standard unitrust, in which the donor receives annual payments based on a fixed percentage of the trust assets, as determined each year. The percentage determined when the trust is established remains constant for the term of the trust. Upon the death of the last surviving beneficiary (or after the twenty-year maximum time period for payments), the trust is terminated and the assets are transferred to the charity for its use. The payout must be at least 5 percent of the trust value, though higher percentages may be used if desired.

2. A net income unitrust with makeup. If actual income is less than the stated percentage, the trustee pays only the income, and deficiencies in distribution are made up in later years if the trust income exceeds the minimum payment.

3. A net income unitrust without makeup, in which deficiencies in later years are not made up.

While all three plans have the same tax benefits, the first plan is probably most desirable for the donor, while the charity would probably prefer the third plan.

As a general example of a unitrust, assume that Mr. Donor, age 65, owns shares in XYZ Growth Company. It has proved an excellent investment. His cost basis for the shares is $20,000; their market value is now $200,000.

However, Mr. Donor, who is about to retire, would like to sell his stock to obtain a higher cash flow. At the same time, he has a favorite charity he would like to benefit and would not mind having recognition for this financial aid during his lifetime.

He is reluctant to sell the stock because of the high capital gain tax to which he would be liable: the tax bite on the sale for federal tax purposes alone could be as much as $58,000, leaving only $142,000 available for reinvestment after tax.

Impact of Tax Without Trust

Cost (tax-free return of capital)	$ 20,000
Capital gain	180,000
Total capital	$200,000
Tax (assumes maximum capital gain tax of 25% × $50,000, plus 35% × $130,000) (Excludes minimum tax at 15% of tax preference income.)	58,000
Leaving a net to invest of	$142,000

Mr. Donor decides to give the stock to a charity through a charitable remainder unitrust: The trust instrument provides that he reserve to himself income from the trust for his lifetime with the charity receiving the property at his death. The amount the trust is to pay him is to be equal to 6 percent of the trust's assets valued at the end of each year for the rest of his life.

IRS tables show that the percent value of a remainder interest in property under a unitrust for a male age 65 is .50015. Thus Mr. Donor could be entitled to a charitable deduction for income tax purposes of $100,030 ($200,000 × .50015 = $100,030), subject to the 30 percent limitation.

• Cash flow from trust property: The trust in turn sells the stock of XYZ Growth Company, realizing the $180,000 in profits. Since the trust is tax-exempt (provided it does not have any unrelated business income), the trustee is able to liquidate the securities without incurring a capital gain tax.

The trustee then reinvests the entire proceeds.

• Taxing the beneficiary: Assuming a 6 percent unitrust, with trust property worth $200,000, Mr. Donor would receive $12,000 in payments. If in its first full year the unitrust received $2,000 in dividends and $4,000 in capital gain distributions, payments to Mr. Donor would be taxed as follows:

Current year's income dividends	$ 2,000
Prior undistributed capital gains (from the $180,000 gain realized when stock was sold and the current $4,000 gain)	10,000
Total payments	$12,000

If in the next year the trust value dropped to $180,000 and $1,000 was received by the trust from dividends and $2,000 from current capital gains, the payments to Mr. Donor would be taxed as follows:

Current year's dividends	$ 1,000
Prior year's undistributed capital gains (now $176,000)	9,800
Total payments (6% × $180,000)	$10,800

If, on the other hand, in that next year the trust value increased to $220,000 and $1,000 was received by the trust in dividends and $2,000 from current capital gains, payments to Mr. Donor would be taxed as follows:

Current year's dividends	$ 1,000
Prior year's undistributed capital gains ($176,000)	12,000
Total payments (6% × $220,000)	$13,200

If the unitrust had not received any dividends, then all Mr. Donor's payment would have been charged against prior undistributed capital gains. When amounts from prior undistributed capital gains paid out are equal to the total amount of the gain, Mr. Donor would then begin to receive back an amount attributable to his original cost basis ($20,000).

Charitable Remainder Annuity Trusts

These trusts are similar to unitrusts, but the donor receives a fixed dollar amount each year. There is no annual evaluation of the trust's market value and no variation in the amount of payment.

Income not paid out is added to the principal, and all payments must be at least 5 percent of the initial fair market value of the property placed in trust. Section 664 of the Internal Revenue Code covers these trusts.

Suppose that Mr. Donor (from the unitrust example) had elected to set up an annuity trust rather than a unitrust. Instead of receiving a fixed percentage of principal each year, he would then have received a fixed dollar amount with a tax deduction as follows:

Value of trust	$200,000
Payout rate	6 percent
Annual payment	$ 12,000
Charitable deduction	$103,577

This deduction is equal to the worth of the property, $200,000, less the value of the right to receive $12,000 every year for the rest of the donor's life. The value of receiving $12,000 each year for life is obtained by multiplying $12,000 by the annuity factor for a male age 65—8.0353—as found in IRS estate and gift tax tables for a result of $96,423 ($200,000 − $96,423 = $103,577).

As noted, the amount deductible is subject to the 30 percent limitation. However, Mr. Donor may carry forward the balance of any unused portion of his deduction for the next succeeding five years.

POOLED INCOME FUNDS

Section 1.642(c)(5) of the Internal Revenue Code defines a pooled income fund as a trust maintained by a charitable organization that receives irrevocable gifts of money or securities and commingles such gifts with the gifts of other donors who have made similar transfers for the purpose of investment, administration, and income distribution.

Donors retain a life income interest in their gift to the pool for themselves and beneficiaries. The pool does not make distributions from the body of the fund, but distributes pro rata shares from the overall investment income. When the last surviving beneficiary of an income interest dies, the assets representing the interest are turned over to the charity.

Each year the donor or beneficiaries receive their share of the earnings, and the income is fully taxable.

The donor receives several important advantages besides the tax savings and the satisfaction of helping the charity. Investments are made by the experienced counselors at the charity, property after death is better controlled, and the property is removed from the probate estate.

Internal Revenue Code Sections 170(b)(1)(A)(i) through 170(b)(1)(A)(v) explain what organizations are qualified to be pooled income fund charitable remaindermen. Included are churches, educational organizations, hospitals, organizations holding and administering property for colleges and universities, and governmental units.

One word of caution: tax-exempt securities cannot be transferred to pooled income funds.

Based upon the gifts involved, each donor receives a specific number of units in the fund. A charitable deduction is allowed in the year of the gift, and the institution benefits from knowing how much money it will eventually receive and by having donors more closely tied to their organization.

As we mentioned earlier in this chapter, there are other forms of deferred giving as well as these five popular types. Depending on your particular situation and your donors, you may wish to inquire further into the other types of donations.

J. Robert Sandberg, vice-president of planned gifts for the University of Nebraska Foundation, says that there is a form of wealth more common than securities in his part of the country. Nebraska has thus prepared a booklet entitled *Gifts from the Land*, which describes the various ways appreciated agricultural land and other real property could be given to the university. The booklet points out that outright gifts of parcels of appreciated land are frequently the most advantageous method of giving for donors with substantial assets other than the gift property. The donor receives an income tax charitable deduction for the full market value, no capital gains taxation, and a reduction of the donor's taxable estate. The booklet describes how such gifts can be made outright, through a life income trust, through place of residence given with the retained right to use the property, through a "bargain sale" of the property, by will, and by will establishing a life income trust for a beneficiary.[14]

Another area growing in popularity is life insurance, as more people are learning of the benefits of these gifts. For the organization, such gifts are usually larger than would be possible through outright grants. If ownership of the policy is given to the charity, no estate taxes are due after the donor's death. As the donor pays the annual premiums on the policy, now owned by the charity, he or she receives a tax deduction, as well as a deduction when the gift is given (usually for the policy's full replacement value).

Gifts of policies already in existence provide excellent benefits for donors who no longer need the protection offered by the policy. If a donor gives you a $100,000 policy that he has had for many years, he is entitled to a deduction for the present value of that policy, deductions when he pays the annual premiums in the future, and when he dies, the full amount of the policy ($100,000) comes to the charity and is not taxed as part of his estate.

If your organization is interested in building extensive support for the future, you should be thinking of starting a deferred gifts program. You will need to spend money now to establish the office and train the personnel, but the rewards will come to the organization in the future.

Your donors will benefit from increased income, money management, and the opportunity to help your organization. In turn, you can better plan for the future and raise substantial gifts from many people who are not capable of giving large amounts of money during their lifetime. It's an investment you can't afford to pass up.

The Capital
Campaign

A capital campaign is designed to raise a large amount of funds over an extended time for a building, equipment, special project, or other major event. Readers who have gone through the chapter on the annual fund already have the basics for planning a capital campaign. The two programs differ in the purpose of the money (usually a capital campaign raises funds for a specific purpose, while an annual campaign stresses unrestricted giving and gifts for ongoing support); the length of the campaign (capital campaigns typically run three to five years, while an annual campaign begins anew each year); amount of money sought (capital campaigns usually have multimillion-dollar goals because of the huge expenses associated with construction of new facilities, while annual funds have widely varying goals usually tied to the organization's expenses and general needs); and the preparation for the campaign (capital efforts need in-depth study and various levels of feasibility studies to determine if the time is right for such an effort, while annual funds often begin with nothing more than an existing program and bills that need to be paid).

But capital campaigns differ the most from other types of fundraising in that you shouldn't even *begin* such a major effort until your development organization and program are quite well established. The entire board must be behind you; you must have the best possible volunteer leadership ready to go to work; you must feel confident that you have enough big gifts lined up to insure a success; and you must have the skills and time to conduct the campaign. Many other fundraisers add another essential ingredient: you should have prior commitments for at least one-third of the goal *before* you ever make the public announcement of the campaign. If you haven't already raised a substantial portion of the goal, and if you haven't identified the dozen top givers and two or three dozen other large prospects, then you aren't ready to conduct a capital campaign.

When these requirements have been met, and when the time comes to expand your present facility, upgrade your current equipment, invest in new property or build a brand new structure, you should begin thinking seriously about a capital campaign.

You don't want to hold them often—perhaps only once every ten years. You don't want everything else in your office to come to a stop. You want to do some long-range planning for your group's next five to ten years, even if you haven't done long-range planning previously. You want to make this a big effort with a huge goal, even if you have never had a big goal before. And you will want to consider using professional consultants, even if you do all other aspects of fundraising yourself.

There is something else you need to consider before the campaign begins. If you're seeking funds to put up a new building, can your current budget assume the expense of operating the facility? More than one small organization has faced major budget problems when it designed a capital campaign to raise construction money, and then found it lacked the funds to pay the utility bill, cleaning expenses, furnishing costs, and other needs. If you plan this beforehand, you can include your estimated budget in the campaign goal. If you forget to include these costs, the gift may cost you more than it gives you.

You may also wish to include the costs of running the campaign in your budget. A good rule of thumb is that you'll need about 5 percent of the campaign goal for the expenses of conducting your capital effort.

A successful capital campaign can provide you with that unique facility or special building or needed office space that your organization just cannot afford otherwise. Many groups apply creativity to their need for a special building and find that raising the money can be enjoyable as well as profitable.

TWO SUCCESSFUL APPROACHES

Michigan State's Enrichment Program

When Michigan State University sought construction funds for a performing arts center as part of its $17 million enrichment program in the late 1970s, they treated the campaign as a play in production. James McIntyre, the university's assistant director of annual giving, reports that the following solicitation letter was sent to performing arts patrons in the mid-Michigan area:

Dear Cast Member:

The stage is set. The production manager, lighting manager, music arranger, script writer, lyricist, costume designer, prop mistress, and choreographer all have been working overtime revising this great new production at Michigan State University for the State Center for the Performing Arts. All that is needed is for the cast of thousands to act for this great performance to be a success.

You've read the script and know the plot. The setting is the Great Hall and the Main Theatre of the new center. An opening is now being held for you to become a member of the cast of this great theatre production today.

Here's what you have to do:

1. Again review the synopsis of the production and make your decision.
2. Take a pledge card from the outside right pocket, fill in your pledge, enclose and seal in an envelope, and insert it on the inside right pocket.
3. Check off your name from the cast list and call the next member of the cast and make arrangements to drop off the synopsis.
4. Call your production associate and tell him/her who now has the synopsis.

Do not delay in your decision. Ten members of the cast should see this synopsis in ten days.

A producer knows that the cast is at the heart of any great performance. The spot light is on you as the curtain rises. Act as though it were impossible to fail. Do not delay.

Producer

This letter was sent to those considered most likely to use the new facility. Prospects were chosen according to past association with the arts, and distribution of materials was according to zip code—one director for each zip code area, a number of production associates for each area, and the supporting cast (the prospects).

Those with potential to contribute $2,000 or more were solicited through personal contact.

Materials further explained that the donor could "achieve stardom in the *Great One-Act Play* for recognizing the importance of the *$17 Million Enrichment Program* and the *State Center for the Performing Arts* to the Mid-Michigan community. Through your personal pledge for a seat in the center you will be named a *Star* or *Co-Star* of this premiere performance. Stars will be recognized for their personal commitments of a seat in the *Great Hall* through a five-year pledge of $200 annually. *Co-Stars* have expressed their personal commitments through pledges for seats in the *Main Theatre* by pledging $150 annually for five years."

The solicitation package consisted of brochures, question-and-answer sheets, a business reply envelope, pledge cards for each supporting cast member, and a check-off list with names, addresses, and telephone numbers of supporting cast arranged in a folder called the Synopsis.

The production associates were responsible for circulating the Synopsis among the cast and returning it to the director.

The Synopsis included an attractive four-page brochure, with information detailing the cost of naming seats, a description of the proposed facility, and a discussion of the tax advantages of making a gift (Figure 43). It was noted that most alumni and friends cannot make the large gifts required for having a building named after them. But "MSU has not forgotten its roots—the tens of thousands of alumni, parents, and friends who earlier have been touched in a special way by the University and are now rendering their service to society." Thus, for a relatively modest commitment, these people are offered the chance to have seats named for them or their loved ones in the State Center for the Performing Arts. Seats in the Great Hall "cost" $1,000 each; seats in the Main Theatre could be named for $750 per seat, with all gifts payable over a five-year period. The seats were designed to contain a permanent recessed metal plate with the donor's choice of inscription.

Furthermore, donors had the first option to occupy their seats at theater events. Series tickets could be bought for their own seats, or they were invited to choose seats elsewhere if they perferred. Campaign planners even included a provision for placing name plates on guide railings defining wheelchair spaces in the theater's handicapped seating area. They noted that these spaces "are especially attractive gift opportunities for civic, social, and veterans' clubs and organizations to consider."

The campaign went right according to schedule, and the goal was reached by mid-1981. The theatre opened in June 1982, with the grand opening set for fall of 1982.[1]

Certainly much of the success of this campaign was due to the well-planned effort and effective use of volunteers. The campaign's structure enabled even inexperienced volunteers to make their solicitations without asking for money. The format of taking part in the play invited the donors on its own.

Furthermore, they had put together a solid strategy of co-ordinating the various campaigns within the total capital program. The trend in such campaigns is the growth of a major effort that brings together deferred giving, foundation support, and other forms of gifts within the structure of a capital or all-inclusive fund drive. Colgate University, for example, used "flexible pledging" in its highly successful $30 million Essential Resources for Achievement Campaign in the late 1970s. They invited prospects to participate through a variety of extended and deferred-payment pledges. Spreading payments over a longer period of time allowed many prospects to make larger gifts than would have been possible otherwise. If you do the necessary research to define your target audience and match the best possible volunteers with each prospect, you will find that you can adjust the many variables to best suit the needs of your campaign.

Niagara University's Chapel Restoration

Niagara University saw the need for a capital campaign when its century-old Alumni Chapel had to be restored. A concerned alumnus pledged a substantial gift to restore the facility if the college would conduct a fund drive between fall 1976 and June 30, 1978. Niagara's development director, Nicholas Pettinico, Jr., explains that they received this challenge with less than a month to go

$17 Million
Enrichment Program
Michigan State University

An Invitation

You are cordially invited to participate in a rare gift opportunity—the naming of individual seats in the State Center for the Performing Arts. A plate with your choice of inscription will be affixed to a seat as a permanent tribute to the donor or as a memorial to a loved one.

Your Legacy at MSU

Gift opportunities for naming items at any University are usually beyond the reach of the majority of its alumni and friends—much to the disappointment of these loyal supporters.

While large donations are being sought from individuals, foundations and corporations throughout Michigan and the nation, MSU has not forgotten its roots—the tens of thousands of alumni, parents, and friends who earlier have been touched in a special way by the University and are now rendering their service to society.

MSU is calling upon its alumni and friends to assist in attaining this $17 million goal and to enjoy the satisfaction of establishing a permanent legacy on campus. For a relatively modest commitment, payable over one to five years, you are offered the opportunity to having one or more seats named for you or your

loved ones in the State Center for the Performing Arts.

The Cost of Naming Seats

The Great Hall (seating 2500): a minimum contribution of $1,000 per seat
The Main Theatre (seating 600): a minimum contribution of $750 per seat

The seats are designed to contain a permanent recessed metal plate with the donor's choice of inscription. This is indeed a most fitting legacy for all alumni and friends of MSU to consider during this historic campaign.

A Note about the Center

The construction of a new performing arts center at MSU will have a special impact not only on academic programs, campus and community life, and the continuing ability to attract and retain first-rank faculty, but also on the University's very reputation. The Center will stand as a major achievement of the Michigan State campus. It will enable MSU to do full justice to its extensive academic obligations in music, drama, and dance. And because there is no comparable facility in the area, the Center will also meet a pressing cultural need of the mid-Michigan public.

Figure 43. This attractive brochure was printed in brown ink on ivory paper. It covers many details of Michigan State's Enrichment Program. Courtesy Michigan State University, East Lansing, Mich.

The Great Hall

This will be the largest theatre in the Center, seating 2,500 persons and providing excellent sight lines from all locations. The Great Hall features "acoustical columns" designed to enhance the sound quality of symphonic, operatic, and dramatic productions. A magnificent and inviting lobby will provide a welcome showcase for arriving audiences.

The 600-seat Main Theatre

This will be used primarily for drama productions, and also serve for recitals and chamber music performances. Designed to foster performer-audience intimacy, the Main Theatre features a thrust stage which fans out into the seating area.

All 3100 seats are available as gift opportunities.

Seat Availability

The Faculty and Staff of MSU in its record shattering $1 million campus Pathfinder campaign have individually selected more than 10 percent of the seats in the Great Hall and 20 percent of the seats in the Main Theatre.

This invitation to participate is now extended for your consideration. Simply sign the pledge/reservation form and send it in today. MSU will hold your seat(s).

Donors of Named Seats

Donors will have first option to occupy their designated seats. They may secure this privilege by notifying the Lecture-Concert Office of their preference when they purchase subscription series tickets. If the option is not exercised by a deadline date, the named seats will be of-fered to regular season subscribers who may then renew them each season. When possible, donors of named seats will be notified of non-subscription performances or events for which they may wish to purchase tickets in advance of public sale. However, donors are not restricted to their named seats; they may, if fact, prefer seats elsewhere. Couples or families should consider naming a pair of seats as a permanent gift opportunity in the Great Hall of the Main Theatre.

Facts about the MSU Enrichment Program

Michigan State University has embarked on one of the most important projects in its 123-year history: a $17 million program for academic and cultural enrichment. The program will enable MSU to accomplish four important objectives:

- Build and equip a major new performing arts center $12,500,000
- Complete the first construction phase of a new natural/cultural history museum building   2,750,000
- Strengthen the MSU Library's holdings in key areas, and establish a "Library of Tomorrow" on campus   1,500,000
- Endow several faculty chairs in various pivotal academic disciplines   1,750,00
          TOTAL GOAL $18,500,000

Attractive Gift Opportunities are available for each of these four components and are outlined in the Enrichment Program brochure, which is available upon request.

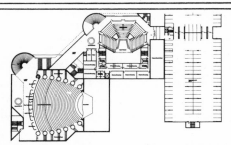

First Nighters

The opening of the State Center for the Performing Arts is planned for the fall of 1981. As a donor of a named seat or of other gift opportunities within the Center, you will be invited to attend one of the premiere performances in the theatre where you may actually occupy the seat which exhibits your inscription plate. Inscription plates will be affixed to your seat(s) upon the completion of your pledge.

Inscription Plate Charges

As the Center nears its final completion stage, and prior to placing the order for your inscribed plates, the Office of Development will reconfirm the original wording you specified when your pledge commitment was made. Perhaps a name change or additional name would alter your previous designation.

Handicapper Seating Accommodations

Both theatres are designed to accommodate theatre goers in wheelchairs. Level floor areas are provided for easy access and egress. Attractive, protective guide railings will define each handicapper space. The surface of the railing will be upholstered and the inscribed plate imbedded in the plush-lined railing.

The Great Hall (35 handicapper spaces avail-able): a minimum contribution of $1,000 per space.

Main Theatre (12 handicapper spaces available): a minimum contribution of $750 per space.

Handicapper spaces are especially attractive gift opportunities for civic, social, and vetran's clubs and organizations to consider.

Tax Information

Contributions to the $17 Million Enrichment Program are tax deductible. Individuals residing in Michigan receive favorable tax treatment, not only through the Federal Income Tax, but also in the form of a Michigan Tax Credit. Tax savings realized from a gift to MSU can enable a donor to give a larger contribution than initially thought possible.

Please make checks payable to Michigan State University of MSU Foundation.

Contributions or pledge payments 'should be addressed and sent to:

Michigan State University
Office of Development
220 Nisbet Building
East Lansing, Michigan 48824
Phone: (517) 355-4566

Figure 44. The front and back of the campaign pledge card. Note how easy it is to designate gifts and set up a pledge schedule. Courtesy Michigan State University, East Lansing, Mich.

before kicking off the regular annual fund program. "We decided to run both the Annual Fund and Chapel Fund programs concurrently," he says, "so we 'improvised' an alumni mail campaign to raise the needed funds."

The campaigns were officially announced at the alumni reunion in early October and were promoted by four direct mail appeals requesting both Annual and Chapel gifts.

The first letter, from the university's president, explained the two campaigns. It included the following:

Dear Niagaran:

As a graduate of Niagara University, you are an essential partner in our future as well as an indelible member of our past. This year we are engaged in two programs: one to assure a stable future for Niagara, and the other to preserve a most treasured tradition from the past.

The first is the Annual Fund, which provides operating funds indispensable to the financial stability of the University. Without the Annual Fund, the activities and operations of Niagara would be seriously hindered.

In addition, the University's major priority is the restoration of Alumni Chapel. The Chapel is the heart of our campus and a program of basic repair and improvements is planned to provide a setting where students can lead active sacramental and liturgical lives. The enclosed brochure describes the restoration process.

I welcome your participation in the Annual Fund and the restoration of Alumni Chapel. Each are vital to Niagara University.

No payment is necessary at this time. Annual Fund pledges are payable by June 30, 1977, while Chapel subscriptions are payable by June 30, 1978. A pledge card and postage-paid return envelope are enclosed for your convenience.

The second letter, sent from the Alumni Fund general chairman, talked about the great challenge of supporting both programs. One month later, the chairman and the alumni association president signed a variation of the "Who Cares?" letter, a popular fundraising technique. It began as follows:

Dear Niagaran:

You might think that with over 12,000 Niagara University alumni we wouldn't care if you aren't among the supporters of this year's Annual Fund and Alumni Chapel restoration drive.

But we do!

The fact is that with University expenditures for 1976–77 anticipated at over $12.5 million, there will be an alarming gap between income and expenses without your participation in the Annual Fund to help bring these more closely into balance.

We also urge you to give special consideration to the restoration of Alumni Chapel. At a cost of $425,000 this project is the University's major priority. Your help is needed to renew this grand old building as the spiritual center of the campus.

Finally, the university's vice-president for development sent a letter emphasizing the need for repair of the chapel, adding, "At the same time, I urge you to participate in the University's Annual Fund. Gifts to the Annual Fund make up the difference between tuition and ever-rising operating expenses."

An important part of the chapel restoration fund was a 12-page brochure that included a letter from the university president, a history of the chapel, the major stages of the restoration and their cost (e.g., Exterior and Interior Entry, $25,000; Electrical, Heating and Lighting, $35,000), questions and answers about the campaign, and a section concerning an honor roll plaque entitled "Names that will live . . . ."

> Commemorative gifts are important to any institution and at Niagara University they have special significance. At Niagara the roots are deep and strong in heritage and tradition.
>
> Commemoration is not for the wealthy alone. Contributions of $1,000 or more, made by June 30, 1978, will be acknowledged on a special Honor Roll Plaque.

"The response among alumni exceeded even our most optimstic expectations," Pettinico said. "Though we set June 30, 1978, as the official end of the chapel campaign, we never really stopped trying to raise funds for the project. Unexpected expenses and the effect of inflation on construction costs proved our goal of $425,000 to be lower than what was actually needed. As of May 30, 1979, we had received pledges totaling more than $560,000."

An interesting aspect of the program is the fact that not only did the chapel drive exceed its goal, but the Annual Fund reached its second highest total ever.[2]

EFFECT ON THE ANNUAL FUND

The Niagara campaign expertly handled the difficulty of running a capital campaign while other efforts were under way. Nelson Cover, Jr., of Johns Hopkins University, explains that his university was able to conduct both campaigns because they timed their efforts to the productivity levels. "By completing efforts for the annual fund in February, the capital campaign could operate productively in our 'down' times in the spring and summer," he says. The development office was thus able to operate The Hopkins Hundred—their centennial campaign for $100 million—while still conducting a successful annual drive. The annual fund leaders deleted capital prospects from their mailing lists, and completed follow-up mailings early in the year before the spring capital campaign mailings. They also did not call areas where the capital campaign was actively in progress when the phonothons were held.

Cover explains that the capital campaign actually challenged the annual giving program to improve itself, rather than compete with it. "The biggest change," he says, "came in our phonothon program, which we had formerly used as a follow-up. To expand our effort, we had to look up all telephone numbers, redesign forms, and store all information so that it would be available to us by computer printout. We also totally revamped addressing, record keeping, and mailing procedures, gaining better control and knowledge of what we were doing and why."[3]

Some institutions avoid the problem by running one major fundraising campaign, and use some of the money raised for the annual fund. This is a simpler approach that avoids the necessity of clearly separating the campaigns and continually explaining their different purposes, but it does weaken the cases for support by watering down the appeal.

The best approach seems to be separating the annual fund from the capital effort either by dividing your prospect list in half and sending one appeal to each group each time, or keeping a unified list and "double asking." Donors are asked to give more frquently during the year, but the purposes are clear and the major reasons for giving are spelled out.

It has been our experience that the worry of running two "competing" campaigns is unfounded. Most institutions that continue their annual giving program while implementing a capital campaign find that there is room for both within their fundraising structure. Hope College, for example, raised more than $10 million from 1972 through 1976, for "bricks and mortar projects," while their annual fund increased from $597,000 to $795,000.[4]

CONDUCTING THE CAMPAIGN

Russell Kohr of Kalamazoo College explains that the strategy for today's capital campaigns consists of five major elements: a blueprint covering the immediate and long-term plans of the organization; identified and evaluated prospective benefactors; a volunteer organization; a staff to serve the volunteers; and a plan of action including a timetable and a budget.[5]

He notes that such a campaign must begin by addressing the fundamental purpose of the group and its objectives, then convert those objectives into "gift packages." Equipment can be itemized, buildings expressed in total cost, and facilities identified as commemorative opportunities. Kohr adds that the logical prospects for these gifts are the people and corporations that will benefit or profit from the facility.

For a capital campaign, David B. Hanaman of the Alta Bates Foundation suggests that you aim for the following gift distribution: 8 to 10 gifts should provide 35 to 45 percent of your total; 80 to 100 gifts should provide another 35 to 45 percent; the rest of the gifts will provide the remaining needed funds.

In particular, experts suggest that your top gift equal at least 10 percent of the goal, and the next two gifts should equal 5 percent of the goal.[6]

John Carlson of Marts & Lundy believes that good volunteers are people who can provide leadership and who offer giving potential. This is especially important, since he feels as many others do that you will need to raise 90 percent of your money from 10 to 15 percent of your donors—and even more important, successful campaigns should have 1 percent of the donors who will give 50 percent of the money.[7]

In the words of Goettler Associates, "A campaign's success depends upon the right people, asking the right prospects, in the right way, for the right amount of money, for the right reason, at the right time."[8] They are strong believers in planning for a campaign, noting that an institution must first audit its current situation, analyze its long-term needs, develop a long-range financial plan, research and evaluate prospects, choose the best volunteers, market the campaign, build the case, and consider a formal feasibility study before launching the campaign.

Just as the case statement is essential to the annual fund, it is also a vital part of the capital campaign. When the Kimball Union Academy began its three-year fund campaign in 1977 to raise $2.25 million, it prepared a case booklet covering the entire effort. Naming the campaign "Kimball Union Looks Ahead," it set up the campaign to raise $1.2 million to increase endowment, $990,000 for construction, and $60,000 to improve academic programs. The case booklet included a statement of the Academy's preparations for the future, signed by the headmaster and the chairman of the trustees; a history of the school in words and pictures; a statement of the institution today; details of how the money would be used; a message from the campaign chairman; and a list of the trustees and national volunteer organization. Figures 45 and 46 show pages from the booklet, and will give you some idea of the way they set up their campaign. C. Parker Jones, who was director of public information at the time, prepared the booklet.

In March 1981, the Academy issued campaign progress report number seven, officially reporting that they had passed their goal and had raised more than $2,407,000 in less than 35 months. It took 47 dinners, luncheons, and receptions, 600 individual visits with prospects by staff and volunteers, and more than 200,000 miles of travel, but they raised the needed funds. David G. Pond, the Academy's director of development, offers the following break-down of gifts from the campaign's final report:

Kimball Union Looks Ahead
What was needed, and given, by size of gifts

Size of Gift	No. Needed	No. Given	Total Amount
$250,000 and larger	2	2	$508,958.00
$100,000–$249,999	5	4	$587,000.00
$50,000–$99,999	8	4	$261,898.00
$25,000–$49,999	10	7	$184,535.00
$10,000–$24,999	20	24	$278,461.00
$5,000–$9,999	30	38	$203,714.00
$1,000–$4,999	100	107	$327,283.00
under $1,000	hundreds	528	$ 55,932.20
Total		714	$2,407,781.20

Kimball Union's careful preparation and planning before the campaign began was evident in its success.

Looking Ahead

The Task

For the first time in its long history, Kimball Union Academy has embarked on a capital fund-raising effort — Kimball Union Looks Ahead. This campaign seeks to raise $2,250,000. It will focus on alumni, parents, and friends of the Academy; it also welcomes the support of the public at large. This openness is based on a conviction that there are many who may not know the Academy well, but would like to do their part to ensure the survival of high-quality independent school education. Kimball Union Academy has been preeminent among private schools in maintaining a tradition of excellence in the education of young people; it is to enable the School to continue this tradition that Kimball Union Looks Ahead is being launched.

Goals

The goals of the campaign are modest by present standards. They do, however, reflect present needs. Of the $2.25 million which must be raised, 1.2 million dollars will be used to increase endowment, $990,000 will be used for construction, and $60,000 will be used to improve academic programs.

Need for An Increased Endowment

A $1.2 million increase in endowment will enable the School to maintain its present financial aid program, to set up faculty chairs, and to implement a sabbatical leave program for teachers.

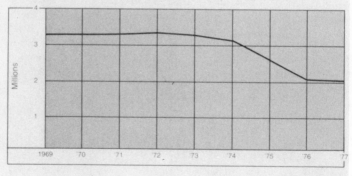

Kimball Union's Endowment, 1969-1976

Figures 45 and 46. Sample pages from the Kimball Union case

St. Joseph Hospital (Stamford, Connecticut) put together a clever case statement for its $125 million capital campaign by printing a prospectus similar to one used to sell stock. Its format clearly followed the notice of a stock offering, which would be familiar to the corporate prospects the campaign sought. The simple printed piece conveyed a very businesslike image for the campaign and enabled it to raise three-year pledges from corporations and industry in the area.

Kimball Union Looks Ahead
Goals

Amount: $2,250,000.00
Campaign period: Gifts and pledges of 3 years; to be completed by December 31, 1980

Endowment

Financial Aid (ten Funds of $50,000 each)	$ 500,000
Faculty Chairs (two of $250,000 each)	500,000
Faculty Advancement	200,000
	$1,200,000

Construction

New Library Building	$ 300,000
Faculty Housing (two new family-style dorms and enlargement of two existing dorms)	250,000
Energy Conservation	115,000
Garage & Maintenance Shop	50,000
Heating Plant Modernization	75,000
Carpeting — DR Halls and Lounge Areas	50,000
Reconstructing of H.M.S. Gym Floor	25,000
Campus Landscaping	10,000
Ski Room Renovation	25,000
Baxter Renovation (seven rooms @ $10,000)	20,000
	70,000
	$ 990,000

Programs

Music	15,000
Drama	10,000
Art	10,000
Audio-visual Equipment	5,000
Computer	20,000
	$ 60,000
TOTAL	$2,250,000

atement booklet. Courtesy Kimball Union Academy, Meriden, N.H.

In setting up the budget for your capital campaign, there are a number of expense items that must be considered. Howard R. Mirkin includes the following: city or state licenses and fees, staff salaries, taxes, insurance, office expenses, promotional material, travel expenses, office space (many capital campaigns set up separate headquarters), site inspections, and such costs as luncheons and dinners, meetings and legal papers that need to be filed.[9]

If your feasibility study shows that you have the potential for success; if your budget shows that you can support the campaign and the facility; and if you have the leadership—both staff and volunteer—to carry out a campaign lasting from three to five years (or even longer), you are probably ready to begin a capital campaign. Implement all of the strategies and tactics of the annual fund—draw up a prospect list, rate and cultivate the donors, assign prospects to each volunteer, put together the promotional material, build the case statement, and begin the campaign. Follow-up is much like the annual fund plan as well—you need accurate records, prompt acknowledgments, and detailed reports on the campaign and how the money was used to benefit the community, the alumni, or the organization.

Fundraising counselor David Ketchum has offered some predictions of what changes we can expect in this decade in capital fundraising. They may help you better plan where your organization is heading and decide whether your campaign is likely to succeed. Among his ideas are the need to identify, inspire, and train new leadership from the volunteer ranks; identify and reach new donors; monitor the continuing legislation affecting fundraising; stress people giving to other people; use the technological advances to handle record keeping, pledge payments, and prospect lists; and continue to explore new and expanded avenues of giving, including more deferred gifts and more support from the corporate community.[10] During the 1974–79 Campaign for Yale, for example, most of the major gifts ($53.7 million of the $374.3 million total) were made in some form of deferred giving.[11] Future capital campaigns will need estate planning literature as part of their basic fundraising materials.

It takes a long time to run a capital campaign. But the time you spend planning it may have a far greater impact on its success than does the time spent operating the program itself.

CASE STUDY

Northwestern University—A Buy-A-Seat Campaign

In late 1979, a number of Northwestern University alumni returned to campus to help dedicate a theater that replaced an outdated one in which they had all studied during their college days. And when your alumni list includes people like Charlton Heston,

McLean Stevenson, Robert Conrad, Paula Prentiss, Cloris Leachman, Patricia Neal, Peter Strauss, and dozens of other celebrities, it makes for a very special occasion.

The $9 million campaign for the new theater had passed the $5 million mark in 1977 when administrators decided that an intensive campaign was needed to reach their goal. A theater had been sought for the university since 1912, and this major capital campaign was about to satisfy a 65-year quest.

Terry A. Wood, associate director of development, noted that Northwestern used direct mail and a telephone campaign to supplement its other printed material, and launched a minicampaign as part of the total effort to "sell" the building's 825 seats at $1,000 each.

The development staff began by going through lists of the university's School of Speech graduates and identifying 3,000 "Buy-A-Seat" prospects, none of whom had been considered as prospects for a separate major gift to the theater campaign.

In May of 1977, the first Buy-A-Seat mailing was sent to all 3,000 prospects and resulted in the sale of 325 seats in four months (Figure 47).

In August, a second mailing was sent by Theatre Campaign National Chairman Charlton Heston to all nonrespondents (Figure 48), advising them that a national phone campaign would be held during the following month. The telephone campaign was for the exclusive purpose of selling the additional seats. Special stationery and envelopes were prepared for Mr. Heston's mailings.

Along with the letter, the staff enclosed a copy of the brochure for the June theater groundbreaking, including an insert with the groundbreaking program agenda, a small cellophane packet containing a teaspoon of soil from the groundbreaking, a printed Honor Roll of those alumni who had already purchased seats, a pledge card, and a reply envelope addressed to Charlton Heston, c/o Northwestern University Theatre Campaign.

After the packets were assembled at the university, they were shipped to California for mailing from the Beverly Hills post office.

The overall objectives of the campaign were to "sell" as many of the 825 seats as possible, to encourage a broad base of support for the theater campaign, and to supplement the major gifts effort.

Preparation for the campaign involved faculty review of the alumni lists to identify former students who were likely prospects, writing support and promotional literature, and recruiting of student volunteers for the four-night phonothon. The phone effort supplemented the print campaign and put the final touches on the conclusion of the campaign.

The results? Six hundred and twenty-five seats were sold (thus bringing in $625,000 for the theater). The names of the seat purchasers appear on plaques in the lobby, along with the names of the stars who performed at the grand opening. These stars waived their usual fees and instead "accepted" seats in their names for the new theater.

Terry Wood notes that the remaining seats are still for sale,

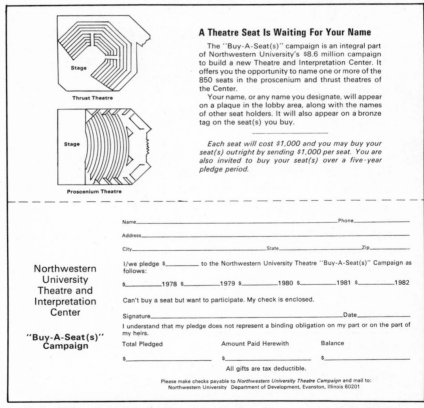

A Theatre Seat Is Waiting For Your Name

The "Buy-A-Seat(s)" campaign is an integral part of Northwestern University's $8.6 million campaign to build a new Theatre and Interpretation Center. It offers you the opportunity to name one or more of the 850 seats in the proscenium and thrust theatres of the Center.

Your name, or any name you designate, will appear on a plaque in the lobby area, along with the names of other seat holders. It will also appear on a bronze tag on the seat(s) you buy.

Each seat will cost $1,000 and you may buy your seat(s) outright by sending $1,000 per seat. You are also invited to buy your seat(s) over a five-year pledge period.

Stage

Thrust Theatre

Stage

Proscenium Theatre

Name_____ Phone_____

Address_____

City_____ State_____ Zip_____

Northwestern University Theatre and Interpretation Center

I/we pledge $_____ to the Northwestern University Theatre "Buy-A-Seat(s)" Campaign as follows:

$_____1978 $_____1979 $_____1980 $_____1981 $_____1982

Can't buy a seat but want to participate. My check is enclosed.

"Buy-A-Seat(s)" Campaign

Signature_____ Date_____

I understand that my pledge does not represent a binding obligation on my part or on the part of my heirs.

Total Pledged	Amount Paid Herewith	Balance
$_____	$_____	$_____

All gifts are tax deductible.

Please make checks payable to *Northwestern University Theatre Campaign* and mail to:
Northwestern University Department of Development, Evanston, Illinois 60201

Figure 47. The first mailing for Northwestern's capital campaign. The cover of this flyer featured a simple picture of theater seats with large type stating "Buy-A-Seat." Courtesy Northwestern University, Evanston, Ill.

and the spaces left on the wall where the plaques are displayed
serve as a constant reminder to theater guests that giving opportunities still remain.

NORTHWESTERN UNIVERSITY THEATRE CAMPAIGN

Charlton Heston, National Chairman

Dear Fellow Alumni:

Few roles I've played as an actor were as gratifying to me as the part
I took in the ground-breaking ceremony for Northwestern's new Theatre and
Interpretation Center. My only prop was a silver shovel; the rest was
sheer enthusiasm.

Yes, it finally happened. The promise to construct a new theatre
building that was made decades ago was kept on June 17, 1978. I know that
some of you have waited as long, or even longer, than I have for this day to
arrive. So, to assure you that this dream we've shared is now a reality, I'm
enclosing a brochure about the building and a copy of the ground-breaking
program. Finally, for the real skeptics, as well as for all of us who
appreciate meaningful souvenirs, you'll also find a small package of soil
taken from one of the half-dozen shovelfuls I turned at the ground breaking.

By far the most important thing you'll find in this envelope is a list
of alumni and friends of the School of Speech who have purchased or pledged
to "Buy-A-Seat" in the new theatre. Were it not for the generous support of
the men and women on this Honor Roll of Donors it may have been necessary to
postpone the ground breaking until a later date. We are still some $3.5
million short of the total cost of nearly $9 million, however; so, my job as
Campaign Chairman is far from over. There is still work to be done.

Now that construction is under way, I hope you will give serious
consideration to buying one or more seats in the theatre to ensure that the
number one Departments of Theatre and Interpretation in the country have a
facility to match. Each seat costs $1,000, and each will bear the name of
the donor or donors, or the name you specify. You may satisfy your pledge
over a five-year period, if you wish — that's well under a dollar per day.
Of course, all gifts to the University are tax deductible.

During the week of September 18, Dean Wood has scheduled a phon-a-thon
to Speech alums nationwide. This will be our last big effort to close that
$3.5 million gap. When a volunteer calls, I hope you will make a pledge for
a seat in the theatre so we can demonstrate that the alumni of the School of
Speech are solidly behind this project. More important, your gift will help
to ensure a healthy future for the American theatre and theatre education
because the best actors, artists and technicians of tomorrow very likely will
learn their arts and skills in Northwestern's new Theatre and Interpretation
Center — or they will be taught by someone who did.

Think about it. Better yet, fill out the enclosed pledge card and mail it
to Dean Wood this week. When the new theatre building is dedicated in 1980,
we hope you'll be there and that your name will be on one or more of its seats.
And I hope the next time I write you will be to thank you for your gift.

Charlton Heston

Charlton Heston

Figure 48. The second letter, from Charlton Heston. Courtesy
Northwestern University, Evanston, Ill.

NU THEATRE &
INTERPRETATION CENTER
Soil from ground broken
by Charlton Heston on
June 17, 1978

*Figure 49. This cellophane
packet contained dirt from
the location of the new
theater.* Courtesy North-
western University, Evan-
ston, Ill.

Wood advises any group seeking to build a new facility or re-
model an existing one to try the Buy-A-Seat program. "It's a
marvelous way to broaden your base of support," he explains.
"We had lots of cooperation from people who had not previously
been involved with the university. This type of program encouraged many people to participate and become a part of the university community."

What major problems did he face during the campaign? "None,
really," he says. Because of careful planning and a well-thought-
out program, everything went smoothly. "About the only thing
that went wrong was that the plaques for the seats didn't arrive
until ten hours before our dinner introducing the donors to the new
theater. I had to run around like crazy gluing the plaques on the
backs of the seats."

The program has carried an added benefit for the development
staff. Wood notes, "It's fun to have people make special trips to
the campus just to see where their seat is. It makes the donor feel
good to see where the money has gone." Showing donors what
their gift has been used for is a great way to encourage repeat gifts,
and Northwestern's program makes it particularly easy.[12]

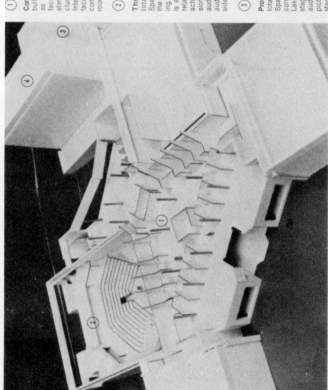

Core Area — The Theatre Building will be built around a Core. The Core will function as the central communal space where faculty and students can interact in a stimulating environment. The Core will include the administrative offices of the Interpretation and Theatre Departments, faculty and graduate student offices, a commons area, and special purpose classrooms.

Thrust Performance Space — Seating totals 500 in the Thrust Performance Space, which has a separate entrance at the northeast corner of the Theatre Building. The rise of interest in the Thrust Stage is a result of trying to find newer, freer relationships between the audience and actor. The design provides a multi-dimensional confrontation between actor and audience, a sculptural effect with the audience surrounding the stage on three sides.

Proscenium Performance Space — Seating totals 350 in the Proscenium Performance Space, which is located at the southeast corner of the Theatre Building overlooking Lake Michigan. The traditional proscenium staging creates a face-to-face actor-to-audience relationship, a two-dimensional pictorial experience. A fully functional stage house provides production support.

Figure 50. A sample page from the case statement brochure. Note how it uses the model of the theater to highlight the features, thus creating giving packages for donors. The brochure also contained aerial views of the campus location, the project budget and space summary information, and detailed explanations of the benefits of the new facility, including enrollment and curriculum of the school. Courtesy Northwestern University, Evanston, Ill.

Foundation Support

You may know the classic Willie Sutton story. America's best-known bank-robber of the twentieth century, Sutton was once asked why he robbed banks. His simple reply: "That's where the money is."

The money is in foundations, too, which is why so many fundraisers spend so much time researching private foundations, putting together grant proposals and requests, and communicating with those foundations most interested in supporting their particular projects. A recent study, for example, found that the average annual grant to colleges and universities from private foundations was $72,000. And while few foundations made general endowment awards, those they did make averaged $110,000 each.[1]

Obtaining money from a foundation is really not a difficult task . . . if. *If* you have a project the foundation is interested in supporting. *If* you have met its deadlines and properly submitted your proposal. *If* you have shown that your organization is capable of providing the service you are proposing. *If* you have built a strong case for support and shown that you deserve it. *If* you are asking for an amount consistent with the support levels of the foundation. *If* you are willing to maintain a relationship with the foundation and report regularly on your progress after the grant is received. *If* you have shown that you have done your "homework" and know your budget, time constraints, staffing needs, and other details. If . . . if . . . if.

If you can do all these things—and more you'll read about later—you have a good chance of receiving foundation support.

Many people think it's as easy as telling a foundation you need money and they should send it quickly. But seeking foundation support is actually a specialized, detailed, systematic process that combines extensive research with detailed communications.

Is there really that much money in private foundations? Consider that in 1979 the top fifty foundations alone paid out more than $703 million in grants, and still had assets of more than $13 billion. Leading the 1979 payments were the Ford Foundation ($109.6 million), Andrew W. Mellon Foundation ($50.7 million), Rockefeller Foundation ($44 million), W. K. Kellogg Foundation ($43.6 million), and the Pew Memorial Trust ($41.4 million).[2] Overall, foundations gave $2.24 billion to charities in 1979, with 29 percent of the grants going to education, 20 percent to the health field, 19 percent to the sciences and technology, 13 percent to welfare agencies, 11 percent to the humanities, 6 percent to international activities, and 2 percent to religion.[3]

In the United States today, there are more than 21,500 foundations with assets of more than $35 billion. They give about $2 billion in grants each year.

The Foundation Center defines a foundation as "a nongovernmental, nonprofit organization, with funds and program managed by its own trustees or directors, and established to maintain or aid social, educational, charitable, religious, or other activities serving the common welfare, primarily through the making of grants."[4] This definition includes both charitable trusts and corporations. Keep in mind that other sources of funding not included in this discussion (e.g., governmental agencies) are also potential sources of revenue, and many of the principles discussed in this chapter apply to fundraising from these other sources.

Working with foundations has been called the most rational part of the entire fundraising business. While it often helps you get your foot in the door (and your proposal looked at more closely) if someone on your board knows someone on the foundation's board, the bulk of the process centers around a cogent, well-written proposal showing that the organization is ready to handle the project and deserves support.

It's more than just a matter of writing a proposal, of course. You have to begin with a need (though there are still fundraisers who think they can write to a number of foundations and ask what types of projects they support, then write up proposals seeking aid for these projects. It just doesn't work as well that way). You have to know who will support your idea. The "shotgun" approach of sending out form letters (and even form proposals) to dozens of foundations proves futile in most cases.

In the advertising business today, with intense competition for the consumer, marketing people know that "if you try to sell to everybody, you will sell to nobody." You have to tailor your appeal to a particular type of consumer with a particular need. The same holds true for grant seekers. If you can match your organization and your need with a foundation interested in the project, you will have a much better chance of receiving funding than if you send out more general, broader-based appeals to a number of foundations.

Each year, approximately one million proposals are submitted to foundations, but less than 7 percent of them are funded. Knowing how to approach a foundation can make your chances of success better than average. Forget about relying on a trustee's phone call to a former school chum and put together a total plan for the foundation to consider.

You begin, of course, with a program at your organization requiring funding. It may be a specific need (e.g., a bus or bookshelves, a new building, a refurbished auditorium) or it may just be general endowment support. If the sum is so large that you can't pay the costs from your annual fundraising efforts, you may consider seeking a grant from a foundation that has supported similar projects in the past.

Just as in other forms of giving, you begin preparing the case for your needs. It helps to dwell on "opportunities" rather than sheer needs of the group. You may want a new hospital wing, but that will provide the opportunity to serve two hundred more patients in the coming year. You may want three new vans or busses, but they will allow your group to take one hundred senior citizens to certain activities each week. Foundations care much more about what their money will do for the organization and the people you serve than what the money will do specifically for you. Then you need to consider the type of foundation interested in your activity. In general, there are five basic types of foundations in the United States today:

General purpose foundations. The most widely known type, these include foundations with large endowments, professional staffs, and governing boards with a wide range of interests.

Special-sponsored foundations. These are set up for specific purposes and only fund specific types of projects (e.g., scholarship aid for students of a certain religion going to a specific college).

Company-sponsored foundations. Many profit-making companies set up foundations to channel their contributions to charitable organizations. Most company foundations make gifts to geographical areas where they have operations or to institutions whose work can benefit the company or its employees.

Family foundations. There are approximately 15,000 family foundations in the United States today. They are usually easier to deal with than the larger foundations since you are appealing to the family or donor for a gift, and their interests are usually better known.

Community foundations. These exist to serve organizations in their own community only. There are approximately 235 community foundations today, offering excellent potential for nonprofit organizations.[5] In 1979, community foundations made 12,000 grants totalling $90 million.[6]

According to *The Grantsmanship Center News*, there are four major forms of community foundations: the Single Bank Trust (one bank, which has sole responsibility for the management of the funds); Multiple Bank Trust (several banks are involved, receiving and administering gifts and bequests for the foundation—more than half of the nation's community foundations are this type); Trust Form with an Incorporated Distribution Committee (similar to the others, but the distribution committee is incorporated); and Corporate Form (an incorporated community foundation, similar to any other type of nonprofit organization).[7]

The Ford Foundation publishes a booklet describing its current interests. The June 1980 report notes that the foundation "works mainly by giving funds for educational, developmental, research, and experimental efforts designed to produce significant advances on selected important problems."[8] Note that the foundation stresses its interest in the accomplishments and results of your work rather than the work itself.

It is important to research the foundations to find the best prospects for your project. Many newcomers find the job almost overwhelming at first, with information available in libraries on thousands of foundations, corporations, and governmental agencies. Your job is to narrow down the list to the handful who are your best prospects—the foundations whose interests match your project, whose funding level is consistent with your needs, and those requirements fall within your framework (e.g., geographical area, type of organization, etc.).

A trip to one of the Foundation Center libraries (the national collections are in New York and Washington, D.C., and the local collections are listed in Appendix B) might be the best starting point, for they carry tremendous files of information on foundations and grant writing.

The regional offices in most of the states contain a great deal of information you'll find useful. Almost every state has a library that keeps files on IRS tax returns for selected foundations.

These tax returns—the 990 ARs—are annual reports submitted by foundations to the IRS, and they are the best sources of information on most foundations. The forms, which must be completed by all foundations with assets of at least $5,000, are sent to the IRS and to the attorney general's office of the state in which they are incorporated and in which they maintain their principal office. If you have trouble locating copies of 990s from your state attorney general's office (many people find this a difficult process), you can obtain copies from the Foundation Center collections, the national and district IRS offices, and even from the foundations themselves, who must make their 990 available for inspection for 180 days after the filing date.

Why is this information so valuable? Ten general categories of data must be included in these reports: the foundation's address and location of its books, total contributions and gifts received that year, gross income for the year, annual disbursements, expenses attributable to gross income, the names and addresses of its managers, names of managers who are substantial contributors, a balance sheet, an account of all securities and other assets, and all grants made during the year, with the name and address of each recipient, the amount and purpose of the grant, and the relationship (if any) between the recipient and the foundation's managers or contributors.

In addition to copies of these reports, you'll find a great deal of information in several of the popular reference books available in many libraries. *The Foundation Directory* and the *Annual Register of Grant Support* are two of the best, containing information on thousands of private, company-sponsored, and community foundations. Good sources of information on federal programs are the *Catalog of Federal Domestic Assistance* (which describes more than 1,000 programs administered by fifty-five federal agencies), the *Federal Register, Commerce Business Daily*, and other standard reference works.

While there seems to be more information available than you'd ever need, most of it is actually quite useful and important, since it covers so many different aspects of the foundations. If a particular foundation gives grants between $5,000 and $10,000, for example, your request for a $100,000 grant has little chance of being funded.

PREPARING THE PROPOSAL

One of the most important tasks in obtaining foundation grants is putting together the proposal. This involves deciding what is to go into the cover letter, into the proposal itself, and into supporting documents (e.g., budgets, statements of goals, etc.).

In his book *Getting a Grant*, Robert Lefferts has noted that there are five distinct types of proposals to be considered by fundraisers:

- *Program proposals*—for services to people or organizations
- *Research proposals*—for study of a problem, group, or service
- *Planning proposals*—for planning and coordination of a problem, group of organizations, or services
- *Training proposals*—for education and training of people or groups
- *Technical-assistance proposals*—for assistance to people and

groups establishing and implementing programs, research, and administration.[9]

Your job is to decide what type of proposal needs to be written to obtain funding for your project, then transfer your enthusiasm for the program into words for a proposal. First outline a number of items that foundations will need to know, including what you hope to accomplish, how much it will cost, who will be served, what is unique about your program, what the credentials are of the people involved in the project, how long it will last, how your program will be evaluated, and why your organization is best suited to conduct this work. You have previously identified the best prospects for your proposal. Now you should make sure that your project is in the geographical area, the field of interest, the budgetary limitations, and the type of population of interest to the foundations you have selected.

Edwin Dieckmann of the Cleveland Institute of Art has outlined the criteria for evaluating proposals used by The Cleveland Foundation. Their guidelines include the following areas, and give an idea of the type of things considered by foundations:

1. Substantive quality of the proposal:
    *   Is there a clear statement of goals?
    *   Are the proposed techniques suitable and adequate?
    *   Is the project of sufficient scope for results anticipated?
    *   Is the project too broad?
    *   Is highly competent personnel available locally? Can it be recruited?
    *   Is the budget adequate?
    *   Are the time estimates reasonable?

2. Priorities among proposals:
    *   How important is the problem being attacked?
    *   Is the project duplicating work being done elsewhere?
    *   Will the project facilitate other work in the field?
    *   Will the project attract permanent talent to Cleveland?
    *   Will the results be of general use or value to one organization only?
    *   Will the project facilitate beneficial community action?

- Is the request made to allow completion of a project already started?

3. Funding:
   - Are other sources of support available?
   - Will a local grant make available other support?
   - Will other funds be likely to be attracted by a grant?
   - Can the project be divided into piecemeal funding?
   - Should some support be recommended if the entire project cannot be funded?
   - Where will future support come from if needed?[10]

The Ford Foundation publishes a small brochure, "Applying for Grants," that helps applicants prepare their proposals.

Other detailed information on foundations can come from their annual reports. The 1979 report of The Kresge Foundation, for example, included a list of their trustees and staff, a chairman's statement, policies and procedures, their 1979 grants, information on appropriations and disbursements for the current and previous years, and detailed financial statements.

One final word on foundations. Don't be confused when you hear a college, university, or other group talking about its foundations. These are quite different from the typical private or corporate foundation.

Organizations such as state universities often set up independent corporations called foundations, so that gifts to the university come to the separate company and not to the state institution. Some schools use foundations so they can receive federal or special grants that the school does not wish to seek or cannot accept. Foundations often inspire additional donor confidence because specialists are managing the funds. And organizations with budgets requiring all funds to be spent before the year ends often find that foundations allow them to carry over money from year to year.

The typical relationship today is to have someone from the organization, either paid directly by the group or by the foundation itself, manage the activities of the foundation. The purpose, though, is strictly to serve the interests of the college or other group setting up the foundation. They do not give grants, but instead accept and disburse them for the betterment of the organization.

The flexibility offered by a foundation often makes it an attractive alternative to having all money come directly to the organization.

WRITING THE PROPOSAL

There are a number of companies and consulting firms offering intensive workshops on writing grant proposals, and courses in this are offered at colleges and universities throughout the country. In addition, your library probably contains several good books on the subject—and certainly dozens of articles on the ways to write a foundation grant.

Probably the best way to learn how to write a grant is to study a sample proposal. But first, here are a number of guidelines suggested by most experts in grant-writing. They all tie in with the need to find the most appropriate foundations and build the strongest possible case for support. Once you've done your homework, you're ready to begin the writing. Keep the following points in mind:

- Tell the purpose of your proposal early—in the first paragraph, if possible. Building a case does not mean keeping the reader in suspense until the end. Tell right away what you want, who your organization is, and what the grant will accomplish.
- Remember that you are writing to people, not just a "cold" foundation. If you know something about these people from checking the names of trustees in foundation directories (and then looking them up in *Who's Who*), it may help you put yourself in their places. But even if you don't know anything about them, try to personalize your proposal and make it as interesting as possible.
- Try to explain clearly how your proposal fits in with the foundation's interests as stated in guideline booklets or from previous grants they have made. Why would this particular foundation want to fund your project? Why have you asked them to take their time to consider your request?
- What exactly will your project accomplish? What is the purpose of your work? As previously explained, no one cares that you

need the money to build a new gymnasium. But the new building may mean that too hundred inner-city children will now have a recreational facility instead of playing on a city street. Talk in terms of expected results.

- If you feel there are unique situations regarding your grant request, explain them fully. Maybe you're the only organization of your type in the city, and no one else can offer what you do. Or maybe your most important building burned down last year, and services cannot be offered until it is restored.
- What other support do you have for the project? Many foundations are especially interested in helping if you can show that you have additional support as well. Do you have a challenge grant, or have certain expenses already been met, or will subscriptions or sales provide for a certain percentage of the total expenses? If you're seeking money for a building do you have the funds to pay the utilities and buy the furniture?
- If you're asking for a renewal of an earlier grant, you need to reaffirm your appreciation for the initial grant, and explain why you did not accomplish everything the first time. Many times a follow-up grant is a natural continuation of an earlier project, and you can capitalize on a successful start. What will this additional grant enable you to do?
- Make sure your budget is well prepared and covers all items. This is an extremely important part of any grant proposal, and foundations are especially interested in how your budget is set up. All costs of the project, including salaries and expenses, should be clearly presented and projected for the duration of the grant time period.
- What exactly will the foundation gain from making this gift? Will it have helped make the world better, students smarter, or sick people healthier? Even though your organization will actually do the work, the foundation is sharing in the accomplishment of the goals.
- Perhaps most important of all, you need to be honest. You must talk about deadlines that are workable, goals that are feasible, budgets that are realistic. The worst thing you can do is mislead the foundation in your proposal, receive the grant, then realize that you cannot meet unrealistic expectations and have the project fail. Writing a proposal is not the time for wishful dreaming.

Some foundations welcome personal visits to discuss your proposal, while a number are definitely against them. But if you think a personal visit by you or your president or board member would help better present your case and answer questions, you may wish to telephone or write for an interview. Keep in mind that if you write, the purpose of the letter is to request an interview—not ask for money. Your letter should be brief, to the point, and tell why you want the meeting. A sample letter might take this format:

> Dear *(Foundation Director):*
> I would like to meet with you to discuss a project *(organization)* has been planning for the past six months to help us serve an important segment of our community not currently receiving recreational services.
> Because you have supported projects dealing with this service in the past, I think your foundation would be interested in helping the people of our community with this need. I would like to talk with you in person about some of our plans and how *(foundation)* can help the people of *(city)*.
> I will be in *(city)* during the week of April 13, and can meet with you at your convenience. Please let me know what day and time would be most suitable. I look forward to talking with you about this exciting program.

Obviously, the letter should be as personalized as possible, with your organization's name, the foundation's name, and specifics about the accomplishments you forecast for the program.

The case study at the end of this chapter gives a sample proposal. We are not suggesting that this is *the* way to write a proposal. Rather, it is one way to approach a small foundation with a simple, clearly stated need. Some foundations require, and more involved projects would call for, a more in-depth proposal. Federal agencies require certain forms filled out, while many corporate and private foundations specify that you use their application forms.

Your research will help you prepare the best way to approach each individual foundation. Then you can write an individualized proposal to mesh with its interests and specifications. Your job isn't done then, of course. First there is the wait for a response. It's not uncommon for a six- to nine-month delay between the submission of your proposal and a response from the foundation, though many will acknowledge receipt of your proposal immediately.

Then after you receive the grant (think positively!), be sure to follow its requirements for updates and reporting, and keep the foundation posted on your progress.

Applying for foundation grants calls for attention to detail, organization, research, and clear writing ability. But the possible rewards make all the work worthwhile.

Finally, consult Appendix B (page 295) for Foundation Center collections available in your area. These libraries are the best places to begin your in-depth research.

CASE STUDY

A Sample Foundation Proposal

The following fictitious proposal may give you a starting point for your next request.

Each situation is different, of course, but many smaller foundations prefer brief proposals that state the case, give the budget, tell what the funds will accomplish, and provide related information. Use this as a general guide to proposal writing.

Mr. John Philanthropist
The Philanthropist Private Foundation
P.O. Box 711
Miami, Florida 33130

Dear Mr. Philanthropist:

I am writing to ask the Philanthropist Private Foundation for a grant of $13,000 to construct an astronomical observatory on the campus of Central Technological University.

Because your foundation has shown an interest in projects dealing with astronomy and celestial observation, I believe that our project would further enhance your commitment to such studies.

These funds would enable us to provide a permanent, accessible observing facility for our existing telescope equipment, and would allow us to purchase a needed 16″ telescope.

While the University receives funds for basic academic needs from the State, we are not funded for many areas that would benefit our students and the surrounding community.

For these needs, we must look for funding from outside sources.

If we had the new telescope and observatory, we could provide a balanced program including practical observational experience for 400 astronomy course students each year. In addition, this facility would help promote the establishment of a future astronomy program.

Most important, such a facility would provide enrichment of any student or member of the community with a curiosity for learning more about the universe. Moreover, the facility would serve the community via observing sessions for scout troops, high school students, junior colleges, and other groups.

Our current telescope equipment is about four years old, and includes one 10″ Celestron reflecting telescope (approximate current value: $1,800); four 6″ Edmund reflecting telescopes ($880 current value); one 4″ Questar reflecting telescope ($800 current value); and 10 orthoscopic oculars ($200 current value).

Presently, during observing sessions, it is necessary to manually transport this equipment both to and from the observing site. This is not only an inconvenience, but it also presents a considerable risk of disturbing or damaging precisely aligned optics. A permanent equipment storage and observing facility would alleviate both inconvenience and hazard of transporting the equipment.

In order to meet both the general enrichment and academic interests of this facility, a 16″ f/5 or f/6 Rich Field Newtonian reflector is greatly preferred to our existing 10″ Celestron. A 16″ offers not only 156% more light-gathering power, but also a marked increase in resolving power of double stars and planetary details.

In addition, the shorter focal length of the Rich Field 16″ will provide a wide angle field of view unattainable with the existing 10″ telescope. These details mean a light-enhanced, well-defined, wide-angle view of large star fields, galaxies, and nebulae. From an academic standpoint, a 16″ instrument would be amenable to serious astrophotography utilizing cooled emulsion techniques, variable star photometry, and precise occultation and transit observations. A 16″ telescope thus appears to be the minimum instrument capable of serving both the casual and serious observer.

The facility would be supervised by Dr. Phillip P. Phillips of our physics department. Dr. Phillips is a faculty member with considerable interest in astronomy. He has spent five summers as a visiting scientist for NASA, and has received two fellowships to further his study in astronomy. His major research interest currently is with radio observation of the remote planets.

Dr. Phillips and other faculty members in the physics department are very interested in helping our students develop an adequate astronomy observatory, and are willing to lend their expertise and contribute use of the department's observational equipment for this effort.

Dr. Phillips says that "We have many fine students at Central Technological University who are very serious about observations and are extremely capable. It is unfortunate that they cannot carry out many studies that are original in concept. Also, we have hundreds of students every term who would be delighted to observe the heavens."

Following is a cost breakdown on the needed items:

16" Astrola Rich Field Reflecting Telescope	$4,700.00
26' Diameter Geodesic Dome Kit	2,400.00
Circular Track Mechanism	1,000.00
Slit Construction w/Roll Away Covering	300.00
Air Vent Turbines and Sky Lites	200.00
Electrical Conduits and Outlets	50.00
Electrical Hook-up 300'	1,000.00
Insulation (Fiberglass)	200.00
Floating Concrete Pier Mounting	50.00
Land Preparation	200.00
Concrete Flooring 4" Thick 30' Diameter	500.00
Steel Fire Door	200.00
Bathroom Facilities	1,800.00
Miscellaneous	400.00
Total	$13,000.00

Please do not hesitate to contact me if you need any further information on this proposal. I have included photographs showing the proposed astronomical observatory along with a floor plan and cross section plans, and detailed fact sheets on the University and our physics program.

Sincerely,

John Fundraiser

APPENDIX A

Government Regulations on Fundraising

Over the years, a variety of organizations has issued guidelines covering gift solicitation. The National Information Bureau, Inc., the Council of Better Business Bureaus, Inc., and the federal government have all published statements of their criteria for ethical fundraising. We include the federal government even though it has not formally published restrictions on fundraising, since the various tax reform acts have all spelled out rules and regulations.

More than two-thirds of the United States have laws regulating charitable solicitations. The chart on page 278 shows the various restrictions as they apply to charitable organizations and to fundraising counsel.

The importance of fundraising restrictions has been clearly spelled out by the National Health Council in its 1976 booklet "Viewpoints: State Legislation Regulating Solicitation of Funds from the Public": "In the past several decades the multiplicity and complexity of tax-exempt activities for charitable purposes in the United States, the willingness of the general public to financially support them, and the failure of many of these organizations to provide adequate financial information created an atmosphere favorable to fraudulent activities by unscrupulous groups."

The unscrupulous organizations (and though they fortunately are few, they do attract a great deal of media attention) not only victimize the public and siphon off funds from legitimate organizations, but they also give the entire business an image of dishonesty and poor handling of funds. The state laws are a step in the direction of standardizing proper procedures for fundraisers to follow. Readers are urged to write the National Health Council for this booklet (cost to non-NHC members is $3, and it is available from the NHC, 70 West 40th Street, New York, New York 10018). It includes a detailed discussion of the various types of regulation along with a recommended form for uniform financial reporting.

In addition to noting the regulations printed here, you should check with your state's attorney general or secretary of state to see if there are additional guidelines covering fundraisers in your state.

It is essential that fundraisers keep up with the ever-changing laws and regulations affecting their work. On February 20, 1980, for example, a major case reaffirmed that charitable solicitation is an activity that enjoys the constitutional protection of free speech. In this case, *Village of Schaumberg (Illinois)* vs. *Citizens for a Better Environment et al.* (popularly called the Schaumberg Decision), the Supreme Court ruled that a community may not impose a flat percentage limit on the fundraising costs of organizations raising money in its area.

We feel strongly that legitimate fundraisers will welcome additional guidelines and laws regulating our business, which will help keep the unscrupulous, fly-by-night solicitors away, and clearly establish procedures by which nonprofit organizations can seek the public support they need and deserve.

STATE LAWS REGULATING CHARITABLE SOLICITATIONS
(As of December 31, 1981)

State	Registration or Licensing	Regulatory Agency	Cost Limitations
Arkansas	Registration	Secretary of State Little Rock Arkansas 72201 501-370-5166	25% for Fund-Raising
California	Registration	Department of Justice P.O. Box 13447 Sacramento, CA 95814 916-445-2021	None
Connecticut	Registration	Department of Consumer Protection 165 Capitol Hartford, CT 06115 203-566-3035	25% to 50% depending on total raised
District of Columbia	Licensing	Department of Licenses, Investigations & Inspections 614 H St., N.W. Washington, DC 20001 202-727-3666	None
Florida	Registration (Names of all fund-raising employees must be registered)	Department of State Division of Licensing The Capitol Tallahassee, FL 32301 904-488-5381	25% to a professional solicitor

Charitable Organizations

Fund-Raising Counsel

Annual Financial Reporting Requirements	Monetary Exemption Ceiling	Charitable Solicitation Disclosure	Registration or Licensing	Bonding Requirement
By March 31 or within 90 days after close of fiscal year	$1,000*	None	Registration	$5,000
End of year	None	"Sale for charitable purpose card" must be shown if merchandise is sold for charity	None	None
In form described by department within 5 months of close of fiscal year and must be audited by an independent accountant if public support exceeds $100,000	$5,000*	None	Registration	$10,000
Within 30 days after the end of a licensing period and 30 days after a demand by the mayor (formerly the commissioner)	$1,500*	Solicitors must present solicitation information card to prospective donor. Card is issued by Department of Economic Development	Licensing	None
With annual registration process on forms audited by an independent public accountant if in excess of $25,000	$4,000*	Organizations must furnish authorization to solicitors which must be exhibited on request	Licensing (Statute refers only to professional solicitors)	$10,000

* If all soliciting is done by volunteers.

STATE LAWS REGULATING CHARITABLE SOLICITATIONS

State	Registration or Licensing	Regulatory Agency	Cost Limitations
Georgia	Registration	Secretary of State State Capitol Atlanta, GA 30334 404-656-2859	30% for administration and fundraising unless exemption is given
Hawaii	Registration	Department of Regulatory Agencies Hawaii State Capitol Honolulu, Hawaii 96813 808-548-4740	10% to professional solicitors
Illinois	Registration	Attorney General State of Illinois 188 West Randolph Room 1826 Chicago, IL 60601 312-793-2595	At least 75% of gross receipts must be used for charitable purposes and not more than 25% for the cost of unordered merchandise
Iowa	(Iowa Code Annotated Sec. 122.1 et seq. (1967) ruled unconstitutional in Federal Court.)		
Kansas	Registration	Attorney General 301 West 10 St. Topeka, KS 913-296-3751	At least 75% of gross receipts must be used for charitable purposes and not more than 25% for the cost of unordered merchandise

Charitable Organizations   Fund-Raising Counsel

Annual Financial Reporting Requirements	Monetary Exemption Ceiling	Charitable Solicitation Disclosure	Registration or Licensing	Bonding Requirement
Within 90 days after close of fiscal or calendar year. (Quarterly Reports required in first year of operation. Report must be verified by independent certified accountant if over $50,000.)	$15,000 if costs are below 30%	Organizations must furnish donor with name of solicitor and purpose for which solicitation is being made	Registration	$10,000 or 50% of total income of PFR for preceding year, whichever is greater
With registration statement	$4,000*	Solicitors must furnish authorization on request	Licensing	$5,000
Within six months after end of fiscal or calendar year	$4,000*	None	Registration	$5,000
Appropriate form pursuant to the Kansas Statutes Annotated Sec. 17-7500 et. seq. as part of registration	$5,000*	None	Registration	$5,000

* If all soliciting is done by volunteers.

STATE LAWS REGULATING CHARITABLE SOLICITATIONS

State	Registration or Licensing	Regulatory Agency	Cost Limitations
Kentucky	Registration (only organizations that receive state funds must register)	Bureau of Corrections and Attorney General Frankfort, KY 40601 502-564-6607	15% of gross contributions of money and property received and net proceeds for sales of goods and services
Maine	Registration	Attorney General Augusta, ME 04333 207-289-3716	See disclosure
Maryland	Registration	Secretary of State State House Annapolis, MD 21414 301-269-3421	25% unless higher is authorized

Charitable Organizations			Fund-Raising Counsel	
Annual Financial Reporting Requirements	**Monetary Exemption Ceiling**	**Charitable Solicitation Disclosure**	**Registration or Licensing**	**Bonding Requirement**
None	None	Registration receipt must be shown to donor	Registration (with county clerk)	None
If more than $30,000 raised, within six months after close of fiscal year. Must be audited by independent public accountant	$10,000*	No professional fund raiser or solicitor shall solicit funds for a charitable purpose without full disclosure to the prospective donor the estimated cost of solicitation where less than 70% of amount donated will be expended for the specific charitable purpose	Registration	$10,000
Most recent completed fiscal year. If in excess of $100,000 an audit is required by an independent certified public accountant according to the standards of accounting and financial reporting of voluntary health and welfare organizations	$5,000†	None	Registration	$10,000

* If all soliciting is done by volunteers.
† If all soliciting is done by volunteers and 500,000 or fewer mail solicitations are sent.

STATE LAWS REGULATING CHARITABLE SOLICITATIONS

State	Registration or Licensing	Regulatory Agency	Cost Limitations
Massachusetts	Licensing	Attorney General Division of Public Charities Boston, MA 02108 617-727-2235	15% to a professional solicitor; 50% overall solicitation expense; unless higher is proven to be in public interest
Michigan	Licensing	Attorney General Law Building Lansing, MI 48913 517-373-1152	None
Minnesota	Registration	Asst. Attorney General 515 Transportation Bldg. St. Paul, MN 55155 612-296-6438	30% for administration, general and fund-raising costs is presumed to be unreasonable
Nebraska	Certificate granted on basis of letter of approval obtained from county attorney of home-office county	Secretary of State Lincoln, NE 68509 402-471-2554	None
Nevada	None	Attorney General Carson City, NE 89701 702-855-4170	None

Charitable Organizations   Fund-Raising Counsel

Annual Financial Reporting Requirements	Monetary Exemption Ceiling	Charitable Solicitation Disclosure	Registration or Licensing	Bonding Requirement
On or before June 1 or before 60 days following a fiscal year ending in April or May on prescribed forms organizations receiving over $100,000 annually must file audited financial statement	$5,000*	Solicitors must exhibit authorization on request	Licensing	$10,000
With application for license or renewal for 12-month period immediately preceding the time it files	$8,000†	License or registration number must be written on solicitation materials	Licensing	$10,000
Within six months of the fiscal or calendar year. CPA statement needed if more than $25,000 is raised	$10,000*	Solicitation card must be shown prior to solicitation	Licensing	up to $20,000
Within 6 months after the close of the calendar or fiscal year	None	Solicitor must carry and show certificate and issue receipts	None	None
By July 1 with Secretary of State	None	None	None	None

* If all soliciting is done by volunteers.
† If all soliciting is done by volunteers and annual report is given to contributors.

STATE LAWS REGULATING CHARITABLE SOLICITATIONS

State	Registration or Licensing	Regulatory Agency	Cost Limitations
New Hampshire	Licensing	Secretary of State Division of Welfare Concord, NH 03301 603-271-4297	85% must be applied to a charitable purpose
New Jersey	Registration	Charities Registration Sec. 1100 Raymond Blvd. Newark, NJ 07102 201-648-4002	15% to professional fund-raiser and professional solicitor; 50% for mail solicitation via unordered merchandise
New York	Registration	Office of Charities Registration Department of State Albany, NY 12231 518-474-3720	50% for mail solicitation via unordered merchandise
North Carolina	Licensing	Department of Human Resources Raleigh, NC 27605 919-733-4510	None
North Dakota	Licensing	Secretary of State Bismarck, ND 58501 701-224-2901	35% re-solicitation of fund-raising expenses (including pay-

Charitable Organizations

Fund-Raising Counsel

Annual Financial Reporting Requirements	Monetary Exemption Ceiling	Charitable Solicitation Disclosure	Registration or Licensing	Bonding Requirement
When requested by the director of the division	None	None	None	None
Within 6 months after close of fiscal or calendar year	$10,000*	None	Registration	$10,000
Within 90 days after the close of its fiscal year. If in excess of $50,000 for preceding year, report must be accompanied by an opinion signed by an independent public accountant	$10,000*	None	Registration	$5,000
With application for registration CPA Audited Reports are required if more than $250,000 in support and revenue is received	$10,000*	Percent of fund raising expenses and the purpose of the organization must be published in newspaper with largest circulation in each county where funds are solicited	Licensing	$5,000
Within 60 days after the close of the fiscal or calendar year if	None	None	Registration	None

* If all soliciting is done by volunteers.

STATE LAWS REGULATING CHARITABLE SOLICITATIONS

State	Registration or Licensing	Regulatory Agency	Cost Limitations
North Dakota (*continued*)			ment to professional solicitor or fund-raiser) 15% to fund-raisers or solicitors, unless higher authorized
Ohio	Registration	Attorney General Columbus, OH 43215 614-466-3180	None
Oklahoma	Registration	Commission of Charities and Corrections State Capitol, Rm. 8 Oklahoma City, OK 73105 405-521-3495	Payments to professional fund-raisers or solicitors limited to 10% of totals raised
Oregon	Registration	Attorney General Portland, OR 97201 503-229-5278	25% for solicitation, 50% overall, unless higher authorized
Pennsylvania	Licensing	Commission on Charitable Organizations Dept. of State Harrisburg, PA 17120 717-783-1720	35% re-solicitation & fund-raising expenses (including payment to professional solicitor and fund-raiser) 15% to professional solicitor, unless higher authorized

Charitable Organizations

Fund-Raising Counsel

Annual Financial Reporting Requirements	Monetary Exemption Ceiling	Charitable Solicitation Disclosure	Registration or Licensing	Bonding Requirement
any contributions were received during the previous calendar year				
By March 31 if on a calendar year; if on a fiscal year 90 days of close of fiscal year	None	None	Registration	$5,000
Within 90 days of the end of the fiscal or calendar year	$10,000	Receipts must be given for contributions over $2	Registration	$2,500
Within four months of close of calendar or fiscal year	$250	None	None	None
Submitted with annual licensing process	$7,500*	Solicitor must produce authorization on request	Licensing	$10,000

* If all soliciting is done by volunteers.

STATE LAWS REGULATING CHARITABLE SOLICITATIONS

State	Registration or Licensing	Regulatory Agency	Cost Limitations
Rhode Island	Registration	Department of Business Regulations Providence, RI 02903 401-277-2405	50% re-solicitation of fund-raising expenses, 15% to professional solicitor, unless higher authorized
South Carolina	Registration	Secretary of State Columbia, SC 29211 803-758-2244	Reasonable percentage to professional solicitor
South Dakota	Registration	Department of Commerce and Consumer Protection State Capitol Bldg. Pierre, SD 57501 605-773-3696	30% to professional fund-raiser
Tennessee	Registration	Secretary of State Capitol Hill Bldg. Nashville, TN 37219 615-741-2555	25% for fund-raising costs; 15% to professional solicitor, unless higher authorized

Charitable Organizations   Fund-Raising Counsel

Annual Financial Reporting Requirements	Monetary Exemption Ceiling	Charitable Solicitation Disclosure	Registration or Licensing	Bonding Requirement
Within 90 days after end of fiscal year audited by an independent certified accountant	$3,000*	Solicitor must produce authorization on request	Registration	$10,000
Within six months of the close of the fiscal year	$2,000*	Solicitor must produce authorization on request	Registration	$5,000
An independent audited annual report for contributions received of $10,000 or more as prescribed by National Health Council, National Assembly of National Voluntary Health and Social Welfare Organization Standards and forms	$2,000	None	Licensing	$20,000
Submitted as part of annual registration process, independent public accountant audit required for over $10,000 in annual contributions	$5,000†	None	Registration	$10,000

* If all soliciting is done by volunteers.
† With no restrictions; $10,000 if all soliciting is done by volunteers.

STATE LAWS REGULATING CHARITABLE SOLICITATIONS

State	Registration or Licensing	Regulatory Agency	Cost Limitations
Virginia	Registration	Administrator of Consumer Affairs Richmond, VA 23219 804-786-1343	See disclosure
Washington	Licensing	Department of Licensing Olympia, WA 98501 206-753-1966	20% unless higher is approved
West Virginia	Registration	Secretary of State Capitol Bldg. Charleston, WV 25305 304-348-2112	15% to professional solicitor
Wisconsin	Registration	Department of Registration & Licensing Madison, WI 53702 608-266-0829	None

Charitable Organizations   Fund-Raising Counsel

Annual Financial Reporting Requirements	Monetary Exemption Ceiling	Charitable Solicitation Disclosure	Registration or Licensing	Bonding Requirement
Submitted as part of annual registration process	$2,000*	Donors must be told minimum percent of donation which will be received by organization for its own use if less than 70% of total donation. Solicitors must produce authorization on request and furnish receipts for contributions of $5 or more	Registration	$5,000
Within 90 days after the close of the fiscal year also at discretion of Dept. within 30 days after close of any special solicitation	$10,000*	Solicitors must identify themselves	Registration	$5,000
Financial report must accompany annual registration statement and if in excess of $50,000 required to have an audit by an independent public accountant	$7,500*	None	Registration	$10,000
Within 6 months of the close of the fiscal or calendar year	$500*	None	Registration	$5,000

* If all soliciting is done by volunteers.
Source: *Giving USA*, Bulletin No. 9, December, 1981. Reprinted by permission.

APPENDIX B

Foundation Center Collections

National Libraries

The Foundation Center
888 Seventh Avenue
New York, New York 10019

The Foundation Center
1001 Connecticut Avenue N.W.
Washington, D.C. 20036

Field Offices

The Foundation Center—San
  Francisco
312 Sutter Street
San Francisco, California 94108

The Foundation Center—
  Cleveland
Kent H. Smith Library
739 National City Bank Building
629 Euclid Street
Cleveland, Ohio 44114

National Cooperating
  Collection

Donors Forum of Chicago
208 South LaSalle Street
Chicago, Illinois 60604

Regional Collections

ALABAMA
Birmingham Public Library
2020 Seventh Avenue, North
Birmingham 35203

ALASKA
University of Alaska
3211 Providence Street
Anchorage 99504

ARIZONA
Tucson Public Library
Main Library
200 South Sixth Avenue
Tucson 85701

ARKANSAS
Little Rock Public Library
Reference Department
700 Louisiana Street
Little Rock 72201

CALIFORNIA
University Research Library
Reference Department
University of California
Los Angeles 90024

San Diego Public Library
820 E Street
San Diego 92101

COLORADO
Denver Public Library
Sociology Division
1357 Broadway
Denver 80203

CONNECTICUT
Hartford Public Library
Reference Department
500 Main Street
Hartford 06103

FLORIDA
Jacksonville Public Library
Business, Science, and Industry
    Department
122 North Ocean Street
Jacksonville 32202

Miami—Dade Public Library
Florida Collection
One Biscayne Boulevard
Miami 33132

GEORGIA
Atlanta Public Library
126 Carnegie Way N.W.
Atlanta 30303
    (also covers Alabama, Florida,
    South Carolina, and
    Tennessee)

HAWAII
Thomas Hale Hamilton Library
University of Hawaii
Humanities and Social Sciences
    Division
2550 The Mall
Honolulu 96822

IDAHO
Caldwell Public Library
1010 Dearborn Street
Caldwell 83605

ILLINOIS
Sangamon State University
    Library
Shepherd Road
Springfield 62708

INDIANA
Indianapolis—Marion County
    Public Library
40 East St. Clair Street
Indianapolis 46204

IOWA
Des Moines Public Library
100 Locust Street
Des Moines 50309

KANSAS
Topeka Public Library
Adult Services Department
1515 West Tenth Street
Topeka 66604

KENTUCKY
Louisville Free Public Library
Fourth and York Streets
Louisville 40203

LOUISIANA
New Orleans Public Library
Business and Science Division
219 Loyola Avenue
New Orleans 70140

MAINE
University of Maine at Portland
    —Gorham
Center for Research and
    Advanced Study
246 Deering Avenue
Portland 04102

MARYLAND
Enoch Pratt Free Library
Social Science and History
   Department
400 Cathedral Street
Baltimore 21201
   *(also covers District of
   Columbia)*

MASSACHUSETTS
Associated Foundation of
   Greater Boston
294 Washington Street, Suite 501
Boston 02108

Boston Public Library
Copley Square
Boston 02117

MICHIGAN
Henry Ford Centennial Library
15301 Michigan Avenue
Dearborn 48126

Purdy Library
Wayne State University
Detroit 48202

Grand Rapids Public Library
Sociology and Education
   Department
Library Plaza
Grand Rapids 49502

MINNESOTA
Minneapolis Public Library
Sociology Department
300 Nicollet Mall
Minneapolis 55401
   *(also covers North and South
   Dakota)*

MISSISSIPPI
Jackson Metropolitan Library
301 North State Street
Jackson 39201

MISSOURI
Kansas City Public Library
311 East 12th Street
Kansas City 64106
   (also covers Kansas)

The Danforth Foundation
   Library
222 South Central Avenue
St. Louis 63105

Springfield—Greene County
   Library
397 East Central Street
Springfield 65801

MONTANA
Eastern Montana College
   Library
Reference Department
Billings 59101

NEBRASKA
W. Dale Clark Library
Social Sciences Department
215 South 15th Street
Omaha, 68102

NEW HAMPSHIRE
The New Hampshire Charitable
   Fund
One South Street
Concord 03301

NEW JERSEY
New Jersey State Library
Reference Section
185 West State Street
Trenton 08625

NEW MEXICO
New Mexico State Library
300 Don Gaspar Street
Santa Fe 87501

NEW YORK
New York State Library
State Education Department
Education Building
Albany 12224

Buffalo and Erie County Public
    Library
Lafayette Square
Buffalo 14203

Levittown Public Library
Reference Department
One Bluegrass Lane
Levittown 11756

Rochester Public Library
Business and Social Sciences
    Division
115 South Avenue
Rochester 14604

NORTH CAROLINA
William R. Perkins Library
Duke University
Durham 27706

OKLAHOMA
Oklahoma City Community
    Foundation
1300 North Broadway
Oklahoma City 73103

Tulsa City–County Library
    System
400 Civic Center
Tulsa 74103

OREGON
Library Association of Portland
Education and Psychology
    Department
801 S.W. Tenth Avenue
Portland 97205

PENNSYLVANIA
The Free Library of Philadelphia
Logan Square
Philadelphia 19103
    (also covers Delaware)

Hillman Library
University of Pittsburgh
Pittsburgh 15213

RHODE ISLAND
Providence Public Library
Reference Department
150 Empire Street
Providence 02903

SOUTH CAROLINA
South Carolina State Library
Reader Services Department
1500 Senate Street
Columbia 29211

TENNESSEE
Memphis Public Library
1850 Peabody Avenue
Memphis 38104

TEXAS
The Hogg Foundation for
    Mental Health
The University of Texas
Austin 78712

Dallas Public Library
History and Social Sciences
    Division
1954 Commerce Street
Dallas 75201
    *(also covers Arkansas,
    Louisiana, New Mexico,
    and Oklahoma)*

El Paso Community Foundation
El Paso National Bank Building,
    Suite 1616
El Paso 79901

Minnie Stevens Piper Foundation
201 North St. Mary's Street
San Antonio 78205

UTAH
Salt Lake City Public Library
Information and Adult Services
209 East Fifth Street
Salt Lake City 84111

VERMONT
State of Vermont Department of
    Libraries
Reference Services Unit
111 State Street
Montpelier 05602

VIRGINIA
Richmond Public Library
Business, Science, & Technology
    Department
101 East Franklin Street
Richmond 23219

WASHINGTON
Seattle Public Library
1000 Fourth Avenue
Seattle 98104

Spokane Public Library
Reference Department
West 906 Main Avenue
Spokane 99201

WEST VIRGINIA
Kanawha County Public Library
123 Capitol Street
Charleston 25301

WISCONSIN
Marquette University Memorial
    Library
1415 West Wisconsin Avenue
Milwaukee 53233
    (also covers Illinois)

WYOMING
Laramie County Community
    College Library
1400 East College Drive
Cheyenne 82001

PUERTO RICO
Consumer Education and Service
    Center
Department of Consumer Affairs
Minillas Central Government
    Building North
Santurce 00908
    (covers selected foundations)

MEXICO
Biblioteca Benjamin Franklin
Londres 16
Mexico City 6, D.F.
    (covers selected foundations)

Notes

CHAPTER 1

1. James F. Bender, *How to Sell Well* (New York: McGraw-Hill Book Co., Inc., 1961), pp. vii–viii.
2. Richard D. Cheshire, "Strategies for Advancement." *New Directions for Institutional Advancement: Presidential Leadership in Advancement Activities*, edited by James L. Fisher (San Francisco: Jossey-Bass, Inc., 1980), p. 14.
3. John G. Kemeny, "Why a president might refuse a million-dollar gift." *Case Currents* (Jan. 1978, vol. IV, no. 1), p. 28.
4. Irma L. Rabbino, "The Many Roles in Public Relations." In *New Directions for Institutional Advancement, op. cit.*, p. 27.
5. H. Sargent Whittier, Jr., "Presidential Commitment to Educational Fund Raising." *Ibid.*, p. 62.
6. Thomas E. Broce, *Fund Raising: The Guide to Raising Money from Private Sources* (Norman, OK: University of Oklahoma Press, 1979), p. 188.
7. Lynn Phillips, "Interested donors can determine breakdown of charity dollars." *Orlando Sentinel Star*, Feb. 24, 1981, p. 3E.
8. Russell V. Kohr, "Capital Campaigning." In *Handbook of Institutional Advancement*, edited by A. Westley Rowland (San Francisco: Jossey-Bass, Inc., 1977), p. 242.
9. Fred Schnaue, ed., *Giving USA* (New York: American Association of Fund-Raising Counsel, Inc., 1980), p. 42.
10. *Ibid.*
11. "How to ask for money and get it." *Ms.* (April 1980, vol. VIII, no. 10), p. 51.

12. Robert B. St. Lawrence, "Volunteers in the spotlight." *Case Currents* (March 1979, vol. V, no. 3), p. 42.
13. Arthur C. Frantzreb, "Management of Volunteers." In *Handbook of Institutional Advancement, op. cit.,* p. 132.
14. Frank Ashmore, "The Trustee and the Development Program." Speech to Indiana University Workshop on Higher Education, Summer 1965.
15. Paul Davis, "20,000 Potent People." Speech to Indiana University Workshop on Higher Education, Summer 1965.
16. H. Sargent Whittier, Jr., "How much access? The chief development officer's relationship with trustees." *Case Currents* (April 1981, vol. VII, no. 4), pp. 22–24.
17. Michael Radock, "Getting good advice." *Case Currents* (Feb. 1981, vol. VII, no. 2), p. 22.
18. Scott M. Cutlip and Allen H. Center, *Effective Public Relations,* 5th ed. (Englewood Cliffs, N.J.: Prentice-Hall, 1978), p. 487.
19. Harold J. Seymour, *Designs for Fund Raising: Principles, Patterns, Techniques* (New York: McGraw-Hill, 1966), p. 178.

CHAPTER 2

1. "Despite Poor Economic Climate, Many Colleges Report Successful Campaign." *The Chronicle of Higher Education* (Nov. 17, 1980, vol. XXI, no. 13), p. 6. Also information provided by Yale's development office.
2. John G. Johnson, "Is the Bedrock Firm?" *Case Currents* (Nov. 1976, vol. II, no. 10), pp. 8–10.
3. "Fact-File." *The Chronicle of Higher Education* (May 21, 1979, vol. XVIII, no. 13), p. 3.
4. Daniel Lynn Conrad, *The Big Gifts Planner* (San Francisco: The Institute for Fund Raising, 1977).
5. G. T. Smith, "How to issue an invitation to significant giving." *Case Currents* (April 1978, vol. IV, no. 4), p. 6.
6. Howard R. Mirkin, *The Complete Fund Raising Guide* (New York: Public Service Materials Center, 1972), p. 23.
7. James G. Lord, "Make your case statement a potent marketing tool." *Case Currents* (Feb. 1981, vol. VII, no. 2), p. 12.
8. James F. Oates, as quoted in Robert E. Nelson, "Ready for a campaign?" *Case Currents* (March 1979, vol. V, no. 3), p. 23.
9. Russell V. Kohr, "Capital Campaigning." In *Handbook of Institutional Advancement,* edited by A. Westley Rowland (San Francisco: Jossey-Bass, 1977), pp. 256–57.
10. David M. Thompson, "Challenging your donors." *Case Currents* (Dec. 1978, vol. IV, no. 11), pp. 14–15.

11. Charles W. Miersch, "Corporate development: market and method." *Case Currents* (Dec. 1977, vol. III, no. 11), pp. 14–17.

12. Robert L. Graze, "You *Can* Get More From Your Call." Speech to First National Fund Raising Conference, University of Chicago, August 7, 1974.

13. Clearinghouse on Corporate Social Responsibility, *1980 Social Report on the Life and Health Insurance Business* (Washington, D.C.: Clearinghouse on Corporate Social Responsibility, 1980), p. 1.

14. James A. Avery, as quoted in William E. Sheppard, *FRI Annual Giving Idea Book* (Plymouth Meeting, PA: The Fund Raising Institute, 1972), p. 27.

15. H. Perk Robins, "Personal Solicitation." Speech to CASE conference on the Annual Fund, 1978.

16. Lynda Boyer, "What I wish they'd told me about personal solicitation." *Case Currents* (June 1979, vol. V, no. 6), pp. 14–16.

17. Arthur C. Frantzreb, "Solicitation Strategy." *Personal Solicitation* (March 1979), microfiche, CASE Reference Center.

18. Scott Van Batenburg, "New Fund Raising Mode: Preauthorized Payments." *Fund Raising Management* (March 1981, vol. 12, no. 1), p. 32.

19. Jon Cosovich, "After you land the big gift." *Case Currents* (Sept. 1979, vol. V, no. 8), pp. 22–23.

20. John G. Kemeny, "Why a president might refuse a million-dollar gift." *Case Currents* (Jan. 1978, vol. IV, no. 1), p. 26.

21. James B. Martin, "When to say No, Thank You." *Case Currents* (Dec. 1980, vol. VI, no. 11), p. 9.

22. Material provided by and used with the permission of Marion College.

23. Material provided by and used with the permission of Edward S. Tobias, Director, Oberlin Annual Fund, Oberlin College.

24. Material provided by and used with the permission of Douglas Geddie, Brock University.

25. Material provided by and used with the permission of John N. Reynolds III, director of development, Winter Park Memorial Hospital.

CHAPTER 3

1. David C. Ferner, "The Gift of Belonging." *Case Currents* (Nov. 1980, vol. VI, no. 10), p. 8.

2. "Tasteful Tailoring." *Case Currents* (Nov. 1980, vol. VI, no. 10), p. 18.

3. Robert D. Sweeney, "Building Gift Club Membership." *Case Currents* (Nov. 1980, vol. VI, no. 10), p. 19.

4. We appreciate the assistance of Ed Coll, vice-president for development affairs at the University of Miami, for sharing this material with us.
5. Kathy Huffer, "Dressing Up Your Gift Club." *Case Currents* (Nov. 1980, vol. VI, no. 10), pp. 24–27.
6. Sweeney, *op. cit.*, p. 16.
7. Paul H. Schneiter, "Paying Attention to the 'After' of Asking." *Fund Raising Management* (June 1980, vol. 11, no. 4), p. 35.
8. Huffer, *op. cit.*
9. Schneiter, *op. cit.*, pp. 36–37.
10. Frank A. Logan, "The Gift Club That Isn't." *Case Currents* (Nov. 1980, vol. VI, no. 10), p. 29.
11. The dollar amounts and names of these clubs have since changed slightly. The Chancellor's Associates includes those who give $1,250 or more; the Chancellor's Circle, Sustaining Level, gifts of $600–$1,249; the Chancellor's Circle, gifts of $300–$599; and the Blue and Gold Circle, gifts of $100–$299. The operation of the clubs remains the same, however.
12. Material provided by and used with the permission of Lynda Boyer, director of the UCLA Chancellor's Associates program.

CHAPTER 4

1. Perri and Harvey Ardman, *Woman's Day Book of Fund Raising* (New York: St. Martin's Press, 1980), p. 268.
2. Special thanks to Don Lemish, vice-chancellor for institutional advancement and planning, East Carolina University, for his assistance and ideas.
3. We appreciate the help of Adelaide Snyder, vice-president of university relations at Florida Atlantic University, for allowing us to use this material.
4. *A Practical Guide to Phone Etiquette.* Winter Park [Florida] Telephone, 1978.
5. Material provided by and used with the permission of Bruce D. Newman, chief executive officer, Rutgers University Foundation, and Rose Migliaccio, assistant director of planned and annual giving.

CHAPTER 5

1. Deborah Baldwin, "Ideology by Mail." *The New Republic* (July 7 and 14, 1979, vol. 181, no. 1), p. 19.
2. Helen Dudar, "Neither Snow, Nor Rain, Nor Gloom of Night Can Stop Sanky Perlowin." *Ms.* (April 1980, vol. VIII, no. 10), p. 54.

3. *Ibid.*, p. 56.
4. Nick Kotz, "King Midas of 'The New Right'." *The Atlantic* (Nov. 1978, vol. 242, no. 5), p. 53.
5. This material, originally obtained through the Direct Mail Marketing Association, is available in CASE's *Creative Direct Mail* booklet, used in their workshops.
6. *Direct Mail*, undated publication of the S. D. Warren Co. We appreciate the cooperation of Mark Myers, who wrote the material, for allowing us to use it.
7. Robert and Joan Blum, "Direct Mail and Development: Pyramid to Campaign Success." *Fund Raising Management* (May/June, 1972, vol. 4, no. 2), p. 44.
8. Virginia L. Carter, "The ABCs of Raising Money by Mail." *Case Currents* (June 1978, vol. IV, no. 6), pp. 6–8.
9. "Tip of the Month." *FRI Monthly Portfolio* (Ambler, PA: Fund-Raising Institute, Feb. 1981, vol. 20, no. 2).
10. Carter, *op. cit.*
11. Robert I. Headley, "Colored, Textured Paper Increases Direct Mail Results." *Direct Marketing* (June 1980, vol. 43, no. 2), p. 38.
12. Carter, *op. cit.*
13. *Ibid.*
14. Susan Wallgren, "Writing Letters that Sell." *Case Currents* (June 1978, vol. IV, no. 6), pp. 12–13.
15. Speech by Robert Blum to CASE Creative Direct Mail Conference, San Francisco, Oct. 5, 1978.
16. Francis S. Andrews, "White Smoke on the Fund Raising Horizon." Speech to National Catholic Development Conference, Chicago, Sept. 20, 1978.
17. Material provided by and used with the permission of Sandra U. Thorpe, associate secretary, Phillips Academy, Andover.
18. The information in this case study was used by permission of C. Edwin Davis, director of development, Berkshire Medical Center.

CHAPTER 6

1. Edwin R. Leibert and Bernice E. Sheldon, *Handbook of Special Events for Nonprofit Organizations* (New York: Association Press, 1972), p. 15.
2. Lee Sinoff, "Special Events: In Theory and Practice." In *The Nonprofit Organization Handbook*, edited by Tracy D. Connors (New York: McGraw-Hill, 1980), pp. 5–89.

3. Kathleen L. Rydar, "How to Sleep at Night: Check it Out." *Case Currents* (June 1980, vol. VI, no. 6), pp. 41–46.
4. Heather Ricker Gilbert, "The entertainer's guide." *Case Currents* (June 1980, vol. VI, no. 6), p. 32.
5. *Ayer Fund-Raising Dinner Guide* (Philadelphia: Ayer Press, 1974), pp. 15–21.
6. *FRI Monthly Portfolio* (Ambler, PA: Fund-Raising Institute, 1977).
7. Material provided by and used with the permission of John C. Butler, director of planning and development, Edgewood College.
8. Perri and Harvey Ardman, *Woman's Day Book of Fund Raising* (New York: St. Martin's Press, 1980), pp. 202–3.
9. Leibert and Sheldon, *op. cit.*, pp. 204–19.
10. Joe Little, "TV Fund Raising: Does Every One Belong On The Tube?" *Fund Raising Management* (Sept./Oct. 1979, vol. 10, no. 4), pp. 37–38.
11. Jim LaMont, "Annual Telethon Meets Needs of Hospital, Local Cable TV." *Fund Raising Management* (May/June 1979, vol. 10, no. 2), pp. 16–25. The material is from an interview the magazine conducted with Mr. LaMont.
12. Material provided by and used with the permission of Joseph Curley, Roger Pynn, and Truman "Duffy" Myers of the Orlando Chapter, F.P.R.A.

CHAPTER 7

1. Scott M. Cutlip and Allen H. Center, *Effective Public Relations*, 5th edition (Englewood Cliffs, N.J.: Prentice-Hall, 1978), p. 487.
2. James E. Murphy, "The Campaign Needs PR." *Case Currents* (March 1979, vol. V, no. 3), p. 44.
3. *Ibid.*, pp. 44–45.
4. Peter Arnold, "PR Plan Boosts a Campaign." *Case Currents* (Sept. 1976, vol. II, no. 8), p. 25.
5. We appreciate the assistance of Joyce Chumbley, executive director of the Council of Arts and Sciences, Orlando, Florida, for allowing us to use material from the Council's 1980 *Publicity Handbook*.
6. Material provided by and used with the permission of the American Red Cross.

CHAPTER 8

1. This story, typical of Conrad Teitell's many humorous anecdotes, is from a flyer entitled "Estate Planning Has Nothing To Do With

Crabgrass," published by the Philanthropy Tax Institute, Old Greenwich, Conn., 1981.

2. William B. Dunseth, *An Introduction to Annuity, Life Income, & Bequest Programs* (Washington, D.C.: CASE, 1978), p. 1.
3. Leonard W. Bucklin, "Deferred Giving." In *Handbook of Institutional Advancement*, edited by A. Westley Rowland (San Francisco: Jossey-Bass, 1977), p. 217.
4. Dunseth, *op. cit.*, p. 3.
5. "A Gamble for High Stakes." *Forbes* (Feb. 5, 1979, vol. 123, no. 3), p. 49.
6. C. Ray Clements, "A Guide to Deferred Giving." *Case Currents* (May 1976, vol. II, no. 5), p. 23.
7. Another great letter from John E. Dolibois of Miami University; we appreciate his tremendous support.
8. Greg Olberding, "Personal Touch Establishes Relationship With Donors." *Fund Raising Management* (Dec. 1980, vol. 11, no. 10), p. 20.
9. The material in this section has been made available courtesy Adelaide Snyder, vice-president of university relations, Florida Atlantic University.
10. C. Ray Clements, "In Planned Giving, Put Policies in Writing." *Case Currents* (Jan. 1977, vol. III, no. 1), pp. 18–19.
11. M. Jane Williams, "Four Expert (And Different) Views on What Constitutes the Key Basic Element of Your Deferred-Giving Program." *FRI Bulletin* (Ambler, PA: Fund-Raising Institute, Sept. 1977).
12. Norman S. Fink, "The Planned Giving Profession: Perspective for the '80's." *Case Currents* (Nov. 1979, vol. V, no. 10), p. 10.
13. Charles W. Patterson III, "Mutual Benefits in Promoting Bequests." *Case Currents* (Nov. 1979, vol. V, no. 10), p. 30.
14. The booklet mentioned is entitled *Gifts From The Land*, part of "The Nebraska Campaign: A Commitment to Excellence." Published by the University of Nebraska Foundation, 1978.

CHAPTER 9

1. We appreciate the assistance of James McIntyre, assistant director of annual giving at Michigan State University, for providing this information.
2. Nicholas Pettinico, Jr., development director at Niagara University, allowed us to include this material in this chapter. We are indebted to him for his help.
3. Nelson Cover, Jr., "How the Hopkins Hundreds Helped Our Annual Fund." *Case Currents* (April 1979, vol. V, no. 4), p. 19.

4. In "Proof of the proposition," *Case Currents* (March 1979, vol. V, no. 3), p. 35.
5. Russell V. Kohr, "Capital Campaigning." In *Handbook of Institutional Advancement*, edited by A. Westley Rowland (San Francisco: Jossey-Bass, 1977), pp. 237–38.
6. David B. Hanaman, "Capital Campaign Basics Promise High Visibility." *Fund Raising Management* (July 1980, vol. 11, no. 5), p. 15.
7. John I. Carlson, "Six Steps that Lead to a Good Capital Campaign." *Case Currents* (Sept. 1976, vol. II, no. 8), p. 24.
8. Goettler Associates, Inc., "Ready! Set! Go!: The Essentials of Preparing for a Campaign." (Columbus, Ohio: Goettler Associates, no date).
9. Howard R. Mirkin, *The Complete Fund Raising Guide* (New York: Public Service Materials Center, 1972), p. 101.
10. David S. Ketchum, "Fund Raising: What's In The Cards." *Case Currents* (Sept. 1980, vol. VI, no. 8), pp. 40–42.
11. From a note in the *FRI Monthly Portfolio* (Ambler, PA: Fund-Raising Institute, Dec. 1980).
12. Material provided by and used with the permission of Terry A. Wood, associate director of development, Northwestern University.

CHAPTER 10

1. H. Judith Jarrell, "The Foundation Stakes: It's No Horse Race." *Case Currents* (May 1980, vol. VI, no. 5), p. 27.
2. "Fact File—Grants of 50 Leading Foundations," *The Chronicle of Higher Education* (June 9, 1980, vol. XX, no. 15), p. 10.
3. Fred Schnaue, ed., *Giving USA* (New York: American Association of Fund-Raising Counsel, 1980), pp. 14–17.
4. Marianna O. Lewis, ed., *The Foundation Directory*, fifth ed. (New York: The Foundation Center, 1975), p. xi.
5. Thomas E. Broce, *Fund Raising: The Guide to Raising Money from Private Sources* (Norman, OK: University of Oklahoma Press, 1979), pp. 107–11.
6. Schnaue, *op. cit.*, p. 15.
7. Jack Shakely, "Community Foundations." *The Grantsmanship Center News* (1976), p. 9.
8. *Current Interests of the Ford Foundation* (New York: Ford Foundation, June 1980), pp. 5–10.
9. Robert Lefferts, *Getting a Grant* (Englewood Cliffs, NJ: Prentice-Hall, 1978), p. 10.
10. Edwin Dieckmann, "Approaching the Foundation." *Case Currents* (Oct. 1977, vol. III, no. 9), p. 21.

Selected Bibliography

The following bibliography covers a number of the major books and materials on the fundraising business. Readers are urged to consult the Notes section (pp. 301–8) for additional articles and speeches that pertain to specific subjects.

American Alumni Council. *Some Methods of Telephone Solicitation.* Washington, D.C.: AAC, 1967. Microfilm.

American Association of Fund-Raising Council, Inc. *Giving USA.* New York: AAFRC, 1980.

Arthur Andersen & Co. *Tax Economics of Charitable Giving.* Chicago: Arthur Andersen, 1979.

Anderson, Ronald D. *Obtaining External Funding.* Boulder, Colo.: Professional Services Institute, 1978.

Andrews, F. Emerson. *Attitudes Toward Giving.* New York: Russell Sage Foundation, 1953.

Ardman, Perri, and Ardman, Harvey. *Woman's Day Book of Fund Raising.* New York: St. Martin's Press, 1980.

Barnes, W. David. *Barnes Fund Raiser.* Phoenix: Barnes Associates, 1975.

————. *Barnes Fund Raiser 2.* Phoenix: Barnes Associates, 1976.

Brodsky, Jean, ed. *The Proposal Writer's Swipe File.* Washington, D.C.: Taft Products, 1973.

Chester, Marjorie F. *McCall's Book of Fund Raising Ideas.* Englewood Cliffs, N.J.: Prentice-Hall, 1963.

Connors, Tracy D., ed. *The Nonprofit Organization Handbook.* New York: McGraw-Hill, 1980.

309

Conrad, Daniel. *Successful Fund Raising Techniques*. San Francisco: The Fund-Raising Institute, 1977.

Cumerford, William R. *Fund Raising: A Professional Guide*. Fort Lauderdale, Fla.: Ferguson E. Peters, 1978.

Cutlip, Scott M. *Fund Raising in the United States*. New Brunswick, N.J.: Rutgers University Press, 1965.

Cutlip, Scott M., and Center, Allen H. *Effective Public Relations*. 5th ed. Englewood Cliffs, N.J.: Prentice-Hall, 1978.

Davis, King E. *Fund Raising in the Black Community: History, Feasibility, and Conflict*. Metuchen, N.J.: The Scarecrow Press, 1975.

Demaris, Ovid. *Dirty Business: The Corporate-Political Money-Power Game*. New York: Harper's Magazine Press, 1974.

Dermer, Joseph, ed. *How to Write Successful Foundation Presentations*. New York: Public Service Materials Center, 1972.

————. *How to Get Your Fair Share of Foundation Grants*. New York: Public Service Materials Center, 1973.

————. *How to Raise Funds from Foundations*. New York: Public Service Materials Center, 1978.

Dunseth, William. *An Introduction to Annuity, Life Income, and Bequest Programs*. Washington, D.C.: CASE, 1978.

Gaby, Patricia V., and Gaby, David M. *Nonprofit Organization Handbook*. Englewood Cliffs, N.J.: Prentice-Hall, 1979.

Goldin, Milton. *Why They Give: American Jews and Their Philanthropies*. New York: Macmillan, 1976.

Gottlieb, Gladys M., *Personal Solicitation*. Washington, D.C.: CASE, March 1979. Microfilm.

Held, Walter J. *The Technique for Proper Giving*. New York: McGraw-Hill, 1959.

Hopkins, Bruce R. *The Law of Tax-Exempt Organizations*. 2nd ed. Washington, D.C.: Lerner Law Book Co., 1977.

Humphries, H. R. *Fund Raising for Small Charities and Organizations*. Newton Abbot, U.K.: David & Charles, 1972.

Katz, Harvey. *Give! Who Gets Your Charity Dollars?* Garden City, N.Y.: Anchor Press, 1974.

Kirstein, George G. *Better Giving: The New Needs of American Philanthropy*. Boston: Houghton Mifflin, 1975.

Knowles, Helen K. *How to Succeed in Fund-Raising Today*. Freeport, Me.: Bond Wheelwright Co., 1975.

Leibert, Edwin R., and Sheldon, Bernice E. *Handbook of Special Events for Nonprofit Organizations*. New York: Association Press, 1972.

Lord, James G. *Philanthropy and Marketing: New Strategies for Fund Raising*. Cleveland: Third Sector Press, 1981.

Mirkin, Howard R. *The Complete Fund Raising Guide.* New York: Public Service Materials Center, 1972.

National Health Council. *Viewpoints on State and Local Legislation Regulating Solicitation of Funds from the Public.* New York: National Health Council, 1976.

Nolte, Lawrence. *Fundamentals of Public Relations: Professional Guide-Lines, Concepts and Integrations.* 2nd ed. New York: Pergamon Press, 1979.

Pride, Cletis. *Organizing, Budgeting and Staffing the Development Office.* Washington, D.C.: CASE, 1971. Microfilm. Kit V-1-4-71.

————. *Public Relations—Special Events: Dedications.* Washington, D.C.: CASE, 1971. Microfilm. XVII-A-AA-71.

————. *Fund Raising by Telephone.* Washington, D.C.: CASE, 1972. Microfilm. XXXVIII-A 10/72.

————. *The Female Donor.* Washington, D.C.: CASE, 1973. Microfilm. XLIX-A 6/73.

————. *Fund Raising: The Big Gift.* Washington, D.C.: CASE, 1973. Microfilm. Kit XLVII-A 5/73.

————. *Fund Raising: Volunteers Make a Difference.* Washington, D.C.: CASE, 1974. Microfilm. Kit 59-A 2/74.

Rowland, A. Westley, ed. *Handbook of Institutional Advancement.* San Francisco: Jossey-Bass, 1977.

Schneiter, Paul H. *The Art of Asking: A Handbook for Successful Fund Raising.* New York: Walker, 1978.

Seymour, Harold J. *Designs for Fund-Raising: Principles, Patterns, Techniques.* New York: McGraw-Hill, 1966.

Sheppard, William E. *Annual Giving Idea Book.* Plymouth Meeting, Pa.: The Fund Raising Institute, undated.

Sheridan, Philip. *Fund Raising for the Small Organization.* Philadelphia: M. Evans, 1968.

Soroker, Gerald S. *Fund Raising for Philanthropy.* Pittsburgh: Pittsburgh Jewish Publication and Educational Foundation, 1974.

Index